The Radio Handbook

D0225126

The Radio Handbook is a comprehensive guide to radio broadcasting in Britain. Featuring two entirely new chapters for this third edition, 'You radio' and 'Sport on radio', as well as sections on making radio adverts and radio drama, this text offers a thorough introduction to radio in the twenty-first century. Using new examples, case studies and illustrations, it examines the various components that make radio, from music selection to news presentation, and from phone-ins to sport programmes. Discussing a variety of new media such as podcasts, digital radio and web-linked radio stations, Carole Fleming explores the place of radio today, the extraordinary growth of commercial radio and the importance of community radio.

The Radio Handbook shows how communication theory informs everyday broadcasts and encourages a critical approach to radio listening and to radio practice. Addressing issues of regulation, accountability and representation, it offers advice on working in radio and outlines the skills needed for a career in the industry.

The Radio Handbook includes:

- interviews with people working at all levels in the industry including programme controllers, news presenters and DJs
- examples of programming, including nationwide and local BBC, commercial radio, community and student stations
- real typescripts and case studies of current stations
- a glossary of key terms and technical concepts.

Carole Fleming is Principal Lecturer at the Centre for Broadcasting and Journalism at Nottingham Trent University. Her previous publications include *The Radio Handbook* (second edition, 2002), *Women and Journalism*, with Deborah Chambers and Linda Steiner (2004) and *Introduction to Journalism* with Emma Hemmingway, Gill Moore and Dave Welford (2006).

Media Practice

Edited by James Curran, Goldsmiths College, University of London

The *Media Practice* handbooks are comprehensive resource books for students of media and journalism, and for anyone planning a career as a media professional. Each handbook combines a clear introduction to understanding how the media work with practical information about the structure, processes and skills involved in working in today's media industries, providing not only a guide on 'how to do it' but also a critical reflection on contemporary media practice.

The Newspapers Handbook 4th edition

Richard Keeble

The Advertising Handbook 3rd edition

Helen Powell, Jonathan Hardy, Sarah Hawkin and Iain MacRury

The Television Handbook 3rd edition

Jonathan Bignell and Jeremy Orlebar

The Photography Handbook 2nd edition

Terence Wright

The Magazines Handbook 2nd edition

Jenny McKay

The Public Relations Handbook 3rd edition

Alison Theaker

The Cyberspace Handbook

Jason Whittaker

The Fashion Handbook

Tim Jackson and David Shaw

The New Media Handbook

Andrew Dewdney and Peter Ride

The Radio Handbook

Third edition

Carole Fleming

Routledge
Taylor & Francis Group

LONDON AND NEW YORK

First edition published 1994
Reprinted 1996, 1999
Second edition published 2002
Reprinted 2006, 2007

This third edition first published 2010
by Routledge
2 Park Square, Milton Park, Abingdon, Oxon OX14 4RN

Simultaneously published in the USA and Canada
by Routledge
270 Madison Avenue, New York, NY 10016

Routledge is an imprint of the Taylor & Francis Group, an informa business

© 2010 Carole Fleming

Typeset in Times New Roman and Helvetica Neue
by Florence Production Ltd, Stoodleigh, Devon
Printed and bound in Great Britain
by CPI Antony Rowe, Chippenham, Wiltshire

All rights reserved. No part of this book may be reprinted or
reproduced or utilised in any form or by any electronic, mechanical,
or other means, now known or hereafter invented, including
photocopying and recording, or in any information storage or
retrieval system, without permission in writing from the publishers.

British Library Cataloguing in Publication Data
A catalogue record for this book is available from the British Library

Library of Congress Cataloging in Publication Data
Fleming, Carole, 1955–
   The radio handbook / Carole Fleming. – 3rd ed.
      p. cm.
      1. Radio broadcasting–Handbooks, manuals, etc.   2. Radio
   broadcasting–Great Britain.   I. Title.
   PN1991.55.F54 2009
   384.54–dc22   2009003518

ISBN10: 0–415–44507–8 (hbk)
ISBN10: 0–415–44508–6 (pbk)
ISBN10: 0–203–87377–7 (ebk)

ISBN13: 978–0–415–44507–8 (hbk)
ISBN13: 978–0–415–44508–5 (pbk)
ISBN13: 978–0–203–87377–9 (ebk)

For my sons:
Dominic, Michael, Tom and Sean Braithwaite,
and my sister Debbie

Contents

·····························

Contents

Illustrations

....

Acknowledgements

....

When I began researching this book I had little idea that the radio industry would be transforming itself in such a dramatic way with mergers, takeovers and closures changing the scene on almost a monthly basis. But despite it being such a period of uncertainty, the enthusiasm and passion for radio shown by everyone I talked to in the industry confirmed my belief that it is the people who work in radio that make it such a fascinating and dynamic medium. I would like to thank everyone who helped me to produce this edition of *The Radio Handbook* and in particular the following people: Trevor Dann from the Radio Academy; Antony Bellekom from BBC Radio 2; Ben Cooper, Piers Bradford, Andy Puleston and James Wood from BBC Radio 1; Phil Dixon from Smooth FM; Lewis Skrimshaw and Mark Dennison from Trent FM; Phill Danks from GCap Media; Phil Blacker from GCap Sport; Stuart Cosgrove from Channel 4; Ross Fletcher from BBC Radio Derby; Aeneas Rotsos, Sophie Stewart and Hannah Kennedy from BBC Radio Nottingham; Philippa TJ; Tim Humphrey from Southern FM; Nick Wilson from Heart 106; Duncan Cooke and Will Nunan from Severn Sound; Andrew David, Sam Kirk and Gavin Roberts from Siren FM; Jim Latham from the BJTC.

In addition I would like to thank my colleagues at the Centre for Broadcasting and Journalism at Nottingham Trent University for their support, in particular Mandy Ball for advice on election coverage and legal matters.

Introduction

....

T he changes in the radio industry in the UK since the publication of the last
edition of *The Radio Handbook* in 2002 show how radio constantly evolves
to meet the challenge of technological advances and shifts in society. Back
then Digital Audio Broadcasting (DAB) radio was struggling to become established,
radio station websites were primitive, podcasting had yet to be invented, and Radio
Authority regulation ruled the airwaves.

Fast forward to 2009 and it is a different world. While DAB is still struggling to
some extent as a platform, the number of people listening to digital radio is
increasing: by the beginning of 2008 25 per cent of people in the UK listened to
DAB radio, while 36 per cent listened to digital radio on digital television, 22 per
cent listened online, and 12 per cent listened on their mobile phone (Ofcom 2008a:
282). Radio stations now actively promote their websites, encouraging the audience
to enter competitions and interact with presenters online, and download podcasts.
The BBC produces hundreds of podcasts every week that regularly appear in the
iPod top ten podcast chart, while 57 per cent of commercial radio stations produce
weekly podcasts (RadioCentre 2008: 19). And in response to the changes in the way
radio is delivered, a softer approach to regulating radio is being taken by Ofcom
with regulations for analogue stations relaxed to bring them in line with digital
stations (Ofcom 2007a).

So the radio industry examined in this new edition of *The Radio Handbook* is
completely different: the big names from the start of the century have disappeared,
replaced by new and relatively unknown players. Global Radio – formed in 2007 to
buy former Chrysalis stations – became the biggest commercial radio group a year
later when it bought GCap for £375 million in June 2008. German media group
Bauer became the second largest radio group in the UK when it bought Emap stations
for £422 million in January 2008. And in May 2008 Virgin Radio was bought by
the Times of India Group ending 15 years of the brand name, which was changed
to Absolute Radio a few months later.

While doom-merchants regard many of these changes as the death knell of radio, others believe the changes show that the radio industry is limbering up, getting ready to reassert itself as it has done so many times in the past when faced with challenges from other media. It is radio's adaptability and ability to reinvent itself, to inspire listeners' loyalty, that make it such a fascinating medium to study. The purpose of this book is to examine the organisational structures and operating principles that produce radio to reveal the complexities behind what is widely regarded as a simple medium: all it needs is a microphone, a transmitter and a voice. Through interviews with a wide range of industry insiders and an analysis of the research produced by those inside and outside the industry, the complexities of radio become revealed and hopefully explained.

With so much upheaval in the radio industry over the past 12 months it is inevitable that between the time of researching this book and its publication the situation has changed. In some cases stations have changed because of new owners, in other cases people have moved on to different jobs. Wherever possible I have tried to take account of these changes. In any event, everyone interviewed for this book was talking about the situation as they saw it at the time, and despite any changes their views are still valid, but should be read within the context of the cyclical changes the industry periodically goes through.

Most people agree that the bedrock of radio in the UK is the publicly-funded BBC, which is listened to by 68 per cent of adults in the UK every week (Ofcom 2008a: 256). But the last few years have seen changes in that organisation as well, with a new Royal Charter that came into effect in January 2007 and restructured the broadcasting giant. For this reason Chapter 1 looks at the new structure of the BBC and analyses how the changes have affected its radio output, including its role as a public service broadcaster. The chapter then moves on to look at the development of commercial radio and analyse its strength as a provider of local and regional radio. It ends with an examination of how listening figures are gathered for UK radio, and how the profile of listeners and the way they use radio is changing.

Without a doubt the biggest change to radio in recent years has been the development of DAB digital radio, and Chapter 2 examines the controversy over the adoption of a system of digital radio delivery that is unique to the UK. The early vision of DAB being the saviour of radio by providing endless choice and superior audio quality has disappeared, and although there is now a tentative timetable for a digital radio switchover, it is widely believed that DAB will be just one system of digital delivery. The chapter then moves on to examine internet radio – including Personal Online Radio – which many believe will be radio's future, before examining more traditional forms of radio delivery – hospital radio and pirate radio.

Another huge change to radio since 2000 has been the development of community radio, which became established as a third tier of radio in the UK through the Community Radio Order of 2004, and Chapter 3 charts its growth and development and analyses its role in the modern media with a profile of community station Siren

FM. The chapter then moves on to another newcomer – podcasting – and discusses how this phenomenon has blurred the definition of radio with its potential to make broadcasters of everyone.

With so many radio stations now available, each one strives to make itself distinctive and offer a unique brand to listeners, and in Chapter 4 we examine the way a station achieves and maintains a brand. In particular the BBC brand and the commercial radio brand are analysed to show how their brands attract audiences. This is followed by a discussion about the role of music on radio and a new section that explains how radio adverts are made by the biggest producer of radio adverts in the UK. The chapter ends by examining how competitions and off-air activities like concerts sponsored by radio stations help promote station brands.

Of course, an important part of any station's brand is the 'voice' it projects, and that is most obviously projected by its presenters. In Chapter 5 the role of the presenter is discussed and different styles of presentation and how they promote the station brand are analysed. On a more literal level, the chapter also has tips for would-be broadcasters from broadcast voice coach Kate Lee on how to maximise the potential of your voice. The chapter ends with a profile of Radio 1, which shows that the success its voice has with its target audience of 15–29-year-olds comes from listening to what their listeners want from radio and applying it.

Another important part of the voice of a radio station – particularly a local radio station – is its news, and Chapter 6 looks at the role of news on radio and how newsrooms operate. While the presentation and duration of news bulletins varies from station to station according to the target audience, essentially the news is compiled in the same way. For this reason this chapter describes the various elements that make a news bulletin and what criteria are applied to the selection of news. It ends with a brief analysis of two news bulletins to show how the same news is shaped to cater for different audiences.

Within all this talk about branding it is easy to forget about the nuts and bolts of radio broadcasting, so Chapter 7 looks at the tools of broadcasting. Although far from an exhaustive account of the technical equipment used in radio, the chapter explains how studios and newsrooms work. It then looks at different types of microphones and their use, before examining different types of interviews and how to get the most from them. The aim of this chapter is not to provide a technical guide, but to demystify the equipment used on most radio stations and show why different tools and approaches are used in different situations.

But while it is undeniable that technology impacts on programming, the fundamental strengths of radio – interaction with the audience and provision of access to distant events and up-to-date information on changing situations – remain the same. In Chapter 8 the way radio incorporates those strengths is discussed through an examination of different types of programming. This includes an examination of phone-ins and how they work; how radio reacts to emergencies; election broadcasting; and drama on radio.

And no discussion about radio would be complete without a look at sport on radio. In Chapter 9 the way that radio deals with sport and its importance to stations is examined. Various sports reporters explain their jobs and give tips on different aspects of radio sport, from covering the Olympics to commentating on football. The chapter ends with a profile of a BBC sports reporter.

From its beginning radio presented a challenge to government who feared its power to influence people. For that reason radio (and other forms of broadcasting) is more heavily regulated than the print media, and in Chapter 10 the way that radio is held accountable is discussed. This includes some of the legal restraints on broadcasting, and a fuller examination of the regulation of radio. In particular the structure of the BBC Trust and Ofcom are examined, and there is an analysis of the Ofcom Broadcasting Code that applies to all radio broadcasters. The chapter ends with an examination of what happens when those regulations are broken, as happened in November 2008 when a telephone prank by two high-profile Radio 2 broadcasters caused uproar throughout the country to the extent that the Prime Minister, Gordon Brown, commented on their behaviour.

The final chapter looks at how to get started in radio with advice from employers and industry trainers. Not all jobs in radio involve being on air, but most of them do need some form of training, and this chapter examines various routes into radio, and gives advice on how to work out which is the best for you.

While this book is by no means an exhaustive account of how radio operates in the UK, it is hopefully an insight into the key issues faced by broadcasters. There are already many books that analyse the theory of broadcasting. There are also books about the practice of radio. What this book attempts is to show how what we actually hear when we switch on the radio is influenced by theory – from the structure of the 'radio day' to the selection of news. The radio industry in the UK has grown so much over the past few years that it is impossible to include every aspect in one volume, but hopefully the main issues have been explored and explained in a way that will inspire a passion for radio. It may be the oldest broadcasting medium, but radio's ability to re-invent itself keeps it eternally fresh and exciting. This book attempts to show both why and how radio manages to be a relevant part of all our lives.

So it seems that despite competition from a huge range of other media, radio is still holding its own, and one reason for its continued popularity may be that by July 2008 there were a total of 397 stations available on AM, FM or DAB (Ofcom 2008a: 243). This means there is even greater competition between stations to get and hold on to listeners.

1 The renaissance of radio

I n the age of an abundance of media it might come as a surprise that the oldest means of mass broadcasting – radio – is still holding its own with almost 90 per cent of the UK population tuning in for an average of 22.5 hours every week (RAJAR 2008a: Q2). Radio is everywhere. There are a total of 397 unique stations available on analogue (AM and FM) and DAB radio (Ofcom 2008a: 4:2:1), over 150 community radio stations, over 80 student radio stations and of course hundreds of internet radio stations.

One of the reasons for such an abundance of radio is that technological advances mean that radio is now available on a range of platforms. As well as the platforms already mentioned above, there were around 80 stations broadcasting on digital satellite in July 2008, with a further 27 stations on Freeview and 34 on cable, although most of these were simulcasts of existing stations (Ofcom 2008a: 4:2:1). And while listening via a mobile phone is still in a minority with only 4 per cent of listeners using it on a weekly basis (ibid.: 4:3:3) there are signs that this will change. Early in 2008 GCap (now Global Radio) announced a deal with Apple whereby it streams its stations live to the iPod touch MP3 player and iPhone. Using wireless broadband, listeners can stream GCap stations, access podcasts, buy music tracks from iTunes or a whole CD from Amazon, with GCap getting a slice of the retail price (Allen: 2008). A month later GCap bought a majority share in the social networking site welovelocal.com announcing that they 'hope to develop online communities around station brands' (Ofcom 2008a: 260). Other developments include WiFi radio with over 40 companies now making WiFi radios. WiFi radio devices link to the web addresses of radio stations without the use of a PC to access an estimated 10,000 stations. Ofcom research in July 2008 showed that only 6 per cent of people have a WiFi radio, but the increasing importance of the internet to radio suggests that this platform will grow.

What this means is that radio is no longer confined to coming from a traditional radio receiver as the director of the Radio Academy Trevor Dann[1] explains:

A number of people are listening to radio in a number of different ways in their listening pattern. I mean, I wake up to DAB radio, then I listen to FM in the bathroom, then I get in the car and usually listen to 5Live on AM then I get on the train and plug in my iPod and start listening to podcasts, then sometimes at work I'll use the 'Listen Again' service on the BBC. So I'm consuming radio from all kinds of different delivery systems. I think that's the modern vision.

In theory more radio stations and different platforms of delivery should provide a variety of different kinds of radio, but in practice the majority of stations have a similar format that is dominated by music, and many people are unaware that some stations broadcast a range of programmes including soaps, drama and comedy. This is shown in the Ofcom report into the Communications Market for 2008, which found that 'the largest share of revenue by station format continues to be held by the Chart-Led and Adult Mainstream genres, which together accounted for 65 per cent of commercial analogue net broadcasting revenue in Q1 2008' (Ofcom 2008a: 249). And despite having so many speech-based stations, even the BBC broadcasts a majority of music on its radio stations with over half the hours broadcast – 51.6 per cent – being music (ibid.: 257).

The reasons people listen to radio will be examined later in this chapter, and the following chapter looks at different kinds of radio. However, given that most people still listen to 'mainstream' radio, that is professionally produced radio for a

Figure 1.1
Trevor Dann, director of the
Radio Academy

mass audience broadcast on AM or FM, it is important to begin by examining those stations.

Broadly speaking, mainstream British radio falls into two categories: the BBC's public service broadcasting and Independent Radio's commercial broadcasting. This division is not a clear-cut one however, and the term 'public service broadcasting' is particularly problematic.

Although the BBC is publicly funded, it still needs to attract audiences to justify its licence fee and its very existence. Since early 2000 the BBC has dominated radio listening in the UK, and in the second quarter of 2008 it held a 55.5 per cent share of listening compared to 42.4 per cent for all commercial radio listening (RAJAR 2008a: Q2). Many commercial radio bosses feel that this is because the corporation is increasingly adopting an aggressive marketing stance and using licence fee money to pay top presenters huge salaries that commercial radio cannot match.

Commercial radio bosses also point out that because a station operates to make a profit that does not preclude it from providing a service to the public. They say that in 2007 commercial radio dedicated over 13,000 hours of air time to community news in *What's On* bulletins and raised over £17 million for charity (RadioCentre 2008: 7).

For these reasons it is worth a closer examination of the two types of broadcasting and a discussion of public service broadcasting.

Public service broadcasting

For the first 50 years of its existence radio broadcasting in Britain was synonymous with the BBC. Originally a commercial company, the British Broadcasting Corporation was created in January 1927 by Royal Charter as a publicly funded organisation with sole responsibility for the provision of broadcasting in the United Kingdom. Its position as a monopoly with assured finance through the licence fee gave its first director general, John Reith, the time and resources to develop it free from commercial pressures, and its charter provided it with full editorial independence (Crisell 1994: 21).

But being publicly funded also brought a responsibility for the BBC to 'serve' the public: its output had to inform and educate listeners as well as entertain them. According to the latest Royal Charter, which came into effect in January 2007 and runs to the end of December 2016, 'the BBC exists to serve the public' (Royal Charter: 3(1)). So although it is independent from the government, it has to justify its programming and spending to it in order to continue to receive public money. The government sets the cost of the licence and what proportion of it is given to the BBC, and ultimately it can decide to discontinue it altogether. For this reason it is important to the BBC that they are seen as the country's public service broadcaster.

The problem is that there is no absolute definition of public service broadcasting[2] (PSB) although the Peacock Commission into broadcasting in 1986 came up with eight principles of 'the public service idea':

> Geographical universality of provision and reception; the aim of providing for all tastes and interests; catering for minorities; having a concern for national identity and community; keeping broadcasting independent from government and vested interests; having some element of direct funding from the public (thus not only from advertisers); encouraging competition in programmes and not just for audiences; and encouraging the freedom of broadcasters.
>
> (McQuail 1994: 126)

However, the media landscape has changed dramatically since 1986 with many more stations now available, and it could be argued that apart from 'direct funding from the public' commercial radio, taken as a whole, embraces these ideas as much as the BBC. Moreover, public backing for the licence fee appears to be diminishing. In a survey by Ipsos Mori for the MediaGuardian in 2008, 41 per cent agreed that the licence fee was the most appropriate way to fund the BBC but 47 per cent felt that it was not good value for money:

> Just as worrying is that many appear not to buy the BBC's argument that it provides programming unavailable elsewhere – and for all the attempts to broaden the justification for the licence fee this remains a key plank of the argument to retain the licence fee, particularly among politicians.
>
> (Gibson 2008a)

But under the latest Royal Charter the BBC was restructured with an Executive Board headed by the director general to deal with the day-to-day running of the corporation, and the BBC Trust to represent the public interest. In the Trust's first annual report in 2007, the chairman, Sir Michael Lyons, said the Trust has three key aims. The first is to ensure the independence of the BBC, the second is to deliver 'distinctive, high-quality services to all the people and all the communities of the United Kingdom' and the third is to 'ensure that the BBC makes a very important contribution to the social, economic and civic life of the UK' (BBC Annual Report 2006/07: 2). As can be seen, these aims are similar to the public service ideas put forward by the Peacock Commission.

Indeed, perhaps because of the debate around the continuation of the licence fee, the BBC Trust is keen to stress that it represents the public:

> The Trust works for the public who pay for the BBC. We listen to a wide range of voices, seeking to understand all opinions and expectations to inform our judgements. We ensure the BBC is independent, innovative and efficient; a creative and economic force for good in the UK, and for the UK internationally.
>
> (BBC Annual Report 2006/07: 9)

In order to achieve this, the Royal Charter laid down six public purposes that govern the way the BBC operates. They are:

(a) sustaining citizenship and civil society;

(b) promoting education and learning;

(c) stimulating creativity and cultural excellence;

(d) representing the UK, its nations, regions and communities;

(e) bringing the UK to the world and the world to the UK;

(f) in promoting its other purposes, helping to deliver to the public the benefit of emerging communications technologies and services and, in addition, taking a leading role in the switchover to digital television.

(Royal Charter: 4)

To make it clear how these public purposes work on each of its stations, the Trust publishes a 'purpose remit' that sets out how the performance of each station will be judged, and it issues service licences based on those remits. Each BBC service has a detailed licence that clearly sets out what is required of it and links those requirements to the public purposes. For example, the service licence for Radio 1 states that in order for the station to contribute towards the public purpose of 'stimulating creativity and cultural excellence' the stations must:

- Broadcast at least 60 hours of specialist music each week.
- Ensure at least 40 per cent of the music in daytime is from UK acts each year.
- Ensure at least 45 per cent of the music in daytime is new each year.
- Broadcast from around 25 major live events and festivals in the UK and abroad each year.
- Broadcast at least 250 new sessions each year.
- Contribute to BBC Radio's commitment to commission at least 10 per cent of eligible hours of output from independent producers.

(Radio 1 Service Licence issued 7 April 2008)

The Trust is also responsible for carrying out Public Value Tests that assess proposals to launch any new service or changes to an existing one. The first part of the process is a 'public value assessment' undertaken by the BBC Trust that looks at the value of the proposals to licence fee payers and includes a public consultation. The second part is a 'market impact assessment' carried out by or for Ofcom to 'measure the likely effect of the proposed changes on other players in the market' (BBC Annual Report 2006/07: 36). This new system should please commercial

Figure 1.2 Antony Bellekom, managing editor of BBC
Radio 2 and 6 Music

broadcasters who have long complained that while they are bound by Ofcom regulations about their performance, the BBC could make changes with no outside consultation. In particular, commercial radio was badly hit by changes to Radio 2 in 1998 when younger presenters and a new playlist were implemented seemingly overnight to attract what many felt was the key commercial radio audience. Moreover the changes worked and Radio 2 is the most listened-to station in the country with over a quarter (27 per cent) of adult listeners (13.6 million) tuning in every week in the first quarter of 2008 (Ofcom 2008a: 256).

Antony Bellekom,[3] the managing editor of Radio 2 and 6 Music, says one of the reasons for the popularity of Radio 2 is that it has a broad approach with something for everyone from veteran broadcasters like David Jacobs and Terry Wogan, to newer ones like Russell Brand[4] and Chris Evans, to specialist music shows and documentaries. He feels this is what the BBC should be doing:

> At the end of the day commercial radio has to be successful at reaching a target audience because it has advertisers who need to do precisely that. The responsibility of the licence fee is to be broader – not to be niche radio but much broader in our approach and that gives us the platform to allow individual passions and insights to turn into really interesting radio.

Indeed, one of the conditions of the station's service licence is that it should 'broadcast a broader range of music than any other major UK radio station with over 1,100 hours of specialist music programming each year' (Radio 2 Service Licence 2008). Although Radio 2 may have broad appeal it is fair to say that some BBC stations are quite niche, but overall the BBC provides for all listeners through what

Stephen Barnard calls 'complementarity'. 'Complementarity in radio services means the provision of radio programming which dovetails, rather than directly competes, with that of other stations' (Barnard 2000: 32). In other words, the BBC designs each of its radio services with a distinct audience in mind so that every interest can be catered for within the BBC family, something Antony Bellekom acknowledges. 'I think Radio 2 takes part of the Radio 1 audience when they feel it's time for them to move on. There's a relationship between all the networks in passing the audience along and that's why the stations need to be separate.'

Providing this stable of radio stations is not cheap and Ofcom say 'BBC expenditure continues to form the largest single source of funding for the radio industry' (Ofcom 2008a: 248). For 2007/08 the total expenditure on radio services was £598.4 million, with £460 million spent on radio content (ibid.: 257) despite the fact that over half of the hours it broadcasts have music content that is recognised as being less expensive to produce than speech.

The BBC's approach to radio shows that while audiences are important to it, it is equally important for it to embrace the public service idea of encouraging competition in programmes and not just for audiences. The remit for Radio 4, for example, is to be a 'mixed speech service, offering in-depth news and current affairs and a wide range of other speech output including drama, readings, comedy, factual and magazine programmes' (Radio 4 Service Licence 2008). This should include at least 2,500 hours of news and current affairs each year, 600 hours of original drama and readings, and 180 hours of original comedy (ibid.). So despite audiences of 9.6 million adults for the first quarter of 2008 (Ofcom 2008a: 256) it has a service budget of £86 million and its programmes are the most expensive on BBC radio costing £9,900 per hour to produce (ibid.: 258).

The high cost of speech radio is also shown in by the second most expensive station in the BBC being 5 Live. Its service licence describes it as the 'home of continuous news and live sports coverage. It should aim to bring its audience major news stories and sports events as they happen, and provide context through wide-ranging analysis and discussion' (Radio 5 Live Service Licence 2008). It is listened to by 12 per cent of the population, with a third of those tuning in via digital radio rather than its unreliable AM frequency, and it costs £6,300 per hour to produce (Ofcom 2008a: 258).

As well as the network stations the BBC has four digital-only stations: 1Xtra, 5 Live Sports Extra, 6 Music and BBC Radio 7. The most popular of these is BBC Radio 7, which is a speech-based entertainment channel designed as the home of children's speech radio from the BBC. In line with most digital-only stations, Radio 7 has a very small audience reaching just 1.6 per cent of the population (RAJAR 2008a: Q1), but because most of its output comes from BBC archives it is one of the cheapest with programming costing £600 per hour (Ofcom 2008a: 258).

Surprisingly the cheapest programming done by BBC radio is its local stations, which cost just £400 per hour to produce, and when the 38 local stations are combined with the three nations' stations – BBC Scotland, BBC Wales and BBC Ulster – they have a reach of 20.4 per cent (ibid.). The local stations have a 60/40 speech/music ratio so it is surprising that they cost so much less than a station like the Asian Network[5], which has a 50:50 speech/music split and costs over three times as much with programming costing £1,300 per hour.

But while the big network stations are the glamorous side of the BBC, it is the local/nations' stations that people really connect to whether as part of their target audience of over-50-year-olds, or as a schoolchild growing up and recognising that BBC Scotland, BBC Newcastle, BBC Guernsey are not only part of this distant and powerful organisation – the BBC – but also part of your community. 'The BBC local/nations' stations reach around one in five UK adults a week (10.3 million listeners); for 2.8 million people their local BBC station is the only BBC station they listen to (ibid.: 256).

And although it might not give financial recognition to local stations, the BBC is aware that they are important, not least because they help fulfil one of the BBC Trust's public purposes of 'representing the UK its nations, regions and communities'. One of the BBC Local Radio service licence conditions is that it should produce at least 85 hours of original, locally-made programming each week (BBC Local Radio Service Licence 2008). The licence also stresses the need for stations to be involved in their communities and to encourage interactivity. 'Programmes should offer listeners the opportunity to contribute, and there should be opportunities for listeners to tell their own stories' (ibid.). As Sophie Stewart[6] the editor of BBC Radio Nottingham says: 'Strategically all we're about is our audience and embracing the audience so that they like us and want to stay with us.'

But while the BBC may dominate radio listening in the UK nationally, there is no room for complacency, especially as at a local level commercial radio is winning the ratings war. More worryingly, there is evidence that parts of the population, including those in lower socio-economic groups, feel the BBC does not represent them. An Ipsos Mori poll for the MediaGuardian in August 2008 also revealed that the London-centric nature of the corporation was a problem:

> The BBC Trust's own research has shown that the further you get from London, the less people feel the BBC represents them. Our results bear that out. For example, in Scotland 35 per cent believe the licence fee is an appropriate funding mechanism, 47 per cent disagreed: in London those figures were 41 per cent and 28 per cent.
>
> (Gibson 2008a)

Commercial broadcasting

Commercial radio, as its name suggests, is run to make a profit by selling air time to advertisers. It began in October 1973 with the news and information London station LBC followed a week later by the 'general entertainment' station Capital Radio, and in the next three years developed a network of 19 local stations overseen by the Independent Broadcasting Authority (RadioCentre 2006: 5). In its early days the stations were similar to BBC stations, partly because so many of the new stations' staff were former BBC employees, but also because of the way it was regulated.

From the beginning the Independent Broadcasting Authority (IBA) imposed certain public service obligations on stations by insisting they carry a full news service and provide programming to appeal to all age groups and reflect the diversity of their community (Barnard 2000: 53). What this meant was that commercial radio could not deliver a specific audience to advertisers so its appeal to them was limited. The prospect of making a profit was further hindered by the charges made by the IBA:

> These costs were high because the IBA rentals – averaging 10 per cent of a station's revenue in the early years – were high in order to cover the costs of regulation, transmission and the forward expansion of the system, and copyright royalties were high, averaging 12–13 per cent. The IBA then required stations to spend another 3 per cent on employing musicians, so that no less than 25 per cent of a station's income was committed before it had paid one employee or met any of the usual costs of operating a business, such as rent, rates, vehicles, power, etc.
>
> (RadioCentre 2006: 6)

On top of this the birth of the new stations occurred during a period of recurrent recession when advertising generally hit a slump, and at a time of increased competition from new forms of television – breakfast television, Channel 4, cable and satellite – as well as an increase in land-based pirate stations who were free from regulation and so could provide advertisers with targeted audiences (Crisell 1994: 37).

The 1990 Broadcasting Act changed all that. Ownership and investment regulations were considerably relaxed, as well as the public service requirement, and three national commercial stations[7] were proposed along with a promise to expand local and regional services. The Act also saw the disbanding of the IBA and the creation of a new regulator, the Radio Authority, which had a much lighter touch and promised to broaden listener choice.

Another development at this time was an end to radio stations – both commercial and the BBC – simulcasting on AM and FM. This had come about because, although Independent Radio had been conceived as a VHF (FM) service, in the early 1970s most radio listening was still through Medium Wave (AM) and, in order to give the fledgling services a better chance, they were also allocated AM frequencies (RadioCentre 2006: 7).

What this meant for most stations was they made their FM service target a slightly younger audience, and started to broadcast a 'gold' service targeting over-35-year-olds on AM.

These moves helped commercial radio to target audiences more effectively than they had been able to in the past. Unfortunately despite the growth of commercial radio throughout the 1990s many stations chose to target if not the same audience, then a very similar one – the one identified by advertisers as having the most spending power and therefore the one they wanted to reach with their message. The size of radio audiences is important to advertisers but equally important is the audience profile that gives the demographic picture of the average listener. There would be little point in advertising disposable nappies, for example, on a station whose audience consisted mainly of 55-year-old men. The most popular audience to target was the 24–35-year-old age group with a skew towards women who are seen as being the main purchasers of disposable goods. This meant that throughout the 1990s although there were more radio stations than ever before, most of them were targeting the same audience and so they sounded very similar.

But in order to continue growing commercial radio needed ever more stations and by the mid 1990s it was clear that the amount of spectrum available on FM was becoming severely limited.[8] This prompted the radio industry – led by the BBC and the biggest commercial radio group at the time, GCap (now Global Radio) – to explore digital broadcasting and the system that was adopted was DAB. With its ability to provide hundreds of stations through digital mutliplexes, DAB was envisaged as being able to provide niche broadcasting to very specific audiences, and in some cases it did just this. But the reality was the high start up costs combined with slow take-up of DAB receivers meant the majority of stations on DAB were simulcasts of existing stations (see Chapter 2 for more on DAB).

So with FM full the only way for commercial radio groups to grow on analogue radio was through buying up existing stations and 2008 saw a frenzy of acquisition and mergers that brought about major changes in the commercial radio sector. Three of the top six radio groups changed ownership and the two largest groups – GCap and Emap – went into private hands. National commercial station Virgin Radio (now Absolute Radio) was sold by the Scottish Media Group to the Times of India Group (TIML) ending 15 years of its brand name (Ofcom 2008a: 251).

By the end of 2008 the biggest commercial radio group was Global Radio with 76 analogue stations including the former GCap and Chrysalis stations, giving them a 25 per cent share of commercial analogue stations. Their portfolio includes five London stations – Capital, Heart, XFM, Choice and Gold[9] – as well as The One Network of former GCap urban stations, Gold, Heart and Galaxy stations, national commercial station Classic FM and the digital only station Chill. Global Radio only formed in 2007 in order to buy the Chrysalis radio group, but by the end of 2008 Ofcom estimated that it could have a weekly reach of 24 million listeners, which is the equivalent of 40 per cent of the population (Ofcom 2008a: 261).

The next largest group is the German media group Bauer who bought out Emap and have 41 analogue licences giving them a 14 per cent share of the market, which means that just two groups control almost 40 per cent of commercial radio. The Bauer portfolio includes Magic, Kiss, Kerrang and Big City stations like Key 103 and Radio City, as well as digital-only stations Heat, Q, Mojo and the most listened to digital only station The Hits (RAJAR 2008a: Q1).

The Guardian Media Group (GMG) is another significant player, and one that dominates commercial regional radio through its Smooth, Real and Century brands. The GMG stations attract a combined audience of almost 5.4 million listeners per week, who listen on average for 10 hours per week, generating a 4.5 per cent share of total listening (Ofcom 2008a: 265).

But as well as changes in ownership, commercial radio seems to be becoming more cohesive in that stations no longer see themselves in competition with other commercial stations as much as they are in competition with the BBC. This makes sense when the radio industry is viewed as a whole: commercial radio has only three national analogue stations (two on AM and one on FM) compared to the BBC's five (one on AM and four on FM). So nationally the BBC can offer listeners more choice and naturally that gives them a bigger share of the audience with BBC network claiming 47 per cent of all listening hours (Ofcom 2008a: 253). But on a local/regional level commercial radio has a total of 305 analogue stations compared to the BBC's 46 local and nations' stations. Predictably commercial radio is strongest at a local level, claiming in 2008 to have a 75 per cent share of local listening:

> The more Commercial Radio stations that listeners have to choose from, the higher Commercial Radio's share of listening is likely to be. In Glasgow, where listeners have approximately 13 stations to choose from, Commercial Radio has a 63% share of radio listening. In both Birmingham and London, where listeners have a choice of approximately 16 and 40 Commercial Radio stations respectively, Commercial Radio enjoys a 51% share of listening.
>
> (RadioCentre 2008: 10)

Some of the credit for the cohesion of commercial radio has to go to the RadioCentre, which was formed by a merger between the Commercial Radio Companies Association (CRCA) and the Radio Advertising Bureau (RAB) in 2006. Almost all commercial radio stations in the UK are part of the RadioCentre, which works as a lobby group for their interests, works with national advertisers, does research into the industry and co-ordinates network programming and radio campaigns (see 'The commercial radio brand' in Chapter 4).

But the strength of commercial radio is in its links to local communities and because of that local news has gained importance. 'The proportion of news bulletins containing local news has increased by almost 5% since 2004: now almost 70% of news bulletins contain news from that station's local community' (RadioCentre 2008:

38). And while chart-led and adult mainstream music stations still dominate, 'specialist music has also seen an increase in share up by almost 7 percentage points from five years ago, as music station choice has increased' (Ofcom 2008a: 249). There are also 33 commercial stations targeting ethnic minorities giving commercial radio a 58 per cent share of ethnic minority listening (RadioCentre 2008: 10).

While all this sounds very positive, Ofcom pointed out in November 2007 that 'over the last three years radio has occupied two parallel universes' (Ofcom 2007a: 1). The first is from the listener's point of view 'for whom things have seldom been better' (ibid.) with a huge range of different kinds of radio available on a number of different platforms. The second is from the point of view of those who run commercial radio where revenues have been declining and 'competition from the wide choice of stations on digital platforms and from the calls other media place on listeners' time is fragmenting audiences' (ibid.). These factors mean the business models of local stations, especially the smaller ones, are no longer viable.

All commercial radio is regulated by Ofcom who award licences for stations to broadcast. In making the awards Ofcom tries to ensure that within any given area there is a diversity of output catering for different tastes and needs. They also stipulate how much of the output needs to be locally made: each licence has a Format for the station that includes a description of the character of the service – for example, the speech/music ratio and a broad definition of the music genre to be used – and specific requirements like the number of hours a station must provide locally-made programming. This varies from station to station and is based on the promise of performance made in the licence application. 'Compliance is ensured by sample content checks and the maintenance of an online public file for each station' (ibid.: 2).

The balance Ofcom tries to achieve is between making sure local communities have output that is relevant to them and allowing stations enough freedom to develop and succeed economically, no doubt being aware that the regulations imposed by the IBA on early commercial radio held it back. Ofcom also acknowledged that the formats for analogue radio were far more detailed than those for digital radio 'while stations on other platforms have no Format regulation at all' (ibid.: 3). For these reasons it decided in 2007 that analogue radio formats should be simplified to bring them more into line with those for digital stations, and that Ofcom would give stations guidance about how much locally produced material they needed to make.

Commercial radio bosses say that networking programmes across a group makes sense. As Mark Dennison[10] of 96 Trent FM explains, 'like it or loathe it networking is here and if it's used in the right way it can be a strong proposition for any station. For smaller stations it's an opportunity to save money and for larger stations it just brings something different.' So groups like Bauer spread their talent with programmes like *Rich and Luce* broadcasting across all their Big City stations from Key 103 in Manchester. Networking also allows stations to pay for big names like Jeremy Kyle, whose Saturday morning music and chat show goes out on 42 GCap stations including Capital Radio, in competition with Jonathan Ross' Radio 2 show.

The argument against networking is that it produces less variety in radio output and it stifles talent. Stations up and down the country start to sound very similar and the distinctiveness of the locality is lost. The schedules become dominated by a few presenters and there is no opportunity for new talent to break into the industry.

Naturally enough commercial stations did not want Ofcom to impose rules about how much local material they had to broadcast. 'They called for self-regulation of localness, focused on the delivery of local material (rather than the regulation of locally-made programming) on the grounds that licensees know best how to serve their listeners' (ibid.: 4). But Ofcom felt that market pressures would lead to an erosion of locally produced programmes as had happened in countries like France and the USA and revised its proposals:

> The revised localness guideline proposals for FM stations are for a minimum of 10 hours a day of locally-made programming during weekday daytimes (which must include breakfast) and four hours per day during the daytime at weekends. Smaller stations may request to be allowed to share some daytime programmes on a sub-regional basis. AM stations should provide a minimum of four hours a day of locally-made programming, but at least 10 hours during weekday daytimes (including the four hours of locally-made programming) should be produced in the nation to which the station broadcasts. No station will be required to produce more locally-made programming or more local material than at present.
>
> (Ofcom 2007a: 4)

But while commercial radio might resent[11] being told how much local programming to provide, they also know that their strength is in their links to local communities. This is particularly noticeable the further away from London you go: the BBC has only one station is Scotland, which makes it difficult to service the entire population, so people living there are more likely to identify with their commercial station because they see it as more relevant to them. According to Ofcom the most popular category of radio in Scotland is local commercial, which has a 43 per cent share of all radio listening (Ofcom 2008a: 281).

Measuring audiences

What is sometimes forgotten is that the purpose of commercial radio is to make money and it does so by selling air time to advertisers. As Alison Winter, the head of Audience Insight at the RadioCentre points out, 'Collectively, commercial radio reaches 30.8 million adults (15+) every week, employs just under 10,000 people, and is funded by approximately £600 million of advertising revenue per annum' (Winter 2008: 30). So the need for accurate listening figures for commercial radio is so that advertisers can know who they are selling to, but the BBC also needs to have accurate listening figures to measure the popularity of their stations and justify the licence fee.

For this reason the BBC and the Commercial Radio Companies Association (now the RadioCentre) set up a radio industry research company – RAJAR Ltd – in 1992. This is an independent company wholly owned by the BBC and the RadioCentre. Prior to this audience data were collected by two separate services: the BBC Daily Survey, which monitored BBC radio, and the Joint Industry Committee for Radio Audience Research for commercial stations. The problem with this was that different methodologies and the fact that the figures were not independently produced cast doubt on their accuracy.

Understandably, measuring radio audiences is complicated: there are about 340 separate stations measured by RAJAR including 60 BBC stations, and radio can be consumed on a huge variety of platforms from digital to mobile phones to listen-again services and podcasts. The annual cost of the service is £7 million (Plunkett 2008c).

RAJAR – which stands for Radio Joint Audience Research – produces listening figures every three months, based on a series of diaries completed by 130,000 adults each year. In RAJAR terms an adult is anyone over the age of 15. They also survey around 5,000 4- to 14-year-olds but the main figures are based on adult consumption.

The radio map of the UK is quite complex so to try to get an accurate picture of the state of the industry stations select the area that they want to be surveyed by selecting a list of postcode districts. The transmission areas are then mapped and overlaid and this produces 550 non overlapping areas called 'segments' that form the framework for the survey. Next, households are approached by interviewers on a rolling basis – each household only does one week so the results are a sample rather than a panel. Although the selection of households is randomly done, in order to make it as representative as possible there are targets for each segment that match the demograph of the area being surveyed to make sure there are enough people from different ethnic backgrounds, age range and gender and so on.

Each respondent is given a paper diary that is personalised to include national stations and those available in that area. The diary is made up of 150 pages – two for each day of the week – sectioned off into 15 minute blocks and the diary keeper has to mark every time they have listened to a station for at least five minutes and also say which platform they used. They are also asked general questions about themselves to establish a profile of the person filling in the diary – things like house ownership, the number of radios and televisions in the house, access to digital platforms and so on, and also about what other media they use. This is so that stations can build up a detailed profile of their listeners to make them more attractive to advertisers. The overall listening figures are available to everyone free of charge, but the more detailed information about audience profiles and what parts of the day get the highest listening figures are only available to individual stations.

The whole process is complicated and time consuming and has obvious flaws as the director of the Radio Academy Trevor Dann points out:

> It's accurate up to a point. Like any opinion survey – and that's what it is, a survey based on recall – it's going to be flawed, but the point about it is how you use it. It's not good at telling you precise figures but you can use RAJAR best for following trends. I think if you can see a radio station's reach or share going up or down over at least four quarters you can probably see a trend that has some meaning.

Because of criticism RAJAR began testing a way of measuring listening using an electronic system. In 2006 it began a pilot of the Arbitron Portable People Meter (PPM). This required users to wear the PPM around their neck or on a belt at all times. But the trial – which cost £3.5 million – was cut short because the data it collected was not always accurate and because it was found people were not wearing their PPMs as much as they should have done, particularly at breakfast when ratings are so important (Plunkett 2008c). It may be old-fashioned but as Alison Winter explains, 'while a handful of countries have moved to a meter-based currency, the paper diary remains the most widely used methodology worldwide' (Winter 2008: 30).

Nonetheless, RAJAR is aware that because of developments in mobile technology and time-shifted listening, a new system for measuring listening is needed and in 2008 it announced that it would begin trialling an online interactive diary, which they believe has the potential to provide a bigger sample size at a reduced cost (Plunkett 2008c).

The listener

But whether it is the BBC or commercial radio, it is clear that the listener is at the heart of everything a radio station does. All radio stations need listeners and the radio industry is aware that in order to survive it has to strive to keep radio as a habit for the population – make it the medium they turn to automatically.

Unfortunately overall radio listening has dropped. In 2002 the proportion of UK adults listening to radio on a weekly basis for at least five minutes was 91 per cent. By 2007 this figure has dropped to just under 90 per cent (Ofcom 2008a: 277). More worryingly, the amount of time people are listening to the radio has also fallen with the biggest drop coming in the 4–24-year-old age group: between 2002 and 2007 their listening dropped by 10.6 per cent (ibid.: 279).

This is a key audience for radio because if young people do not get into the habit of listening to radio, it is less likely that they will become radio users when they are older, so potentially they are lost to radio forever. Interestingly the Ofcom research showed that the only age group to increase their listening in the period between 2002 and 2007 was the over-55-year-olds who increased the amount of time they spent listening to radio by 2.3 per cent. 'This suggests that while almost as many people are listening to radio, they are spending less time as radio competes with other entertainment and information media channels such as the internet' (ibid.).

But of course statistics can be interpreted in different ways and while most people accept that younger people are less interested in radio than older people, research from the Radio Advertising Bureau (RAB) found that radio, and in particular commercial radio, was still a major part of the lives of most 15–24-year-olds. Their research looked at what they called the 'digital natives': young people who developed their media habits in a world that was already digital, and who were completely at ease with the internet and computer technology. Their research found that 88 per cent of 15–24-year-olds tune in to the radio every week and 72 per cent claim it is part of their daily routine (Radio Advertising Bureau 2007: 3).

More encouragingly for radio, the research showed that the traditional strengths of radio are valued by this age group with 71 per cent saying radio kept them company, 37 per cent saying it was like a friend to them, and 46 per cent saying they trusted the medium. 'The high score for "*keeps me company*" might be expected, but the high scores for trustworthiness and "*like a friend to me*" suggest that there is a significant emotional relationship between radio and the 15–24 group' (ibid.: 7). Tim Humphrey[12] of Southern FM says the trust audiences have in radio is one of its enduring qualities:

> People take what they hear on radio as true. Radio is essentially one person speaking to another one and most radio listening is done on your own. With newsreaders and presenters people build up a relationship and they trust them and that's what makes the difference. It's down to trust.

Another traditional strength of radio is that it is portable, and Ofcom research shows that this is helping to maintain audiences with the amount of listening done outdoors or at work up from 13 per cent in 2007 to 16 per cent for the first quarter of 2008. 'This increase might have been helped by the growth in listening to podcasts or on mobile phones while on the move or commuting. In-car listening also increased, up by 3% to 20% over the year' (Ofcom 2008a: 289). Antony Bellekom, the managing editor of BBC Radio 2 and 6 Music, says capturing the market through podcasts is vital to radio's survival:

Radio's traditional strength has been about its portability but it had very limited content because it was live. So what we're doing through the iPod and other similar devices is offering something not dissimilar to a radio experience but giving greater choice. If we're not in that market then we're not in the present and there will be no future.

It can also be argued that radio's role as a secondary medium – one that can be used while doing other things – is also one of its saving graces. As the RAB's research shows, 'young people are more at ease with multi-media consumption than previous generations' (Radio Advertising Bureau 2007: 4) so despite spending more time online, only 11 per cent of 15–24-year-olds are spending less time with radio (Ofcom 2008a: 286) and the RAB found that if they listen online they tend to do so for longer spending 23.7 hours per week on the internet compared to 19 hours on analogue radio (Radio Advertising Bureau 2007: 6).

But radio is a constantly evolving medium and it is perhaps this quality that will secure its future. With the growing choice of stations now available on a range of different platforms, radio in the UK has something that will suit everyone, and this is reflected in the fact that Ofcom found 88 per cent of their survey were either 'very' or 'fairly' satisfied with the choice and range of radio stations (Ofcom 2008a: 289).

So while radio is the oldest broadcasting medium, it has managed to re-invent itself to be relevant to the twenty-first century. The following chapter examines different types of radio and the role they play in keeping radio a relevant medium.

2 Radio revolution

....

R adio is endlessly adaptable. Despite challenges from other media radio continues to be popular because of its ability to adapt to changes. Technological determinists might claim that the changes are due to advances in technology like stereo broadcasting, the transistor radio and the use of FM and DAB for better sound quality. But a closer examination of these technological developments shows that most were available long before they were applied. What brought about their application is what Brian Winston calls 'supervening social necessity' (1995: 68) which act as accelerators in the development of media and other technology.

The transistor, for example, was first discovered in 1948 but it did not become widely used until the 1960s when Britain was more affluent. The new transistors made radio portable at a time when society was becoming increasingly mobile and the younger generation was emerging as a distinct group. Radio responded to this by tailoring programmes to match the lifestyle of the time. Similarly the first FM transmitter was opened in Kent in 1955 but it was not until the 1980s that stations began to switch to the better-quality frequency, mainly because the IBA (the regulating body at the time) insisted on an end to simulcasting on AM and FM. The supervening social necessity in this case was the need to find more spectrum combined with that of producing better-quality audio to meet the expectations of audiences used to ever more sophisticated sound systems. As Stephen Barnard notes, 'radio's ability to survive in a competitive media environment has always depended on how well broadcasters tap into social, cultural and technological change' (2000: 17).

The development of digital radio is another example of this. By the mid 1990s the radio industry realised that spectrum was running out and that computers were playing an increasing role in our lives. They needed a system that would give them room to expand and the ability to broadcast on different platforms to match the changing lifestyle of society. Whether or not the best system was chosen for the UK is debateable, but there was a clear need for a digital system of some kind.

The adaptability of radio is clear not only in the many ways it is broadcast but also in the way it is used for so many different purposes. As this chapter examines, the different forms that radio has make it suitable to reach people in a myriad of ways from mass global audiences to those in closed communities.

Digital radio

There are now over 170 different radio brands broadcasting digitally in the UK and Northern Ireland, and from the start of digital broadcasting in 1995 it has gained audiences year-on-year. By early 2008 almost a third of UK adults – those over 15 – listened to radio on a digital platform (RAJAR 2008a: Q1).

To a large extent the boon in digital radio is due to the variety of platforms it can be received on. As the RAB explains:

> It is sometimes mistakenly assumed that the term 'digital radio' refers only to DAB radio (radio which is transmitted via Digital Audio Broadcasting). Whilst DAB is the fastest growing platform it is important to understand that digital radio is radio via any digital platform, and perhaps in simple terms could be better defined as 'multi-platform' radio.
>
> (Radio Advertising Bureau 2006a: 4)

So as well as DAB digital radio can also be accessed through other platforms including digital television, the internet and mobile phones. In the first quarter of 2008 listening to radio through mobile phones rose to 11.6 per cent compared with 8 per cent the previous year (Plunkett 2008d), with online accounting for 6 per cent of listeners, and DTV 11 per cent (RAJAR 2008a: Q1). Andrew Harrison, the chief executive of the RadioCentre that represents UK commercial radio, says, 'Mobile phones and the internet are a whole new listening opportunity. Technology is allowing radio consumption to take place out and about on the move as well as in the bathroom and in the car and in the kitchen' (quoted in Plunkett 2007a). Nonetheless the majority of digital radio listening is still done through DAB sets (18 per cent), and despite the increasing use of digital radio platforms by the first quarter of 2008 the digital share of all radio listening hours was just 18 per cent (Ofcom 2008a: 285).

One reason for the slow uptake of digital radio is that the vast majority of stations are available on analogue radio. The BBC began digital broadcasting in 1995 by simulcasting its five national stations and only gradually did it introduce digital-only stations. In those days the only reason to listen to digital radio was for its better sound quality, although, as discussed later, this is a debateable point. In November 1999 the first digital national commercial service, Digital One, went on air. It consisted of three existing analogue stations (Classic FM, Virgin Radio and talkSPORT), and five exclusively digital stations aimed at tempting listeners to DAB. Although some of the original digital-only stations have fallen by the wayside, by 2008 there were 38 digital-only stations – 34 commercial and four BBC.

Nationally the BBC broadcasts its existing national stations on DAB as well as six other digital-only stations, including 6 Music, which is aimed at those who fall between Radio 1 and Radio 2, and BBC 7 that plays classic comedies and plays from the BBC archive. Meanwhile commercial digital radio has four national stations – Classic FM, talkSPORT, Absolute Radio and Planet Rock – and it is beginning to exploit the medium in the way it was originally envisaged by providing a range of niche digital-only stations including Bauer's The Hits, which is the most popular digital-only station, Smash Hits – based on the teen pop magazine that closed in 2006 but is thriving as a digital-only station – and Gaydar – with a target audience of predominantly gay young men – which was named best station in the 2007 BT Digital Music awards.

What is DAB?

Digital Audio Broadcasting (DAB) was developed by a consortium of 12 partners during the 1980s with the overall aim of 'co-ordinating industrial hi-tech R & D (research and development) to increase European industry's global competitiveness' (Eureka, 1999; cited in Rudin 2006: 165). It works by using a high frequency spectrum on terrestrial transmitters, known in the UK as Band III, with several services carried in one block of frequencies known as a multiplex. Britain has seven multiplexes divided between the BBC and commercial operators, with each multiplex typically carrying ten services. It works by converting the radio signal into binary digits (0s and 1s) in a way that is resistant to interference using a Single Frequency Network that allows the same frequency block spectrum to be reused throughout a large service area. This means there is more space for extra services, and because all the transmitters are using the same frequency to broadcast the same digital radio signal, there is no need to retune national stations when driving. Digital radio has done away with the need for listeners to remember station frequencies because sets are tuned by the station name, in much the same way as television stations, and it also allows extra information to be sent to the LCD display of radio sets. Each multiplex operator has 20 per cent of its capacity reserved for data services, for example, the latest news, travel and weather, website addresses and potentially even adverts.

By the summer of 2008 90 per cent of the UK was covered by at least one DAB transmitter with most areas covered by three or more (Ofcom 2008a: 270). The BBC has 105 digital transmitters and commercial radio has 133 bringing to an end the domination of the airwaves by the BBC, which has the majority of analogue spectrum. The problem is there is still 10 per cent of the UK that has no DAB signal, most notably in Scotland, and even where there is a signal there are black spots where it cannot be received:

> Each multiplex is licensed to cover a defined geographical area, with the aim of offering services to as many people as possible within that area. However, due to topographical and other local issues such as the location or structure of a building, there are often a number of areas within the multiplex licensed area that are unable to receive a clear DAB signal.
>
> (Ofcom 2008a: 270)

With the FM frequency in the UK now full (the last FM licences were awarded in 2007) DAB was hailed as the saviour of the radio industry giving listeners more choice of stations and CD quality sound. But as so often happens with grand projects involving multiple partners, the reality is not quite as rosy as that, and right from the start there were doubts about the system being used.

As Richard Rudin (2006) convincingly argues, the driving force behind the adoption of the DAB system was the European consumer electronics industry who wanted to be able to manufacture DAB radio sets for sale across the world. In fact, when the UK DAB Forum was set up in 1993 to develop the system, 'of the Forum's 12 founder organisations, only one-third can be considered to be involved in producing or regulating programmes' output of radio services' (Rudin; 2006: 165). This meant that right from the start the idea of digital radio providing a wider range of radio stations became secondary to alleged technical benefits like purer sound quality. In fact, early DAB radio was dominated by simulcasts from both the BBC and large commercial radio groups, so the only selling point digital radio had was its sound quality, and that appealed to a narrow range of usually older listeners. As Andy Puleston,[1] content producer for Radio 1 Interactive, admits, DAB did not inspire younger audiences. 'DAB for young people is a difficult one because if they've only got a certain amount of disposable income to spend on a gadget they're not going to buy a digital radio.'

So what emerged was a chicken-and-egg situation: broadcasters were wary about investing huge amounts of money in digital radio at a time when audiences were very small so there would be no revenue generated by it, so in most cases they simulcast their existing analogue service, but with nothing new being offered on the new sets, take up was slow which further put off stations migrating to digital. In order to kick start the process the Radio Authority (the then regulating body) offered commercial radio an incentive, and any commercial company that invested in digital would have their analogue licences rolled forward again giving them a total of 20 years security in their FM licence. While this encouraged existing stations – at least the big ones that could afford it – to go digital, it did nothing to create stations that were only available on digital.

Then there is the issue of sound quality. Ironically, as more broadcasters go digital the sound quality diminishes because the bandwidth has to be shared out more. This is not a problem for speech-based programming, which does not need as much bandwidth, but it is one for music stations. As media commentator Bobbie Johnson notes:

> The digital versions of Radio 1 and 2, for example, now broadcast at significantly lower rates than when they launched – and now stream at only slightly over 60% of what audio engineers (including the authors of the BBC report first drawn up in 1994) deem 'CD quality'. If you can get good FM reception, it often provides better quality than DAB.
>
> (2006)

It may be that this is the price the UK has to pay for being ahead of the rest of the world in its digital roll out. According to radio expert Jack Schofield 'the UK is still on course to have the worst radio in the world' because it is 'broadcast at low bit rates using an inefficient MP2 codec' (2007). The answer is to switch to a more efficient codec like the one that is being developed in other parts of the world to produce DAB+, and that is also used by Apple's iTunes Music Store, many music players and mobile phones. The problem is that the seven million digital radio sets already sold cannot receive the form of AAC (advanced audio coding) that provides DAB+ although dual standard systems that will receive both DAB and DAB+ are being developed. Another advantage of manufacturing sets capable of receiving DAB+ is that it would allow Ofcom to embrace another digital system called Digital Radio Mondial (DRM). This system uses the AM spectrum and could provide the answer to the need for more useable spectrum. This situation seems to have come about because there was never any real debate about the best way to go digital. As Richard Rudin (2006: 167–8) points out, most broadcasters were not invited to take part in the discussions about digital radio until the essentials of the system had been agreed: the actual system was decided upon by technical specialists and manufacturers.

Trevor Dann, the director of the Radio Academy,[2] admits that mistakes have been made:

> We find ourselves somewhat isolated in the UK – we're the only country that's got the system we've chosen. It may be we opted too soon for what will turn out to be a redundant technology. What worries me most about DAB is that it costs a lot of money to build multiplexes and it costs money therefore to broadcast on it and the money that's being spent on that is coming out of programmes – there's only one budget.

The high cost of broadcasting on DAB for very little return is a constant complaint from broadcasters, and in 2008 the digital system was dealt a blow when GCap –

the radio group that had initially championed DAB – announced it was scraping its digital-only station The Jazz, despite a growing listenership, and selling the award-winning *Planet Rock* to concentrate its efforts on FM and the internet. Industry insiders say it costs £1 million to broadcast on a national commercial digital multiplex (Plunkett 2008e) and overall commercial radio invests £20 million a year in digital radio (Plunkett 2007b).

Part of that investment went into the founding of the Digital Radio Development Bureau (DRDB). This is a trade body funded by the BBC and commercial radio multiplex operators to promote DAB digital radio across the UK and to a wider audience. According to their website they 'work directly with broadcasters, manufacturers and retailers to encourage more and different products, heightened consumer and high street awareness, improved understanding of DAB technology and co-ordination of brand awareness' (www.drdb.org.uk). A lot of the positive spin about the benefits of digital radio comes from the DRDB, and in the main they have done a good job in promoting DAB, but many, like Richard Wheatley, the chief executive of the Local Radio Company, are yet to be convinced that it is the right system. 'I am a total believer that radio listening will migrate to digital radio, but the way everything is moving it is much more likely to move to internet radio than DAB' (quoted in Plunkett 2008e).

In November 2007 the Digital Radio Working Group (DRWG) was formed from representatives of the radio industry and related stakeholders to look at how to promote digital radio and increase its penetration. In its interim report for the Secretary of State for Culture, Media and Sport in June 2008 it acknowledged that the high cost of digital broadcasting was not sustainable, and it identified several barrier to its growth including gaps in coverage and the robustness of the signal within covered areas, and the lack of European harmonisation: France has opted to use DMB-A, a system developed in Korea primarily for the delivery of digital television, and at the beginning of 2008 Germany announced it was pulling out of its DAB experiment and opting for DAB+ (DRWG 2008: 3.6). These barriers have meant that car makers do not fit digital radios as standard, which the DRWG admit is a further blow to digital listening. 'Around 20 per cent of radio listening in the UK happens in cars and although around 30 per cent of new cars registered in the UK during 2007 were offered with DAB products in their ranges, take-up remains low' (DRWG 2008: 3.9).

Despite these barriers the DRWG is agreed that radio must go digital: 'Radio stuck in an analogue world risks becoming increasingly irrelevant, particularly to young listeners, as consumers' expectations for interactivity, quality and choice grow' (2008: 4.1). They also agree that 'DAB, as a broadcast specific platform, is currently the most practical replacement for analogue' because the UK already has a DAB market, it is free at the point of access, and 'as a radio specific broadcast platform it provides the opportunity for the industry to determine its own future' (2008: 4.4). That said, the Group recognised that other platforms including variants of the

Eureka 147 family like those adopted by France and Germany, and particularly the internet: 'The industry should embrace the opportunities of a hybrid technological approach, not least because different technologies suit different listeners' needs' (2008: 4.3).

In order to achieve a migration to digital the Group recommended that DAB should be the primary platform for national, regional and large local stations, with FM used for small local stations and community radio with IP delivery to complement it. Current AM services should be moved to either DAB or FM to allow the medium wave to be used for other things, and research done to consider the future of long wave services. And in order to cover all future developments they recommend that manufacturers should make receivers that are capable of receiving FM, DAB and the other main variants of the Eureka 147 family (DRWG 2008: 4)

In December 2008 the DRWG published its final report into the migration to digital. They concluded that three criteria were needed to trigger the move:

> that at least 50% of total radio listening is to digital platforms; that national multiplex coverage will be comparable to FM coverage by time of digital migration; that local multiplexes will cover at least 90% of the population and, where practical, all major roads within their licensed areas by the time of digital migration
>
> (DRWG Final Report: 2.5)

These conditions are to be monitored by Ofcom who will make regular reports to the government, and when the conditions are met the government should make an announcement of the switchover date two years later. They estimate that this announcement will happen in 2015 and the switchover will be in 2017.

But while the DRWG is positive about the need for radio to go digital they also acknowledge that the process is expensive at a time when advertising revenues are low,[3] and they make several suggestions about how the radio industry could be helped:

> In the short-term we believe the government should consider options for funding to support the reduction of carriage costs. Ofcom should also consider removing the specific requirement for a marketing budget in the national commercial multiplex licence. To provide longer term security the government should pass new legislation to allow the roll-over of the national multiplex licence until 2030. In addition, Ofcom should consider delaying the implementation of AIP ('Administered Incentive Pricing') is an annual fee levied on the holders of spectrum) on DAB multiplexes until after digital migration.
>
> (DRWG Final Report: 4.7)

The report also noted that local multiplexes have particular problems because often there are not enough stations on a multiplex to fill it. To help this problem they want the government to pass legislation so that where there is excess capacity on local multiplexes Ofcom can allow them to merge with an adjoining multiplex 'to create a larger and more sustainable structure' (ibid.: 4.10). They also want new legislation to extend the licence terms of all analogue services, both national and local, which are broadcast on DAB (ibid.: 4.13) and a relaxation of the amount of locally produced material stations are required to carry:

> While we do not believe it would be appropriate for all local services to be produced in a single central location, a model which focuses so heavily on where content is made may not be the best way to deliver either what listeners will most want in the future or allow the industry space to grow

> (ibid.: 4.15)

As Barry Cox, the chair of the DRWG, notes:

> We acknowledge that in some cases the proposed changes are controversial and may be difficult to implement, but we do believe they are essential if the radio industry, particularly the commercial sector, is to be enabled to achieve a digital future.

> (ibid.: Foreword)

In recommending that future radio receivers should be capable of receiving FM, DAB and other main variants of the Eureka 147 family it may seem that the DRWG is backing all horses, but the reality is that DAB does not offer enough in terms of content, station availability and sound quality to drive people to it. And despite huge levels of investment and promotion, even the BBC has doubts about its long-term viability saying, 'digital-only stations – including BBC stations – have yet to make a breakthrough. Although growing, reach and audience awareness remain low' (BBC Annual Report 2007/08: 15).

But the biggest blow to DAB came in October 2008 when Channel 4 – the main stakeholder in the UK's second national commercial multiplex – announced it was closing its radio division and would not be launching its three Channel 4 branded stations. Aside from the fact that this jeopardised the future of a second national commercial multiplex, it meant that in December 2008 the only commercial station broadcasting nationally as a digital only station was Planet Rock. All the others were available on analogue and that gave little incentive for people to adopt DAB.

The second national multiplex was awarded to 4 Digital in July 2007 after a keenly fought contest including a proposal from National Grid Wireless to provide 12 stations. As mentioned, the majority shareholder in 4 Digital was Channel 4 Radio who formed a consortium with Bauer Radio, BSkyB, the Carphone Warehouse Group, UBC Media and UTV Radio. Their plan was to have ten stations on the multiplex – three coming from Channel 4 itself: E4 Radio – a music station aimed at 15–29-year-olds with a commitment to new music and new comedy talent; Channel 4 Radio – a speech-based service aimed at 30–54 year-olds with an emphasis on news, current affairs, comedy, documentaries and debate; and Pure 4 – a music and speech service targeting 30–49-year-olds with an eclectic range of music and discussions about the arts and contemporary culture. Right from the start Channel 4 insisted it would challenge the dominance of the BBC on radio by providing something different. Before the project was ditched, Stuart Cosgrove,[4] Channel 4's director of Nations and Regions, believed they had a winning recipe:

> The multiplex strategy is based on the idea that we're looking for a mix of different programme stations some of which would be done in partnership with people who already have significant content but no radio outlet. Disney for example, who've got a huge family reputation, great brand salience and an amazing archive. So to be able to support and work with them to brand a station with their content is something that's different – it's a new offering. Within our own content if you talk just simply E4, Channel 4's the most successful station with young viewers and we think we can do a lot more with young listeners. Hitherto and up until now they've been treated purely and almost exclusively as ears for music and that's reduced them to merely consumers of music. Now in actual fact, as we know from E4, they're hugely interested in a wide range of other subjects – entertainment, comedy, news and current affairs, political campaigns and a whole range of other things that are part of the youth experience and not just branded music. I think that one of the mistakes that often previous people working in radio have made is to actually say teenagers equal indie music – let's do that. They're good at branding things in terms of the genre of music but not that good at reaching audiences with more diverse tastes.

Doubts about Channel 4 Radio began when the launch of E4 Radio was put back from July 2007 to later in the year, and then to spring 2008. Industry insiders had always been sceptical of the success of the stations, mainly because the existing national commercial multiplex – Digital One – has a capacity for ten channels but only four were broadcasting by the beginning of 2009. At the time of publication the future of the second national multiplex was still unknown, but the planned Channel 4 radio stations have been scrapped and with them the chance for radio in the UK to take a new direction.

There is little doubt that DAB is here to stay, despite its many critics, but as Trevor Dann of the Radio Academy notes, it will not be the only system for delivering digital radio:

> I think it's a problem and the resolution will be the market. Commercial radio bosses who spend their lives not wanting to be regulated suddenly think regulation could solve this. They're looking to the government and Ofcom to

say there will be an FM switch off. Well there won't be in my view because there can't be because DAB isn't good enough yet and it maybe never will be. The market will decide whether people want it and it may be in the end just another delivery system that will sit alongside all the others.

Internet radio

The link between the internet and radio listening is now well established with almost every UK station having its own internet site providing live streaming and listen-again facilities (see Chapter 4). There are also thousands of radio stations across the world that can be accessed through the internet and a huge number of radio station directories available through Google to help you find the station you want.

The use of the internet to listen to radio has grown so much that RAJAR commissioned research in November 2007 and again in May 2008 to find out how widespread the practice is. The survey found that over a quarter of the UK adult population (aged 15 or over) had listened to the radio online – that is 14.5 million people – a rise of 21 per cent on the number listening six months before. Of those, two-thirds (18.8 per cent) listen at least once a week with 5 per cent listening every day or most days. That equates to 2.5 million people, which is a rise of 16 per cent in six months (RAJAR 2008b: 4).

Broadband is now available in 57 per cent of UK homes (Ofcom 2008a: 238) so unsurprisingly the majority of radio listening via the internet is done at home, but almost one in four people listen at work (ibid.: 5). As Stephen Whelan explains, radio complements these activities:

> Searching the net is largely a solitary pursuit, and listening to radio in the background can help create a feeling of connectedness to a larger community while you're exploring the inner reaches of a message board. For listeners at work, the general feeling seems to be that listening to the radio while performing other tasks can help provide relief from something that would otherwise be seen as a chore.

> (Whelan 2007: 7)

Of course traditional radio has always provided connectedness and distraction from tedious tasks but listening online also allows people to select what they want to hear: almost a quarter of listeners (24.7 per cent) listen to programmes at a later time than the original broadcast, and a further 39 per cent use a combination of real-time and listen-again (RAJAR 2008b: 5). What is surprising is that most people in the survey (77.2 per cent) said using listen-again did not affect how much live radio they listened to, and 13.2 per cent felt they listened to more live radio having heard programmes originally on listen-again (ibid.).

The ability to listen online was given a boost in 2002 when the BBC launched its RadioPlayer. Since then the number of people using its listen-again and live streaming services have steadily increased especially for the younger audience of Radio 1:

> In Q4 2007 4.6 million hours of live content were streamed from the Radio 1 website, up by 31% on last year. In addition 1.6 million hours of on-demand content was accessed from the site in the form of listen-again programmes or podcasts.
>
> (Ofcom 2008a: 287)

But internet radio listening is about more than hearing stations you can already access on FM or DAB. As well as being able to hear stations from across the UK and Ireland that broadcast outside your area, the internet allows you to access thousands of stations from all over the world through directories like www.reciva.com. The fun bit about a lot of these stations is that many of them are quite different to traditional stations. 'Lost and Found Sound by the Kitchen Sisters' (www.kitchensisters.org), for example, works with America's National Public Radio and has a selection of old recordings often sent in by the public, including one by a 19-year-old marine in the Vietnam war. The site also has a sonic memorial to the World Trade Centre created by the public:

> The Sonic Memorial Project set up a phone line asking listeners to call in with their stories and audio artefacts. Hundreds of people called in with their sound and messages creating a remarkable archive of personal recordings and remembrances. From this material and hundreds of hours of interviews and archival recordings gathered by producers around the country, the Sonic Memorial Special was crafted.
>
> (Lost and Found Sound)

Other sites feature the 'best' of speech radio from around the world (www. speechification.com) or more experimental audio like Sound Transit (www.sound transit.nl) where you can take an audio trip from one place to another hearing the sound of children playing in the streets of Nice, for example, then moving on to church bells in Paris and ending up with the sound of someone's fridge being opened in London. Perhaps not the sort of station you would listen to 24/7 but strangely compelling nonetheless.

Another twist on traditional radio is Personal Online Radio (POR). This is an online service that combines social networking with a music recommendation system that tracks listening habits and then recommends other music that is similar. The best-known POR in the UK is Last.fm – so called because its owners say it will be the last radio station you will ever need. As Jemima Kiss explains:

The idea is relatively simple: users can create their own profile on the social networking site with the familiar bells and whistles of blogs and friend-finding, but the clever part is that users then start building a profile of their music tastes by tracking what they listen to through their computer, including iTunes and Last.fm's own media player. Last.fm then suggests similar music, based on the listening habits of its 20 million users . . . Enter a favourite band and the site compiles a freakishly accurate array of suggestions.

(Kiss 2007)

Given that commercial radio pride themselves on being guides for their listeners and the place where new music is discovered, a service where the recommendations are coming from a software package and 'ordinary' people could be a challenge. And POR is being taken seriously by big business. After only four years of operating the London-based Last.fm was bought in May 2007 by CBS for £141 million.

Hospital radio

At the other end of the broadcasting scale is hospital radio. This is run entirely by volunteers and has a history as long as radio broadcasting itself. There are currently 231 hospital radio stations that serve almost 400 individual hospitals providing 11,760 hours of radio every week. The stations broadcast within hospitals mainly through a closed-circuit system accessed through bedside headphones, although some transmit over low power AM or FM transmitters.

The first hospital radio in the UK began at York County Hospital in 1926. It came about through the efforts of its chief physician Thomas Hanstock, who wanted to broadcast football commentary, church services and eventually recorded music to patients. From there other hospitals created their own stations until by the 1970s 'virtually every hospital of any size had their own radio service' (Hospital Broadcasting Association (2009)) with as many as 700 services broadcasting at one point. In 1970 the National Association of Hospital Broadcasting Organisations was established to bring all the stations together and help promote a good standard throughout the service. This became the Hospital Broadcasting Association (HBA) in 1992 – a national charity that promotes and supports hospital broadcasting. Through its website every hospital radio in the country can be contacted, and it offers training and support to the 4,373 volunteers who run the service.

As technology improved and the cost of running a radio station became less, the hospital stations became more professional, and often one station will serve several hospitals in a locality. Each station has to find funds to pay for the service, but some funding is available through the National Lottery, and nowadays many hospital radio studios are the same standard as those in the BBC or ILR. This means that volunteers gain invaluable experience behind the microphone, and also learn how to target their particular audience – skills that all radio presenters need. Indeed, many current radio personalities did a stint on hospital radio before going professional, and it is still used as a pool of potential talent by station managers on the look-out for new presenters. For all that, the focus of these stations is the patents who listen to their 24 hour broadcasts. As the HBA says:

> No matter how hi-tech the patient entertainment systems installed throughout hospitals, there will remain a place for the visitor and broadcaster who cares. In the future, as now and in the past, the most successful stations will be those which at all times remember their objectives and their commitment to bring entertainment and cheer to the patients.
>
> (Hospital Broadcasting Association (2009))

Pirate radio

Pirate radio – unlicensed illegal broadcasting – was at its height in Britain in the 1960s when it provided an alternative to the BBC who were the only legal radio broadcasters in the UK. At the time the 'pirates' – so called because they broadcast from ships or disused sea forts – were seen as taking on the stuffy establishment and giving audiences alternative radio formats. But despite huge changes in the number and type of radio legally available, illegal broadcasting continued with Ofcom estimating that there are around 150 illegal radio stations in the UK at any one time, with half of those transmitting in the London area (Ofcom 2007b). This causes problems for existing legal radio stations, can interfere with radio networks used by the emergency services and air traffic control, and can divert advertising revenue away from small legal stations, especially community stations, putting their viability at risk. More worryingly, research by Ofcom into illegal broadcasting says there is a direct link between illegal broadcasting and serious crime including violence, illegal drugs and theft (Ofcom 2007b: 8). This section will examine the history of illegal broadcasting, discuss the reasons behind it, and look at the measures being used to combat it.

Pirate radio: a brief history

The first British pirate station was Radio Caroline, which began broadcasting from a ship off the coast of Essex in March 1964. By 1968, 21 pirate stations were broadcasting, with an estimated total daily audience of between 10 and 15 million (Shingler and Wieringa 1998:24).

The first wave of pirate broadcasters was unashamedly commercial in its output, influenced by the format of Radio Luxembourg and American radio stations. Most followed a top 40 music format with casual, chatty links from DJs so that in both style and content it was the antithesis of BBC broadcasting at the time. It is generally acknowledged that the restructuring of BBC radio with the creation of BBC radios 1, 2, 3 and 4 in 1967 was a reaction to the popularity of pirate radio, and Andrew Crisell believes they also inspired the creation of local radio:

> First they were in some sense 'local' themselves. None of them broadcast over an area larger than the Home Counties, many of them publicised local events and aroused local loyalties, and a few such as Radio London and Radio Essex took local names. Second, although they afforded no broadcasting access to actual members of the public, they broke the BBC's virtual monopoly of radio to fulfil a demand which it had neglected, and so in that sense assumed a 'public' voice.
>
> (Crisell 1994: 33)

Technically the pirate stations were not illegal because they were broadcasting from international waters, but this loophole was closed with the 1967 Marine Broadcasting (Offences) Act, which officially outlawed them. That, along with the creation of pop music station Radio 1 – whose first DJs often came from pirate stations – eventually led to most offshore stations closing down.

The next wave of illegal broadcasters came in the late 1970s and 1980s. This time the stations were land-based and tended to operate in urban areas. As Shingler and Wieringa point out, 'During the 1980s growth in terrestrial pirates was so massive that at one stage illegal operators actually outnumbered legal broadcasters' (1998: 25). Looking at the stations illegally broadcasting at the time it is clear that they emerged for similar reasons as the first lot: some, like Sunshine Radio in Shropshire and Radio Jackie in south-west London, were grassroots community stations serving a need that the relatively new local stations did not. Others, like London stations Kiss (dance), Solar (soul) and Alice's Restaurant (rock), focused on particular music genres ignored by mainstream radio as being too niche to attract big audiences.

Once again the actions of illegal broadcasters forced a change in legal broadcasting, this time in the shape of the 1990 Broadcasting Act. This opened up the development of commercial radio and was designed to encourage diversity in radio. Until then there had been only one commercial radio service for each licensed area, apart from London which had both a speech and a music station. At the time the Act seemed to promise a radical shake-up of radio and a number of illegal broadcasters such as Kiss in London, FTP in Bristol and KFM in Stockport, successfully applied for licences and became legal. But although the 1990 Act did a lot to open up radio, freeing it from regulations that prevented stations targeting a particular audience, the commercial imperative for stations to make a profit inevitably led to them all targeting the audience most sought after by advertisers and so adopting very similar formats. Equally importantly, many felt that the reality of the Act undermined community-orientated stations and small-scale radio entrepreneurs, so that while there were more radio stations, there was less diversity, and by the end of the 1990s illegal stations once again blossomed.

Illegal broadcasting since 2000

Since 2000 the radio industry has gone through many changes and it could now be argued that most tastes can be catered for by legal radio in the UK. Community radio has boomed and is now a successful third tier of radio serving very local areas and communities of interest (see Chapter 3). Digital radio and internet radio have the opportunity to broadcast to less mainstream tastes. But despite this Ofcom estimates there are around 150 illegal broadcasters at any one time in the UK, with half of those based in London, so there still seems to be a demand for this type of radio.

In its research into illegal broadcasting, Ofcom notes that start up costs for a radio station are now cheaper than ever before: a studio can be equipped to a good standard for around £2,000 and a transmitter costs around £350 which is not much when compared to the amount of money an illegal station can make. In its research Ofcom says, 'There is a popular misconception that the people behind illegal radio stations are just enthusiasts with an interest in music and/or broadcasting; in fact many illegal stations turn over large sums of money' (Ofcom 2007b: 5). Most of the income derives from selling on-air advertising particularly about events in nightclubs: 'a large illegal radio station can generate up to £5,000 per week in cash this way' (ibid.). Another source of income comes from stations charging DJs who want public exposure and experience up to £20 an hour to broadcast.

But the stations would not exist if there was not an audience for them and research carried out in June 2006 showed that 16 per cent of all Londoners listen to illegal broadcasts (Ofcom 2007c: 3) but in the boroughs of Hackney, Haringey and Lambeth this rises to 24 per cent – almost a quarter of the population – with a 41 per cent listenership among black ethnic groups (Ofcom 2007d: 1). 'There is a consensus amongst illegal radio listeners (62 per cent) that illegal radio stations offer something different to licensed commercial stations' (ibid.: 7). The main reasons given for listening to these stations was that they play a distinctive style of music, have DJs the audience identifies with, and give information about local nightclub events not available elsewhere. Some listeners (21 per cent) also tuned into illegal stations to hear relevant religious programmes, or because it was broadcast in a language other than English (24 per cent) (ibid.: 10).

Ofcom's research showed that the key drivers of illegal broadcasting and listening in Hackney, Haringey and Lambeth were the urban music scene, grass roots participation and communities who feel underserved by mainstream media. 'Listeners are pushed into the illegal market by the perceived failure of licensed broadcasters to cater adequately for the needs of people from these three interest groups in particular' (ibid.: 13). In particular, listeners to pirate stations felt that the music they played was more up-to-date and innovative, and the DJs more knowledgeable than the 'white, middle-class' presenters on legal stations. They also felt that pirate stations were more interactive and responsive to listeners' views. 'Illegal broadcasting is broadly perceived as being "for music" or "for the community" whereas licensed commercial stations are perceived as "corporate" and "money-centric"' (ibid.: 19). On top of this it was found that many people thought illegal broadcasting was the only way for disadvantaged youngsters to break into broadcasting. 'There appears to be a generally held view amongst those involved in unlicensed broadcasting that the existing radio licence application process is unfair and discriminatory against those from less affluent and less educated backgrounds' (ibid.: 22). This is despite the fact that under the 1990 Broadcasting Act anyone convicted of an unlawful broadcasting offence is barred from working for a legitimate station for five years.

In the past the main arguments against pirate radio stations centred around the loss of music copyright fees for performers and the danger caused by interference to emergency services and air traffic control. This is still the case, but because the spectrum is now full the impact of illegal stations is even more noticeable. For example, in July 2005 London City Airport came close to shutting down because of heavy interference on their ground to air communications system caused by an illegal transmitter. This was just one of 41 'safety-of-life' cases Ofcom dealt with that year (Ofcom 2007b: 7).

Illegal broadcasts can also undermine the viability of small legal stations, particularly community radio stations which transmit on much lower power than commercial radio. With a powerful illegal transmitter the signal of small stations can be entirely obscured. Illegal stations can also be in competition with community stations for local advertising, and with low overheads they can often undercut the legal stations.

Even big commercial stations and the BBC can be affected by illegal stations that cause interference because they are being broadcast on the same or a nearby frequency. '30 per cent of UK listeners say they suffer from interference, with 14 per cent of those attributing this to illegal broadcasters. In London those figures rise to 40 per cent and 27 per cent respectively.' When this happens 41 per cent of listeners switch to another radio station, and 23 per cent switch off altogether (Ofcom 2007b: 8).

More worryingly, Ofcom says there is a direct link between illegal broadcasting and serious crime. 'Raids on studios of illegal broadcasters have uncovered weapons, including firearms. There have also been reports of violent acts committed by members of rival illegal radio stations. These include serious assaults and shootings' (Ofcom 2007f: 4). Raids have also found links to illegal drugs. 'There is evidence that illegal broadcasters send coded messages to dealers and users by playing a particular song to indicate that drugs are ready for collection' (ibid.).

Because of this Ofcom has 70 field officers investigating illegal broadcasting and in 2006 they carried out over 1,000 separate operations including seizing transmitters and raids on studios, and made 63 convictions. In most cases these officers work with local police forces because of the potential violence they face from operators. But even when there is no violence, officers are often put in danger by the way the illegal stations try to evade detection. Examples cited include placing transmitters 'down ventilation flues, or in chimneys on a roof-top, then restricting access to the device through the use of scissor-type car jacks' and 'attaching "live" 240 volt electric cables to the access doors on roof-tops, in an attempt to shock or cause injury' (Ofcom 2007b: 10).

The maximum penalty for someone convicted of illegal broadcasting is an unlimited fine and/or two years in prison, as well as the confiscation of equipment, as laid down in the Wireless Telegraphy Act of 2006, but Ofcom's own research suggests that the penalties are not seen as a compelling deterrent (Ofcom 2007d: 23). Moreover, it is unlikely that the demand for illegal broadcasting will diminish, with listeners identifying it as the 'home' of urban music, a way to break into broadcasting, and a voice for underserved minorities (ibid.: 21). Because of that Ofcom is undertaking a consultation about how to tackle unlicensed broadcasting which will look into ways to deal with it. 'In particular, our work will consider possible spectrum and licensing options' (Ofcom 2007b: 15) and this may well mean that the positive aspects of illegal broadcasting will influence the future structure of the legal industry.

Restricted Service Licences

Restricted Service Licences (RSLs) are temporary licences issued by Ofcom for non-commercial broadcasting and they come in three forms: short-term RSLs, long-term RSLs and audio distribution systems RSLs (ADS-RSLs). The most popular category of short-term RSLs operate on a low-power basis for a limited geographical area, typically to cover a town or a three kilometre radius in a city. Most of these licences are granted for a maximum of 28 days, and outside London groups can apply for two RSLs a year as long as there is a four month gap between the two broadcasts.

Short-term RSLs are used for a variety of reasons but the majority of licences are issued to community stations running a trial of their service prior to applying for a full-time licence, with licences awarded to educational institutions a close second. 'Whilst some of these licences continued to be used for university "freshers" and RAG events, most were for either school or college radio projects or training in radio for young people normally undertaken during school holidays by youth organisations' (Ofcom 2008b: 5). In 2007 these two categories made up almost 50 per cent of the licences awarded (ibid.).

Religious broadcasting is also popular on RSLs and in cities across the country there are regular broadcasts throughout Ramadan. Other reasons for short-term RSLs include sporting events like Wimbledon as well as 'quirkier events such as lawnmower racing, for which there has been an annual broadcast since 2005' (ibid.: 6), and festivals like the Edinburgh Fringe and the Belfast Film Festival.

Long-term RSLs are granted for up to five years and usually broadcast on AM only. These licences usually operate within a clearly-defined site such as a university, hospital, prison or military barracks, but there is also a tourist information service in the Shetland Islands, with transmitters located at six different sites across the islands, providing tourist information for each site. At the end of 2007 there were 96 licences operating.

The new ADS-RSLs were introduced in 2007 following a trial by Ofcom. These five-year licences provide a service within a site such as a sports stadium or conference centre and are broadcast on spectrum other than AM or FM. There are currently only two of these licences operating, one at Arsenal Football Club's Emirates Stadium, and the other at the 02 arena in London.

RSLs were made possible through provision in the 1990 Broadcasting Act and they were designed as a way to allow groups that would not normally be heard broadcasting time, in particular community radio stations. But since community stations now have their own licences, and with the ability for groups to broadcast easily over the internet, their popularity is diminishing: only 432 licences were issued in 2007 compared to 475 the year before (Ofcom 2008a: 274).

One reason for this could be the fact that RSLs are expensive. Each application incurs a £400 fee, which is not normally refundable if the application is rejected, unless the reason is that there is no frequency available. On top of this a tariff is charged for every day of the licence, including any time used for testing and any days when there is no broadcasting. The tariff varies according to whether it is an AM or an FM frequency and the strength of the signal,[5] and must be paid before the licence is issued.

Generally RSLs are issued on a first-come-first-served basis but applications must be received at least six weeks before the proposed service goes on air, and will not be considered more than a year in advance. Usually only one RSL is allowed in any area at the same time and there is a gap between the end of one service and the beginning of another.

Under the 1990 Broadcasting Act (amended by the Communications Act 2003) certain groups and individuals are not allowed to be given licences. Those who are disqualified include local authorities, the BBC, the Welsh Authority, advertising agencies, and anyone convicted for unlicensed broadcasting offences in the previous five years (Ofcom 2008c: 3.8).

As this chapter has shown, radio is much more than a box in the corner of the living room, and increasingly it is becoming available for everyone to broadcast. In the following chapter we examine two of the ways that non-professional broadcasters can use to have their voice heard: community radio and podcasting.

3 You radio

....

I n an age when technological innovations make communicating with other people
easier than it has ever been before, it is easy to forget the magic of radio and the
effect it had on society. Before those early broadcasts in the 1920s the only way
to experience an event – be it a speech from the Prime Minister or a musical concert
– was to physically be there and with the limited transport available that was not an
easy option. Then radio came along and brought the sounds of the world into homes
across the country. By the 1930s it was possible to share the excitement of a football
match as it was going on without actually being there. Political speeches were heard
in living rooms across the country as they were being made. The varied regional
accents of the nation could be experienced without leaving your home. Thanks to
the wireless in the corner it was possible to have some experience of life beyond
your immediate community.

But paradoxically, as communication became easier the truly local level of life
got lost in a battle between radio stations for ever better listening figures that forced
managers to opt for the widest possible appeal at the expense of niche community
news. Local radio opened the airwaves to a wider range of voices, and innovations
like phone-ins meant that the occasional 'ordinary' person was heard, but
broadcasting was in the hands of professionals and the voices of minority groups
were often absent, as Antony Bellekom,[1] the managing editor of Radio 2 and 6 Music
explains:

> Historically radio was a linear exercise where the broadcaster sat in the centre
> of his world, showed off his stuff, and the job of the audience was to consume
> it unquestioningly. It was a single direction exercise. In the 70s the phone-in
> came along and . . . it moved from being a one-way process to being a two-way
> process where the listener could actually talk back and respond to what you
> were saying. That was second generation radio and it had its strengths and its
> weaknesses. I think we're now into a third age for radio.

This third age for radio makes broadcasting more accessible to everyone and restores the magic of the medium. With close to 200 community radio stations across the country, the airwaves are being opened up to previously silent groups of people, from isolated rural communities to young offenders trying to get their lives back on track. As Professor Anthony Everitt, who led an independent investigation into community radio in the UK, noted, 'Community-based broadcasting, where local people produce and present their own programmes, promises to be the most important new cultural development in the United Kingdom for many years' (Fogg *et al.* 2005: 10).

Even more revolutionary, the technology now exits for anyone with a computer and a microphone to make their own radio in the form of podcasts and send it out on the internet for anyone to hear. Broadcasting has opened its doors and now you can make your own radio either as part of a community station or on a laptop from the cosiness of your own kitchen.

This chapter looks at 'you radio' – radio created by non-traditional broadcasters who would formerly have been listeners with little chance to be heard by any audience – starting with an examination of the growth of community radio in the UK. Once regarded as backwater broadcasting, community radio in the twenty-first century is vibrant and exciting, helping to give an identity to previously disconnected groups of people across the country, and to unearth skills and talents in the 'ordinary' people who do it. The authors of *The Community Radio Toolkit* warn would-be broadcasters that community radio has 'the capacity to change your life' but they still think it is worthwhile:

> We think you should do it to express yourself and to fulfil yourself. To empower yourself and engage yourself. Do it for the memories, do it for the fun. Do it for the look on people's faces when you explain it to them and they say 'wow!'. Do it for the thrill of flying by your bootstraps, for the rawness, the immediacy, the buzz.
>
> (ibid.: 10)

Anyone involved in community radio will recognise the emotions conveyed in that quote, and there is no doubt that Andrew David, the managing editor of *Siren FM*, the community radio station profiled at the end of the section, agrees with them all.

Following the section on community radio there is an examination of podcasting, the new kid on the broadcasting block. Traditionalists may argue that this is not 'real' radio, but finding a stable definition for radio in this multi-platformed age is increasingly difficult, and because it has so many radiogenic qualities people like Trevor Dann,[2] the director of the Radio Academy, regard podcasts as just another delivery system for radio, and one that might well help attract new users:

I think radio's healthy but what we need to do is think how to drive new listeners to radio – particularly the younger generation. That's going to be done by making it available everywhere they are and by inventing some interesting new formats and concentrating on content rather than delivery.

As this chapter shows, both community radio and podcasting meet that challenge by producing innovative and engaging audio designed to captivate radio lovers and perhaps even those who until now felt that radio was not for them.

Community radio: the background

The struggle for community radio to be a 'third tier' of broadcasting alongside the BBC and commercial radio began in the 1980s and culminated in the Community Radio Order in 2004. This allowed community radio stations to be licensed by Ofcom for a period of five years, giving stations long term stability and the chance to plan for the future in a way they had never had before.

So what is community radio? In essence it is a radio station owned and operated by a local group for the benefit of the community it is addressing. Community radio is staffed by volunteers – although there may be some paid positions – and operated on a not-for-profit basis, which means any profits made by the station are put back into the business. But community radio is about a lot more than broadcasting. As detailed later, most stations have social goals that include providing access to the airwaves for under-represented groups, providing training and education for volunteers, and helping the audience to identify with their community and feel a part of it rather than feeling isolated and excluded.

It is widely acknowledged that the development of community radio in the UK lags far behind that of other countries. For example, Australia began licensing community stations in 1972, and in France there is a separate licence category for community stations that protects them from take-over by for-profit organisations, and a special fund based on a levy on the advertising revenue of commercial broadcasters provides revenue to support the stations. The reasons for the slow development of community radio in the UK are linked to the way broadcasting evolved in this country, and in particular the role of the BBC, which was the only legal source of radio in the UK until 1972. In 1967 the BBC started to open local radio stations that had a community-based ethos. These stations provided a voice for the community they served, giving access to the airwaves to local groups who otherwise would not be heard. Local radio was further broadened by the Broadcasting Act of 1972, which allowed for the creation of commercial radio, and despite its rocky start by 1980 there were nearly 30 independent local radio stations in the UK. Many of the new independent stations began life as community stations, but because there was no financial support for stations, and no legislation to prevent them being taken over by commercial groups, most of them found they had to choose between closing down or being bought out. At the same time independent stations began to have an impact on local BBC audience figures, and 'recognising the competing force of commercial radio stations [the BBC] began to align its local programming policies with the new independent stations thereby effectively severing the link with community development' (*Looking to the Future* 2006: 2).

This meant that by the 1980s radio in the UK was increasingly the reserve of professional broadcasters aiming to maximise their audience often to the exclusion of minority groups within their transmission area. Naturally enough this led to an increase in the number of unlicensed or 'pirate' radio stations, particularly in urban areas. While many of these stations were music based stations that differed from existing stations by playing 'alternative' music some stations had broader social and political aims catering for ethnic minorities or by allowing communities of interest to be in touch with each other. In 1977 an umbrella group, the Community Communications Group (ComCom) was formed to lobby for community based radio, and in 1983 the Community Radio Association was established with the aim of establishing a legal framework for community radio in the UK.

The growing interest in community radio eventually forced the government to agree to a community radio experiment, and in 1984 it was announced that the Home Office would grant community radio licences for 21 designated locations. The response was overwhelming with 271 applications received from across the country – 64 of those in the London area alone. However, faced with the difficult situation of selecting and monitoring the stations, along with intense lobbying from commercial broadcasters and backbench Conservative MPs, the experiment was abandoned in favour of further consultation about the future of local radio and arrangements for short term Special Event Licences.

The Broadcasting Act of 1990 made special event licences a reality. As well as introducing greater powers to prevent pirate broadcasting, the Act allowed for Restricted Service Licences (RSLs) to be granted for short term events and for low power broadcasts for designated institutions like hospitals, educational establishments and military bases. The RSLs were usually granted for periods of 28 days, and groups were limited to two periods a year, or one a year inside the London area. RSLs proved to be hugely popular not only with community radio groups, but also for festivals and events, and for trial broadcasts by groups bidding for FM licences as they became available in different areas. By the end of the 1990s over 2,000 RSLs had been awarded.

But while RSLs gave community radio groups the chance to broadcast legally they did not provide any security or allow for any long term social goals to be achieved. The Community Radio Association (now known as the Community Media Association or Commedia) argued that a new 'third tier' of radio, distinct from commercial broadcasting or the BBC was needed to make community radio viable, and the then licensing body, the Radio Authority lobbied the government to be allowed to give licences to 15 pilot community services, initially for a year but later extended.

In some ways the experiment that was called 'Access Radio' illustrates the different viewpoints held by those who are involved in community radio and those outside it. The term 'access radio' was primarily adopted because it was felt that existing radio services would be upset if it were implied that they do not provide a service for the communities in which they broadcast. In other words, local radio wanted communities to identify with it rather than a grassroots station. But those involved in community radio were never happy with the term access 'as it only describes at most fifty per cent of a community station's remit – to provide access to the airwaves' (Fogg *et al.* 2005: 12). Moreover, a report that compared the legal and regulatory frameworks for community radio in six countries – *Community Radio in a Global Context* by Eryl Price-Davies and Jo Tacchi – argued that the term access radio put the UK out of step with international radio institutions, and that existing radio services in the UK did not conform to internationally accepted definitions of community radio:

> Commercial stations are operated for the purpose of making profits, and have a primary responsibility to their shareholders in this respect. The BBC, funded by the licence fee, operates under clear public service guidelines, and these are by no means identical to the ethos of community radio. It is also evident from the research that it would be a mistake to equate 'localness' with 'community'.
>
> (2001:62)

In the event, the term 'access radio' was abandoned for the more familiar 'community radio', and under either name it was deemed a huge success. Professor Anthony Everitt was commissioned by the Radio Authority to produce an independent evaluation of the pilot scheme, and his report, *New Voices*, published in March 2003, recommended a third tier of radio for the UK alongside the BBC and commercial radio.

So after two decades of lobbying and overcoming obstacles and objections community radio became possible through the Communications Act 2003, and explicit provision for it was given through the Community Radio Order of 2004, which defines community radio in the following way:

1   It is a characteristic of community radio services that they are local services provided primarily:

  (a) for the good of members of the public, or of particular communities, and

  (b) in order to deliver social gain, rather than primarily for commercial reasons or for the financial or other material gain of the individuals involved in providing the service.

2   It is a characteristic of every community radio service that it is intended primarily to serve one or more communities (whether or not it also serves other members of the public).

3   It is a characteristic of every community radio service that the person providing the service:

(a) does not do so in order to make a financial profit by so doing, and

(b) uses any profit that is produced in the provision of the service wholly and exclusively for securing or improving the future provision of the service, or for the delivery of social gain to members of the public or the community that the service is intended to serve.

4   It is a characteristic of every community radio service that members of the community it is intended to serve are given opportunities to participate in the operation and management of the service.

5   It is a characteristic of every community radio service that, in respect of the provision of that service, the person providing the service makes himself accountable to the community that the service is intended to serve.

(History of Community Radio in the UK; Commedia)

As with a lot of formal definitions, the Community Radio Order makes community radio sound quite dull and worthy. But the reality is that community radio stations are vibrant hubs run by enthusiastic and talented people. Broadly speaking, community stations can be categorised as either communities of place, based on catering to everyone in the transmission area regardless of age, race creed or identity, and communities of interest, like religious groups, cultural groups and age-specific groups that target a particular group within a geographical area. But what all community stations have in common is that they give access to the airwaves to people who might not ordinarily be heard, and that they provide social gain to communities in the form of training, encouraging linguistic diversity, support for vulnerable members of the community, and even some economic impact at a local level.

The largest community radio group in the UK is Radio Regen in Manchester. This is a registered community development charity founded in 1999 with a mission to 'work with communities to enable them to use community radio to tackle disadvantage' (Fogg et al. 2005: 19). Its first step was to set up a Business and Technology Course (BTEC) accredited radio training course in collaboration with Manchester College of Arts and Technology (MANCAT) whose graduates were then able to set up and help to run temporary radio stations under RSLs. Radio Regen also organised the first Community FM conference in 2004, which brought together community broadcasters from across the country to share experience and skills with each other. The conference is now an annual event, and ultimately Radio Regen hopes to establish a national centre for community radio development. Along the way Radio

Regen has published the invaluable 'Community Radio Toolkit', and a linked website, that has a wealth of information to help people start community stations and advice for those already broadcasting.

Radio Regen firmly believes that community radio is '90 per cent community, ten per cent radio' (Fogg *et al.* 2005: 17) and it admits that this can sometimes cause a conflict between allowing access to the airwaves and the impact of the station on the community. But as part of the legislation that allowed the licensing of community radio, in order to get a licence stations must demonstrate that they are providing social gain:

> For better or worse, the UK community radio framework is now structured with the emphasis on social gain rather than access. This perhaps places a duty on stations themselves to remember the importance of access. Any community radio station worth its salt will try to get the most social gain while also offering access to voices which do not appear elsewhere on the airwaves.
>
> (Fogg *et al.* 2005: 18)

So what exactly is 'social gain'? According to the Community Radio Order of 2004 'social gain' is defined as:

(a) Provision of radio services to individuals who are otherwise underserved by such services;

(b) Facilitation of discussion and expression of opinion;

(c) Provision of education or training;

(d) Better understanding of the community and the strengthening of links within it.

Social gain may also include the achievement of other 'social objectives':

(a) Delivery of services provided by local authorities and other public services;

(b) Promotion of economic development and of social enterprises;

(c) Promotion of employment;

(d) Provision of opportunities for the gaining of work experience;

(e) Promotion of social inclusion;

(f) Promotion of cultural and linguistic diversity;

(g) Promotion of civic participation and volunteering.

(Quoted in ibid.: 17)

So far so worthy – but the best way to understand social gain is through real examples of the difference community radio can make to lives, and research done on the initial 'access radio' pilot stations by Anthony Everitt (2003 and 2003a), as well as a report from the Community Radio Sector of Ofcom (Goatley 2007) give many examples of this.

So while all community radio stations can be seen to provide 'radio services to individuals who are otherwise underserved', stations like Takeover Radio in Leicester, that enables children between the ages of 8 and 14 to run their own radio station with minimum adult supervision, gives a voice to a particularly neglected sector. The station runs a training scheme to build up skills in production and presenting for its young broadcasters, and is thought to attract around 72 per cent of young people in Leicester at some point (Goatley 2007). At the other end of the scale, Angel Radio based in Havant, serves older members of the community by only playing music recorded between 1900 and 1959. The station has produced CDs for local schools about the life and times of older people in an effort to encourage intergenerational understanding. 'Greater understanding here may make a difference in helping to prevent old people being neglected or in more extreme cases physically or mentally abused' (ibid.: 2005 12).

Several community stations also work directly with people who are traditionally on the margins of society thereby encouraging social inclusion. For example, Bradford Community Broadcasting (BCB) holds sessions with young offenders, a group not often heard from in mainstream media. Similarly, Down FM, which is situated within Down Patrick's College of Further and Higher Education in Northern Ireland, has a weekly session with 14- and 15-year-olds referred from local schools with behaviour problems. 'The students are from different religious backgrounds and quite often the College sessions represent the first occasion on which they have been required to work closely with people with differing religious beliefs' (ibid.: 12).

But getting the balance between programme production and the needs of the community can be difficult. Wythenshawe FM and ALL FM are two stations based in socially deprived areas of Manchester, which were originally set up with help from Radio Regen who have years of experience in producing successful RSLs. But as Radio Regen's director, Phil Korbel, explains, dealing with large numbers of volunteers brings its own pressures:

> We completely underestimated the need to resource and properly 'do' the community side of it. We didn't set up a radio station, we set up a community centre. By that I mean the needs of the volunteers were nothing to do with radio. We had to go with volunteers to court to stop them from being evicted. We had to advise them on personal issues that were messing up their heads and making them unwelcome in the station . . . We could have had the best programmes being made by a small group of skilled volunteers, but if they weren't representative, if we didn't have the whole range of the community involved, then it wouldn't be community radio.
>
> (Fogg *et al.* 2005:16)

The 'promotion of cultural and linguistic diversity' is another aim that several community stations embrace. Desi Radio based in Southall aims to raise awareness of the Punjabi language as a way to help intergenerational differences. 'This is important with the young people who are born here and who have a "hybrid" way of life quite different from that of their parents' (*Looking to the Future* 2006: 10). And as BCB in Bradford discovered, community radio can help transient and refugee populations feel less excluded. 'Bradford has seen large groups of Belarusian, Polish, Lithuanian, Iranian and African refugees move into the community and BCB has run a number of projects to cover their interests and information needs' (ibid.: 2005: 10) not least by broadcasting in twelve different languages.

At the other end of the scale, community radio can be a life-line for rural areas, providing them with access to information and services, helping to fight isolation, and giving the community, especially younger members, something to do. This is probably best illustrated in the Highlands of Scotland where a number of community stations have formed the Highlands and Islands Community Broadcasting Federation (HICBF). But other rural areas also use radio to help give their community a sense of identity, and the first five-year community radio licence was awarded to Forest of Dean Radio. Its founder, Roger Drury, explains why he set the station up:

> I moved here in 1986 and I soon had the feeling that in an area like this where people are so cut off, radio would be a very good medium. There's a real sense of people being isolated, even invisible. All the media we get comes from other places . . . Even the local press doesn't cover the whole Forest. Nothing was being produced in this area. There's a real need for identity in this area and the longer I lived here the more I felt it.
>
> (Fogg *et al.* 2005: 198)

But although the social gain aspect of community radio is important, it is clear that far from detracting from the quality of programming, this is encouraging stations to find innovative ways to combine the two. This includes many stations working with schools and colleges, collaborative work with local authorities, health organisations, and other advisory and charity groups. Every community station has examples of how they have helped individuals or groups, whether by simply providing a feel-good factor or by directly turning around the lives of volunteers by providing training and encouragement. But as Radio Regen points out:

> A community radio station must never become 'Spokesperson FM' with a succession of official voices telling us to eat up our greens. Community radio is by the people, for the people and of the people, and must always remain so.
>
> (ibid.: 2005: 17)

Of course running a radio station costs money, and there are strict regulations on how a community station can access or generate funding in order to prevent commercial organisations from gaining access to the airwaves 'through the back door' and to protect small commercial stations. So, for example, under the Community Radio Order of 2004 a community station cannot receive more than 50 per cent of its funding from any one source, and where advertising and sponsorship of a station is allowed,[3] no more than 50 per cent of its annual income can come from advertising and programme sponsorship. This means that in practice community stations tend to get their funding from a mixture of places including grants from a wide range of European, national, regional and local agencies, advertising, sponsorship and other commercial activities, and local fund raising. As the *Community Radio Toolkit* advises stations:

> As a general rule, you are unlikely to find many funders that will pay you simply to make community radio, but you will find funds that will pay you to do many of the things you need to do in order to make community radio – training, community development, youth work, tackling joblessness etc.
>
> (ibid.: 174)

However, following a recommendation from the follow-up report made by Professor Anthony Everitt (2003a), the department of Culture, Media and Sport established the Community Radio Fund in 2004 to help with the core running of stations. The fund is administered by Ofcom who undertook a consultation with various radio groups, including community stations, on the best way to allocate the £500,000 pot. Following this it was decided to appoint a three person Community Radio Fund Panel to consider applications from community radio stations, and allocate grants. The panel consists of Kevin Carey, the founder director of humanITy, a charity that focuses on Information and Communications Technologies and social inclusion, and a member of Ofcom's Content Board; Richard Hilton, the treasurer of the Community Media Association (CMA); and Thomas Prag, the Radio Authority's member for Scotland and chairman of its Access Radio pilot scheme, and a member of Ofcom's Advisory Committee for Scotland.

To qualify for a grant a station must have a full community radio licence – in other words those broadcasting on RSLs do not qualify. In the Community Radio Fund Guidance Notes (October 2006), Ofcom outlines what the grants can be used for:

> While some of the activities undertaken by a station such as training, may attract funding more easily than others types of activity, it is recognised that the essential core work involved in running a station is the most difficult for which to find funding for. This is what the Community Radio Fund has been set up to provide help for. These core functions might include, for example:
>
> •   management
> •   administration

- financial management & reporting
- fundraising to support the station (grants and commercial funding)
- community outreach
- volunteer organisation and support.

(Ofcom: October 2006)

There are two rounds of grant awards each year, and those awarded money have to report back to the Panel about how it has been spent to make sure that it is not being used inappropriately. There is no ceiling on how much stations can apply for, but the minimum grant is for £5,000, and Ofcom particularly encourages stations to enter joint bids, for example, to pay for a fund raiser who would work with more than one station in a particular region. The first round of grants was for 2005–6, when 17 eligible applications were received. All 17 stations were given an award, and in some cases more than one.

So it seems that community radio in the UK is now getting the support it needs to be effective, but there are many issues that still cause concern, not least how to attract an audience. As Anthony Everitt noted in his follow-up 'New Voices' report, 'While the actual listenership of the Access Radio pilot projects has not yet been comprehensively measured, there are anecdotal signs of a growing quality and depth of listening' (2003a: 20). These include responses from listeners to appeals for help, or to job adverts. However, increasingly community stations are getting involved in broadcasting live events, and this not only gives them publicity, but just as with traditional stations, it reinforces the station's link with the community. It is also important for stations to know their audience to help tailor their programmes, and to let public sector bodies giving them funding know who they are reaching.

But there is little doubt that community radio in the UK will continue to develop because of the positive impact it makes on those involved in it, whether as broadcasters or listeners. Its blend of innovative programming, training opportunities and social benefit to the community make an important contribution to broadcasting, and in many ways community radio is a good example of the aspirations of early radio enthusiasts. As the Community Radio Sector report *Looking to the Future* notes, 'Long life for the community radio sector cannot be guaranteed, but there is a sense that the stations are only just beginning to scratch the surface in terms of the issues that they help to influence or at least draw attention to' (2006: 28). The following profile of Siren FM, the community radio station for Lincoln, illustrates the challenges and successes experienced in the UK's third tier of broadcasting.

Siren FM

Siren FM is a community radio station with a difference because although it serves the people of Lincoln, and so could be described as a community of place station,

Figure 3.1
Andrew David, managing editor
of Siren FM

because it is based in the University of Lincoln it can also be seen as a community
of interest station because it is physically part of the university and so many students
take part in it. But for managing editor Andrew David the dual identity is what makes
Siren unique. 'One of the things the university here is proud of is its drive to take
the university to the community and the community to the university,' he says. 'They
use the radio station to help do that and there are signs that it's working.'

The station broadcasts 24 hours a day from purpose built studios in the front of
the block that houses the Media, Humanities and Technology faculty, which has
Media Production, Media Communication and the School of Journalism in it. But
even before the university built and equipped the £130,000 studios, the University
of Lincoln had broadcasts that involved people from outside the university. 'Siren's
grown out of a student online radio station that the university ran for six or seven
years,' Andrew explains. Once a year the online station would also apply for an RSL
to broadcast on FM. This was designed to coincide with the climax of a research
and development project by students on Media Production who trained groups of
schoolchildren from across Lincoln to make their own half-hour programmes.
'There's always been a station in Lincoln broadcasting either online or on air which
has had young people and students very much hands-on doing their own thing,' says
Andrew.

As well as building and equipping the studios, the University has agreed to pay for Andrew's position as managing editor. But despite this, Siren faces the same lack-of-cash problems that most community stations battle with, as Andrew explains:

> We're given a £10,000 annual operating budget to cover things like broken microphone clips that cost £40 each. I don't have the problems other community radio stations have of lighting, heating, rent and those sort of things. But in order to do any developmental work I have to fundraise using a whole range of funding bodies.
>
> One of the problems is because we're based in the university we're perceived as being cash and asset rich and we're not. We're asset rich because the studios I designed and which were built along BBC local radio lines are quite impressive. They're designed professionally to give presenters a taste of the real thing because my joy would be for presenters here to be poached by other radio stations.
>
> I'm delighted to have studios like this but the downside is that people won't give us money for programme making and that's essential. It takes cash to develop – putting equipment in or putting people in to train people in communities about how to make radio – it all costs money.

Nonetheless, *Siren* did manage to get sponsorship from the Co-op who are funding the post of a deputy manager whose specific remit is to involve schools and colleges in the area to get involved with the station and make their own programmes, maintaining the station's strong link with schools. 'On our grand opening day we had a primary school from Coleby and they had groups of five schoolchildren who went into the studio, did five minutes playing a tune and moved on,' says Andrew. 'It was fantastic – full of energy and enthusiasm. It may have been a bit rough and ready but it was real and that's the sort of work we're developing.'

Andrew is also proud of the work he has done with Lincoln's Polish community. 'I've been working with a group of young Polish people for about a year, teaching them interview techniques and that sort of thing,' he says. 'They did a fifteen minute all Polish speech programme two days after we went on air and we've now increased that to an hour a week – in Polish, for Polish and by Polish.'

But there is still a slight barrier between the townsfolk and the students, and getting the community to feel that Siren is their station despite it being part of the university is a real challenge, especially as during term time the airwaves are dominated by students. Lincoln nightclub DJ Gavin Roberts started on the station because one of his friends was a student at the university and asked him to help out on his show. The friend has since moved away, and now Gavin presents the lunchtime show every week day. 'I'd like to think that Siren helps the community,' he says:

It certainly provides a voice for community members should they choose to take it, and it's given me experience so it's helped me. A lot of people in the industry say community or hospital radio is really where you've got to start and I think this is where a lot of people cut their teeth and get the experience and knowledge to make that next step. I'm looking at my next step being a job on a commercial station.

Media Production student Sam Kirk, who does the drive-time show three days a week, says as well as getting invaluable broadcasting experience, the station allows him to meet a wide range of people. 'There are a lot of great people that come in to *Siren* from the community that we just wouldn't have met without the station – like the people from the Polish community,' he says. 'We also have a lot of school groups coming in and it's great to see young children take command of a studio desk.

I consider it a privilege to broadcast – not everyone can do it and not everyone wants to do it but I get great enjoyment doing it. We also have good links with the BBC in Lincoln and Lincs FM (the local commercial station) and that's led to me getting paid work at the BBC as a broadcast assistant.

Figure 3.2 Andrew David and a volunteer at Siren FM community radio

Having worked on the BBC since 1972, running a community station is a complete change for Andrew David. As well as dealing with day-to-day problems like replacing broken microphone clips and making sure presenters are there, he has to fund raise, devise strategy, do health and safety, and work with students and school children. 'It's madness but it's what community radio's all about,' he says.

> We could talk about community benefit – we could talk about improving communication skills, confidence – all that stuff. But if you talk to anyone who has broadcasting coursing through their veins, it's when they press the buttons and the needles move and you know you're live on air and that tingle is what I want people to get involved with. I want to myth-bust – stop them feeling it's all too difficult to do. I just want them to get out there and kick radio butt and give me some interesting radio.

Siren FM broadcasts on 107.3 FM in the Lincoln area and is available online at www.sirenonline.co.uk.

From the many to one

Where community radio is very much a team production, podcasting can be regarded as its opposite because it tends to be a solo production. A podcast is a piece of audio in MP3 format that has been downloaded from the internet and is played either through a computer or most commonly on an MP3 player. The term was first coined by *Guardian* journalist Ben Hammersley in 2004 (Berry 2006: 143) and comes from the words iPod and broadcast, and just a year later it was so ubiquitous that it was included in the *Oxford English Dictionary*. By 2008 podcasting was so popular that RAJAR commissioned a special survey into it and found that around 1.87 million people listen to at least one podcast a week. A typical podcast user subscribes to around three podcasts a week and spends almost an hour a week listening to them, with music and comedy the most popular genres. But despite their popularity, the survey found podcasts were not affecting live radio listening:

> Podcasting appears to have a positive effect on live radio listening – almost 18% say they now listen to more live radio since they started downloading Podcasts while only 8% say they listen to less, and 31% say they are now listening to radio programmes that they never used to listen to thanks to Podcasts.
>
> (RAJAR 2008a)

The survey also found that two-thirds of podcast users get their podcasts from iTunes, which offers 100,000 different podcasts from independent creators as well as established media bodies like the BBC and the *New York Times* – all for free.

One of the reasons that podcasts have taken root so quickly is that they are easy to access. Producers[4] simply upload their podcast onto the internet then subscribers sign up to have it delivered to their computers automatically every time there is a new episode. Although users are said to 'subscribe' to podcasts, all that means is they sign up for them – they do not cost anything to receive. Researcher Richard Berry (2006) describes the system as being similar to print subscriptions where you subscribe to a newspaper or magazine and it is delivered to your home for you to read when you want. With podcasts it is the same but done electronically, with the material delivered to your computer for you to access when you want. But as Andy Puleston,[5] content producer for Radio 1 Interactive explains, the term is still not universally understood:

> We stopped calling it podcasting on the [Radio 1] website because research tells us that not everyone knows what it is so we now refer to it as 'free downloads'. Our audience understand downloading and they understand the word 'free' because they don't really have any money yet because they're young. Anything that's free is a real plus in their book. That came out of some research we did and we changed it immediately and Huw Stephens' Unsigned podcast jumped 50% in a week just by referring to it as a free download and not a podcast. It went from 10,000 downloads to 15,000.

Whatever it is called, podcasting is an example of converged media bringing together audio, the internet and portable media devices like MP3 players. It came about when internet developer Dave Winer and American broadcaster Adam Curry wanted to share audio files across the net without having to visit individual sites. Winer developed RSS – Really Simple Syndication – which allows users to subscribe to content and view or download the website content from a single piece of software without revisiting the sites. Curry then wrote a simple program, which he posted on the internet for others to use and develop. As Richard Berry explains, this was key to the growth of podcasting:

> It is this open approach that has made Podcasting the rapidly adopted and popular medium it has been. No one person owns the technology and so it is free to listen and create content, thereby departing from the traditional model of 'gate-kept' media and production tools ... What Podcasting offers is a classic 'horizontal' media form: producers are consumers and consumers become producers and engage in conversations with each other.
>
> (2006: 145–6)

But is it radio?

According to researchers Gary Hudson and Sarah Rowlands 'A radio programme may be live, and a podcast cannot be live, but apart from that there is no difference'

(2007: 371). Indeed, if you compare the core elements of radio with those of podcasting they can be seen to be very similar. As Richard Berry points out, radio is an intimate medium that we tend to listen to on our own rather than in a group, and because it 'talks' to us and allows us to build pictures in our mind it becomes like a friend that we build up trust with and enjoy spending time with (2006: 148). Trevor Dann, director of the Radio Academy, agrees, saying, 'Radio is still a one-to-one communication medium, possibly even more so now with the arrival of podcasts and the iPod in your ears.'

Interestingly, in 2004 when podcasting was just beginning the radio industry became aware that there was a drop in the number of 15–25-year-olds listening to the radio, and they blamed a rise in the use of MP3 players – specifically iPods which were relatively new and had an iconic status. As a result, Ofcom commissioned a special study to find out what that age group wanted from radio, called *The iPod Generation.* They found that most young people resented radio playlists and preferred to listen to music they wanted to hear on their iPod, and they also liked the way iPod listening cocooned them from the outside world while they were commuting or shopping or just out walking. While the report made it clear that younger listeners were dissatisfied with radio's output at that time, it found that they did use radio for companionship, information and access to new music and interesting speech pro-grammes, but too often this sort of content was difficult to access easily. 'Ultimately . . . ease of use is key' (Ofcom 2004: 39).

Just two years later the media landscape had changed, podcasting was becoming established, and listening to radio via the internet was on the increase. In this climate the Radio Advertising Bureau commissioned a study into the complementary roles of radio and MP3 players called *Discovery and Recovery* (RAB 2006a), and far from finding that MP3 players were damaging to live radio, they found that the two technologies work well together. Their survey found that most people used the radio to discover new music, but turned to their MP3 player for recovering music they already knew and liked. More tellingly, the study found that most people used their MP3 players to 'escape' while they were doing mundane tasks like shopping or travelling, while they turned to their radio as a way of 'connecting' with the world – to get news, traffic and travel, and some companionship. As the survey puts it, radio is used 'to avoid boredom, to stave off feelings of isolation, to make the daily grind a bit more bearable, and so on. They use radio as a kind of personal climate controller for the soul' (ibid.: 8). So it could be said that podcasts are the best of both worlds providing connectivity through their radiogenic qualities, and allowing users to feel cocooned through the platform they are delivered on.

But while podcasts may be seen as a way to engage younger people with radio output, in the early days the podcasts being produced by broadcasters like the BBC were clearly aimed at an older audience. In early 2004 Virgin (now Absolute) Radio's 'Pete and Geoff Show' was the first daily podcast produced in this country, and this was followed later that year with a BBC trial, and the first regular programme they offered was Melvyn Bragg's 'In Our Time', which is a Radio 4 discussion programme that looks at the history of ideas including philosophy, history and science. All very interesting but hardly aimed at the 'iPod generation.' Nonetheless, by the end of a month it had been downloaded 70,000 times (Berry: 2006: 150).

There has also been a change in who makes podcasts since they first began. In the early days most podcasts were made by 'grassroots' producers. This included professional broadcasters like Adam Curry, the so-called 'podfather', whose *Daily Source Code* show website proclaims it to be 'the challenge to mainstream media and the voice of independent media' (www.dailysourcecode.com) . While Curry's podcasts are similar to traditional radio shows in some ways – with highly produced jingles mixed with music and DJ chat – because podcasts are not regulated he is free to talk about whatever he wants to and use swear words freely. One of the reasons for the popularity of his podcasts is that they act as an antidote to the rather bland fare available on mainstream radio in the US. Curry also began what became known as podsafe music – which is music where the artists have agreed to waive their royalties in return for free exposure. This added to the popularity of his podcasts that soon gained a cult following.

The whole point of early podcasts was to give a voice to anyone who could be bothered to make one and upload it. It does not require special equipment and there are hundreds of internet sites that can help novices to launch their podcasts. It is now possible to get podcasts from 'ordinary' people sharing their favourite recipes or gardening tips, or simply talking about their lives. Their appeal is very radiogenic: the intimacy of a voice talking directly to you. As Richard Berry (2006) notes, people tend to listen to radio on their own, and they have to actively engage with this 'blind' medium to create pictures in their head, and podcasting goes one step further:

> These characteristics of intimacy and blindness shared by Podcasts enable Podcasting to reach individuals and groups not normally found in mainstream radio, as the listener may feel the producer is 'one of them', a member of their community, whether defined by geography, ethnicity, culture or social group.
>
> (Berry: 2006: 148)

But it did not take long for mainstream media to realise that they could turn their products into podcasts, and while a few years ago the iTunes podcast chart featured people like Adam Curry and early grassroots podcasters Dawn and Drew (www.dawnanddrew.com), in July 2008 the top five listed on the UK site were established media presenters like Stephen Fry, Ricky Gervais, Russell Brand and Chris Moyles. One of the drawbacks at the moment (2008) is that podcasts are not able to use recorded music because of royalty restrictions, although the BBC is allowed to include 30 second clips, and increasingly bands are happy to waive their royalty rights in order to reach a wider audience. Industry insiders, however, think it is only a matter of time before this restriction is overcome. 'I think the rights issue will change and when it does that will open up a whole set of opportunities,' says Ben Cooper,[6] head of programmes at Radio 1.

Commercial radio in the UK also produces regular podcasts for its listeners. According to the Commercial Radio Audit of 2008 done by the RadioCentre 57 per cent of commercial radio stations make podcasts:

> The majority of podcasts are produced on a weekly basis, although 10% of stations provide daily updates. The larger the station, the more likely it is to produce non-live content, but smaller stations also continue to produce high quality podcasts
>
> (RadioCentre 2008: 19)

Examples of the sort of podcasts made by commercial stations include music from unsigned bands, local sport interviews and digital station Chill's 'Living a Chilled Life', which is designed to help listeners relax.

And radio stations are not the only people producing podcasts. The Virgin Atlantic airline has a series of podcast guides for its customers to various major destinations like New York, Shanghai and Cuba. NASA uses podcasts in its educational work with scientists giving talks on various topics – there was even a podcast from the Space shuttle in 2005. Various public service groups like the St John Ambulance, the Scottish Tourist Board and South Yorkshire police use podcasts to give out information. In politics, American politicians were quick to realise that they could reach voters through podcasts and George Bush started doing regular podcasts in 2005 giving a twenty-first-century spin to the hearthside radio talks of Franklin Roosevelt in the 1930s. Now most politicians use them. Google Gordon Brown + podcast and you will get over a million hits.

Education has also embraced podcasting. In 2004 Duke University in North Carolina gave out 16,250 iPods to new students to allow them to record lectures and download course content from the internet and to record themselves or interviews for projects. Some universities make lectures available as podcasts that students can listen again to so that while they are in the lecture they can listen to it rather than take notes, then later they can listen again. It is also a way for researchers to 'publish' their work and make it available to anyone who wants it.

And of course newspapers now all have podcasts covering every conceivable topic. Early podcasts from newspapers tended to be someone reading the content of that day's edition. But very quickly newspapers realised that they could attract people to their websites – thereby getting more hits and making them more attractive to advertisers – by featuring the actual interviews they use in their print edition, or by having guest celebrity podcasts like the ones done for *The Guardian* by comedian Ricky Gervais. Traditionalists may argue that because these audio snippets are not produced in a radio station they are not 'real' radio. But with the BBC's 'listen again' service, the ability of DAB radios to pause or record and store live broadcasts, and the rise of Personal Online Radio (see Chapter 2), the definition of 'real' radio is becoming blurred, and for many experts like the director of the Radio Academy Trevor Dann, podcasts are just another delivery system for radio, and the fact that they are so popular is good news for the industry:

> The great strength of the radio industry can be seen by the people who're doing it now – *The Guardian* for example make a lot of podcasts and they've joined the Radio Academy. *The Times, The FT, Sky* – lots of people we didn't think made radio are making radio they're just distributing it in a different way.

The way that radio has developed in the UK shows that one of its strengths is its ability to adapt to changing technology, and both community radio and podcasting have allowed the medium to reinvent itself so that it still has relevance to users. But while the platform for the delivery of radio may change, it still has key qualities that all broadcasters use to attract an audience, as the following chapter explores.

4 Radio style

E very radio station strives to achieve an identifiable style. Although the style may be similar to others within the same group – for example, BBC local radio or all Global radio stations – every station wants to be heard as offering an identifiable product that is different from other stations available in the area. The most obvious way a station declares its identity is through its choice of music (or lack of it) and the style of its presenters. But the identity of a station is also detectable in its jingles, its logo, the type of competitions it runs, and all its promotional material, as will be examined in more detail later in this chapter. In other words, a radio station is more than just its output: it is a set of attitudes and values that constitutes its brand.

The branding of radio stations and its importance within the industry reflects the increasing commodification of radio. Radio is not just a form of information and entertainment, it is a 'product' to be consumed by the audience through a range of platforms. As with all products it has to fulfil the basic requirements of the consumer. For example, in choosing which supermarket we shop in the basic requirement is that it stocks food and drink. The basic requirement we have for a radio station is that it provides information and entertainment. Beyond that, however, the brand we choose also says something about what is important to us: someone who shops in Aldi is more likely to be interested in the price of goods than someone who shops in Sainsbury's where the price is less important than the perceived quality of the goods. Similarly listeners to BBC 5 Live are more likely to be interested in news and sport than listeners to Classic FM whose taste is for light classical music. And just as supermarket shoppers can be won or lost by a range of features that have nothing to do with the basic service they provide – such as the quality of their trolleys or the attitude of the check-out staff – so too can listeners be won or lost by details like the frequency and style of their jingles or the chat from a particular presenter.

Branding, then, is a way of achieving a consistent identity for a radio station that is delivered through every part of its programming and promotions and as the number of stations available to audiences grows, the importance of having a distinct and attractive brand grows too. Even in the mid 1990s the number of radio stations easily available to most people in the UK was limited to a handful of national stations and two or three local stations. Now through DAB and other platforms there is a seemingly unending choice of stations, and what they all strive for is an identifiable brand that encourages listener loyalty: the station everyone wants to be part of because of the image it projects.

The importance of a brand image can be seen most clearly by looking at how a station changes its brand following a take-over, as happened when the Guardian Media Group (GMG) bought the Saga radio stations in spring 2007 and relaunched them as Smooth radio. Phil Dixon[1] was the managing director of *Saga* Radio for the Midlands, and became the managing director of *Smooth*. *Saga* was already a well established brand catering for the needs of over-50-year-olds, from holidays to insurance, before it went into radio. The regional radio stations it developed helped extend their brand:

> There was no doubt that Saga radio was a huge boost to the Saga business particularly in areas that had radio stations compared to areas where it didn't. They carried out research and found that through the halo effect – people listening to the station, liking it and deciding to buy a Saga product whether it be insurance or a holiday – actually added £5million to the bottom line which was a fantastic achievement.
>
> (Phil Dixon, managing director, Smooth Radio)

Because Saga was so well known, when the stations launched a lot of over 50s identified with the brand and tuned in creating an instant audience. But the strength of the brand also put some people off. 'There were quite a lot of listeners who did listen but wouldn't admit to listening simply because of the stigma of listening to what was perceived as an old person's radio station,' explains Phil.

The target audience for *Saga* radio was the over 50s and the target audience for Smooth is the over 40s so it was not a huge change, but simply changing the name would lose the 'old person's radio' image. Phil says that the weekend before the launch of Smooth the station virtually shut down in terms of speech and simply played the kind of music that the new station would be using. This was combined by a huge advertising campaign using bus backs, taxis and television commercials at peak times. Phil says the changeover was a success:

> We didn't particularly want people to think it was changing from Saga to Smooth – we just wanted to give the impression that this was a brand new radio station starting up. What we had to be careful about doing was not losing our Saga audience because if they suddenly decided 'I don't like this' and switched off we would have been in a bit of a mess. It was a balancing act really – making

sure the music wasn't too revolutionary – making it evolutionary rather than revolutionary.

As well as changing the station's playlist, GMG undertook a lot of market research into their audience's lifestyle, and Phil says this was replicated on air so that a younger brand was created, and everything in the station was made relevant to the new target audience. 'No matter what you do it has to be in keeping with the brand values throughout the business,' he says.

As we will see later in this chapter, all radio stations know the importance of their brand and spend a lot of effort getting it right. But before that it is important to consider the basic blocks that all radio stations have to deal with – the radio day.

The radio day

Radio output is not just a random selection of programmes or segments but a carefully considered blend of audio designed with a particular audience in mind. The basic idea is that radio output should somehow reflect the general mood and activities of listeners, so breakfast shows are bright and breezy to get the audience moving in the morning, and late-night shows are more intimate and reflective. In other words radio tries to complement the real-life activities of listeners with content that suits their needs and moods at a particular time of day, while at the same time providing a schedule that appears new every day. As Paddy Scannell notes:

> The effect of the temporal arrangements of radio and television is such as to pick out each day as *this* day, this day in particular, this day as its *own* day, caught up in its own immediacy with its own involvements and concerns. The huge investment of labour (care) that goes to produce the output of broadcasting delivers a service whose most generalised effect is to re-temporise time.
>
> (1996: 149)

To achieve this, broadcasters break the day into segments, or what Scannell calls 'zones', that match the daily life of most people, making the programmes 'appropriate to who in particular is available to listen at what time and in what circumstances' (ibid.: 1996: 150).

Of course it could be argued that because of podcasting, listen-again and the ability of some DAB radio sets to record programmes for playback later, these 'temporal arrangements' are less relevant than they used to be. Most overnight programmes are now listened to as downloads rather than live, and in the podcast for Chris Moyles' Radio 1 show for 25 July 2008, the breakfast show presenter jokingly blamed people who listen to the podcast only and not the live show for a half million drop in the RAJAR listening figures. Given that Moyles' podcast is regularly in the top five iTunes chart this is not something that will cause him to lose sleep but it does illustrate the fact that a show designed to help you kick-start the day is being listened to at other times and still getting a loyal audience. But the majority of radio listening is still done live, and for that reason the traditional radio day is still valid.

The breakfast show

The most important programme on most radio stations is its breakfast show. This is the time when most people listen to the radio, and as the station's flagship programme, it is used for a number of different purposes, the most obvious being to hook listeners into the station, hopefully for the rest of the day. The total audience for breakfast shows is around 14 million and according to Ofcom 'Breakfast time is the peak time for radio listening and a key time for the national radio stations. Their share at breakfast largely reflects their overall share in the radio market' (Ofcom 2008a: 288).

The breakfast show establishes the station's identity – whether it's a BBC or a commercial station, national or local, speech or music-based. This is done not only through the content of the actual show, but also by trailing programmes scheduled for later in the day. Presenter and deputy programme controller for 96 Trent FM, Mark Dennison,[2] says this is the best time for promoting other shows and the station itself:

Figure 4.1 Mark Dennison, presenter and deputy programme controller at 96 Trent FM

Breakfast is really your front door where you're trying to get people through and hopefully they like the music and style and know they can rely on us to play decent music while they're working or driving. They need to know that come 10 o'clock at night there will not be just a love-song show, but a relationship phone-in, or that there's fresh new music at seven o'clock at night. You need people to know that your station does all these different things, and without overtly being a sales man or woman, your job as a presenter is to highlight the station.

Many breakfast shows, whether speech- or music-based, are done by a team of presenters who each have a distinctive on-air personality. The main presenters on Radio 4's *Today* programme, for example, each have a different style of interviewing. John Humphrys is known for his aggressive, almost bullying approach, while the no less tenacious James Naughtie has a more reasoned way of dealing with interviewees that balances the programme. Similarly, Sheila Foggarty on 5 Live's breakfast show comes across as calm and in control to balance the excitable Nicky Campbell who regularly injects witty texts and emails into the show.

Interestingly, one station that bucks the trend for peak listening at breakfast is the gay and lesbian station Gaydar Radio, and that reflects the fact that although the station is available on DAB, the majority of its listeners access the station online.

Unlike most radio stations, Gaydar's peak audience is not at breakfast, but in the evening, coinciding with maximum traffic on the dating site that spawned it, gaydar.co.uk. The inescapable conclusion is that the internet is driving listening to the radio.

(Paul Robinson, *MediaGuardian*, 2 July 2007)

But for mainstream radio the breakfast show has a distinctive format no matter what its style. That means regular time-checks to keep people on course for getting out of the house, travel and traffic news to help them plan their journeys, and news of what has happened overnight as well as what is likely to happen for the rest of the day. It is generally assumed that most of the audience at breakfast tunes in for around 20 minutes, so a certain amount of repetition is allowed, especially on important news stories or particularly 'hot' show-biz gossip.

Daytime shows

The pace of programmes tends to slow down a little after the breakfast show as it is assumed that most people are where they need to be for the rest of the day by 9 or 10 am. Traditionally this zone of broadcasting was aimed at housewives, but it is now recognised that daytime radio is used by a wide variety of people, with many office workers tuning in online.

Figure 4.2 The studio at 96 Trent FM

Generally, daytime programming assumes a slightly more focused listener and tends to feature requests, competitions and phone-ins. The idea behind them is to provide what one listener describes as 'chewing gum for the brain' (Hargrave 2000: 12) – something to keep people involved and interested without too much effort.

Mark Dennison, who presents the morning show on 96 Trent FM, says although his show is generally aimed at people at work, he is aware that a lot of other listeners have no interest in work at all, and he has to cater for them and try to keep them coming back to the station. 'Radio listening has changed over the years. People grab ten minutes here and ten minutes there and it's our job to try to get them to listen for longer,' he says. 'So if they're not going to listen now for ten minutes more then come back at five o'clock and listen – or tonight, or tomorrow.'

Drive-time shows

The pace picks up again on most stations as the traditional working day comes to an end. Drive-time shows serve the same function as breakfast shows but in reverse. Their job is to provide information about traffic and travel to get people home from work, as well as news of what has happened during the day. Just as breakfast shows trail programmes on later in the day, drive-time acts as a bridge between daytime programmes and those on later in the evening.

Drive-time is also when a lot of what BBC Radio Nottingham editor Sophie Stewart[3] calls 'functional listeners' will tune in to get specific information, perhaps because they are stuck in a traffic jam, or because they need to know what the weather forecast is:

> Functional listeners would be younger people who come to us through need. They want to know what's going on . . . what the weather is . . . what the news is. They'll press that button to find out what they need and then they might go away again. The challenge is to bring that listener to the rest of the output. The emotional listeners tend to have a better relationship with our presenters and will love us more and want to stay with us. They tend to be people who're available to listen to us for longer. Both audiences are really important to us and we need to provide for both and not turn either audience off.

Evening and overnight shows

The audience for radio after 7 pm is generally very small for traditional listening with only an estimated 4 million listeners in total (Ofcom 2008a: 288). Traditionally this is the time when less mainstream programmes are aired. Often these are specialist music shows featuring country, jazz, dance or alternative music. The thinking behind this is that if you have a specialist interest you will make the effort to hear these shows, or where possible download them, and if you do not you will most likely not be listening at that time anyway.

Until a few years ago overnight slots were used by station managers to trial new presenters and new formats. Many mainstream broadcasters started their career on the overnight slot, and the legendary John Peel established a cult following with his late night alternative music show. But overnight shows are now nearly always networked programmes that help smaller stations save money, which they would argue means they can spend more on peak listening times.

Weekend shows

Weekend programmes reflect the fact that for most people this is leisure time so they tend to be more relaxed whatever the style of the station. Traditionally, sport featured prominently on a Saturday afternoon, although this is done in different ways.

Predictably, stations like talkSPORT and BBC 5 Live devote their entire Saturday afternoon to sport but many music-based stations feature match reports and goal updates during the football season (see Chapter 9 for more details about sports programming). Local radio also features sport on a Saturday afternoon often providing commentary on local teams with regular updates from other key games.

For many stations the audience on a Saturday afternoon is different to their weekday one, and as Sophie Stewart, the editor of BBC Radio Nottingham explains, this makes it a time to promote the rest of the station to try to turn 'functional listeners' into 'emotional listeners':

> Football's really important to us because it brings in a different audience that probably don't listen other than for sport on Saturday. The challenge is to bring that audience to the rest of the output. We use a lot of trails and promos for other programmes at that time. At half-time it's important we have a lot of messages but they have to be done in a proper way. The way we do a trail for (inclusion in) sport on Saturday is different to other times because we want to be promoting things that this different audience can access easily.

And even stations that recognise that their attraction on a Saturday afternoon is that they are free of sport tend to carry at least the results of local teams. They realise that even if their audience do not follow sport, they want to be kept up-to-date on local events.

The BBC brand

Although the BBC is publicly funded branding is still important to it for two main reasons. The first is that like all broadcasters the BBC needs to project an image of itself that will inspire loyalty in listeners. The second is that a strong brand image makes it easier for the corporation to sell its programmes abroad, earning money that can be used to supplement the licence fee.

The BBC brand is recognised worldwide as quality broadcasting. It is intimately linked to British society through its history and held up as an example of public service broadcasting (PBS) that attracts large audiences, unlike other parts of the world where PBS is often seen as 'worthy but dull'. Of course commercial radio in the UK also provides public service broadcasting, but because of its history the BBC is regarded by many as synonymous with PSB and fair and impartial broadcasting, as their Editorial Guidelines make clear:

> The BBC is committed to delivering the highest editorial and ethical standards in the provision of its programmes and services both in the UK and around the world. We seek to balance our rights to freedom of expression and information with our responsibilities, for example, to respect privacy and protect children.

> (BBC Editorial Guidelines 2008a)

In practice the BBC consists of a number of different brands all under the BBC umbrella, with each brand targeting a different, and at times overlapping, audience.

This makes it a formidable competitor and led to questions in the summer of 2008 about its use of the licence fee to secure high profile presenters like Jonathan Ross in the face of rival bids from commercial competitors (Gibson 2008a). But while the national and digital BBC stations each have their own identity within the BBC brand, BBC local radio has a consistent identity that inspires loyalty in its listeners, as the BBC Trust acknowledges:

> English local radio provides a highly valued service of local news and information for audiences who can sometimes feel underserved by the rest of the BBC. BBC English local radio attracts more than 7.5 million adults in an average week, although with some decline in reach over time. The service faces some difficult challenges – striving for broad appeal among the target audience of over 50s while maintaining distinctiveness within local markets and within the BBC radio portfolio.
>
> (BBC Annual Report 2006/07: 20)

BBC Radio Nottingham editor Sophie Stewart says their appeal is because they nurture their relationship with the audience. 'It's about being the local currency in the pub – people talking about what they heard on us,' she says. 'People come to us because they know that we'll be telling them about what's going on locally, and that we want to hear their stories and they can interact with us.'

Where the BBC does have a real advantage over commercial radio is in its ability to cross promote all of its services. Although the BBC does not carry commercial advertisements, it does advertise its own products, with BBC television promoting different radio stations, online and digital services and vice versa. They also have pan-BBC initiatives where all the services promote the same thing, and Sophie Stewart admits there are a lot of advantages to centralised initiatives:

> A good example was Springwatch, where there were things on TV, things on radio and to maximise the impact all BBC local stations did big outside broadcasts on the same day so network TV could promote us all at the same time and we all saw the benefit of that. So there are times when we all do the same things to maximise impact and that can be cross promoted across all our platforms.

But whether or not the BBC has an unfair advantage over its competitors, it undoubtedly has a very strong brand that has been built up over a long time. The challenge for commercial radio in the UK is to provide a brand that is more appealing.

The commercial radio brand

For a long time commercial radio in the UK was regarded as a poor relation of the BBC, mainly because it was associated with local broadcasting, which many people regarded as less important than national broadcasting. As Ofcom acknowledges 'The traditional radio policy in the UK, followed by successive legislation and regulators was for the BBC to be the focus of national broadcasting and commercial radio to be the focus of local broadcasting' (Ofcom 2007a: 1.5). More recently however, commercial radio has realised that its strength is in being local and identifying closely with the community they broadcast to while at the same time banding together so that stations can benefit from each other:

> Commercial Radio extends to the four corners of the United Kingdom; its presence is as strong in Norfolk as it is in Newcastle, similarly Belfast and the Borders. There are 36 Commercial Radio stations in Scotland, 17 in Wales and 10 in Northern Ireland. Consequently, Commercial Radio has a 75% share of local listening.
>
> (RadioCentre 2008: 10)

As mentioned earlier, the BBC has several different brands within its portfolio of radio stations, and the same can be said for commercial radio that operate under the umbrella of the RadioCentre who promote all commercial radio as being intrinsically linked to the local community. As Andrew Harrison, the chief executive of the RadioCentre notes:

> There are (also) some extraordinary stories of how, on a daily basis across the UK, the people who work in radio stations literally change their listeners' lives for the better. At a time when the role of the media is under increasing scrutiny, the trust that develops from such a close relationship is more important than ever. I take great heart from the fact that Commercial Radio matters to its listeners because listeners matter to Commercial Radio.
>
> (ibid.: 8)

Cynics might say that listeners are important because that is what stations' income is based upon, and while that is true, local commercial stations realise that their main competition is not other commercial stations but the BBC and in particular Radios 1 and 2 who target the same age range as the majority of commercial stations. As Mark Dennison from 96 Trent FM explains, even the music is similar. 'The fact is our music isn't a million miles away from what Radio 1 plays – it's not a million miles away from what Radio 2 plays,' he says. 'The difference between us is what you put between the songs and how you bring it to life.' And what commercial stations stress in their presenter chat is the fact that they are local and part of the community:

> 25 million adults tune into local Commercial Radio every week. They do so because the UK's local Commercial Radio stations place themselves at the heart

of community life, working with creativity and determination to provide the locally relevant programming which their listeners need and enjoy.

(RadioCentre 2008: 22)

One way stations involve themselves in their locality is by promoting community events, and according to the 2008 audit of 347 stations carried out by the Radio Centre, the average station broadcasts at least five 'What's On' segments a day (ibid.) They also get involved in raising money for local and national charities, with the 2008 audit showing that commercial radio supports 100,000 different charities:

> Charities recognise that the exposure they receive on Commercial Radio not only allows them to access a large audience free of charge, but also to interact with audiences that they may otherwise struggle to reach; in particular, the young and ethnic minorities. The value of the airtime that Commercial Radio donated to charitable causes last year would equal tens of millions of pounds.

(ibid.: 26)

With a record like that it is easy to see why commercial radio bosses get upset when the BBC claims to be the country's public service broadcaster. Across the country local commercial stations promote their communities and local talent, and of course this inspires loyalty in their listeners who feel that they are part of the station. But as Mark Dennison from 96 Trent FM admits, it is not entirely altruistic. 'If we're honest the other big reason for doing stuff with local bands is that when we've done bits before it was the best bit of marketing the station could get,' he says.

One of the big changes within commercial radio in more recent times is its willingness to band together to broadcast as a national network. One such event was in January 2005 when more than 200 stations took part in *UK Radio Aid*, when stations suspended their schedules to raise money for the children affected by the Asian tsunami:

> One single star-studded programme was broadcast to an estimated audience of over 20 million listeners, the biggest ever UK Commercial Radio audience. As well as appealing for listener donations, participating stations donated one day's profits. This one day of radio programming raised an incredible £3.3 million.

(ibid.: 32)

Stations also band together to promote music. For example, in May 2007, 250 commercial radio stations took part in 'UK Music Week', which had special programming promoting new and established UK musicians, and the following year 170 stations took part in the 2008 'Brits Radio Week' that had a series of interviews with Brit nominated musicians, and a three hour show on the night of the awards.

But commercial radio broadcasting as a national network goes against the strong local brand that stations have built up, and Trevor Dann, the director of the Radio Academy, says they need to be aware of why listeners choose local radio:

> I think if you're listening to local radio you've already made the decision that you don't want to listen to national radio. I think local radio at its best is done by local people, is responsive to the local community and is largely staffed by people who at the very least understand the area and largely live there.

The music

As previously mentioned, most radio stations in Britain are music-based, and the style of music each station plays is a crucial aspect of the station's identity. Even stations more orientated towards speech usually broadcast a few hours of music every week. In any event, the music played on most radio stations is not randomly selected by individual presenters or producers, but it is governed by a music policy that has been developed to appeal to the station's target audience. Managing editor of Radio 2 and 6 Music Antony Bellekom[4] says one reason the station is so popular is the range of music they play:

> There's a huge core of music – perhaps 12,000 songs – that we call upon on a regular basis, plus the play lists which feature new music coming through. A mid-range commercial station is probably playing no more than 500–600 tunes in a week. We would play something like 2,000 in a week so there's a breadth of music there. There's a lot of time and energy that goes into making that music work well.

But despite the popularity of music on radio, it is not the easy option it seems on the surface. In the first place it is very expensive. Every piece of music played must be logged and details sent to the Performing Rights Society (PRS) who then charge royalties on behalf of the performers. Another problem is that even if a piece of music is popular, in that it is selling well, it may not be compatible with the overall sound of the station, so each piece of music has to be given careful consideration to ensure it will not make listeners switch off. A third consideration is that the music needs to reflect the time of day and the sequence in which it is played, so that the programme flows from one item to another rather than lurching around. Mellow love songs, for example, are generally regarded as more appropriate to late-night shows, while more upbeat music is used in breakfast shows. For these reasons a carefully considered music policy is vital to every radio station.

Most music-based stations operate a playlist that is updated every week. The playlist determines what will be played and how often it will be played. At small independent stations this is compiled by the programme controller often in consultation with the head of music or other producers. Stations that are part of a group, however, tend to have a group music policy so that their aural brand is consistent across all of their stations. In any event the selection of music is not down to personal taste but is a professional judgement that takes into account a variety of factors including the station's target audience, how appropriate a track is to certain times of day, and increasingly how well it has scored in audience research.

All of the big radio groups undertake audience research about the music they play, and BBC local radio runs auditory tests from Birmingham to create the playlist for the 39 BBC local stations that have a standard ratio of 30 per cent music to 70 per cent speech.[5] The problem is that a lot of commercial radio stations target a similar audience – broadly speaking women between about 25 and 50 – so every station ends up with the same tunes scoring well in tests. According to radio presenter and journalist Martin Kelner 'the slavish adherence to this perceived wisdom' is making radio bland and predictable:

> Music programmers are crazy about testing. The way this works is that a group of people of a similar age and gender to the audience being targeted by the station are played 40 seconds of a series of songs, and asked to give them a score. Popular songs get played on the radio a lot.
>
> (Kelner 2008)

But BBC Radio Nottingham editor Sophie Stewart says even on speech-based stations, getting the music right is vitally important and it should not be left to individuals:

> Twenty years ago people picked their own music and one of my first jobs here was to choose the music. When you think that we agonise over three minutes of breakfast output – three minutes of music is just as important. I welcome the fact that it's tested but not everyone agrees with that. It's something we're all passionate about but our own passions need to be put on the back burner really.

The similar sound of many radio stations is also blamed on computerisation. The most widely used software package in commercial radio is the Selector system. This takes a pre-entered playlist and divides it by various categories like artist, title, tempo, and mood and provides a running order. The running order takes into account how often the piece should be played over the day, which tracks should be played at a particular time of day, and makes sure the tracks flow together well. The advantage to such a system for stations in a group is that it ensures a consistent sound effortlessly. It also gives every station an easy way to log what music has been played without filling out logging sheets and copyright returns.

'No music is ever selected genuinely by computer,' says Radio 2's Antony Bellekom. For him, the software used to programme Radio 2 is a tool for producers and presenters to use to make sure there are no clashes or repeats:

> We give our daytime programmes a musical running order based upon the rules that we set the computer to and the computer chooses the music, but we then ask each programme producer to look at that music, work out whether it's in the right order, and the presenter and the producer will have some free choices. So what they're given is not a finished dish – the lid's not coming off and there's this thing they have to serve at the table. They're given a bag of really interesting ingredients to which they can add more and add their skill to turn it into a compelling programme.

Sophie Stewart from BBC Radio Nottingham agrees, and adds that the computerised playlist gives the station a consistent sound:

> I don't ban people from using music outside the playlist because sometimes it's important to do so. It's about having trust and the reason you would do it is to illustrate a piece well or if you've got a local band coming in. You wouldn't play four minutes of a piece, you'd play enough to illustrate it without people turning off. We've got to be consistent. We've got our specialist music which is fantastic, but if anybody dipped in at any time of the day you'd want them to be having the same product. You don't want every show to be different because it's important that we don't day-part. So while we do allow some use of music to be illustrative, it's something that has to be thought about.

Of course it could be argued that music radio is losing its influence on the music market because so much new music is now launched on the internet bypassing big record companies and their promotions departments. But research by the group that represents commercial radio in the UK, the RadioCentre, found that 'radio remains the number one place to discover new music' (RadioCentre 2008: 44). Their research shows that 83 per cent of 15–19-year-olds and 87 per cent of 20–24-year-olds agree that radio gives them ideas of what songs to buy, and 71 per cent of listeners say they were introduced to a new artist through radio. 'As well being expert at knowing the perfect song to play at the right moment, stations expand their listeners' musical horizons with specialist and live music that challenges and educates, as well as entertains' (ibid.).

The report – which surveyed 347 commercial radio stations in the UK – adds that the majority of stations also have specialist music shows, which it defines as not being based on the station's playlist or listener requests. On average stations play 11 hours a week of specialist music, and in the London area this rises to 25 hours a week.

And commercial radio stations do not simply play well-known, international artists but instead strive to reflect their communities. 10% of stations play local bands on a daily basis and a further 25% do so weekly. Shows which champion local artists and bands include Mix 96's 'Live and Local', Brunel FM's 'The Frequency' and Wessex FM's 'Unplugged'. In fact 83% of Commercial Radio stations include local artists somewhere on their schedule. The liveliness of the Welsh music scene is reflected by the fact that 55% of Welsh stations play local bands and artists every week.

(RadioCentre 2008: 44)

Not to be left out, the BBC launched its own specialist music station – 6 Music – in 2002. The station is available on digital radio and online, and it was the first national music station to be launched by the BBC for 32 years. The station aims to play alternative music as well as live music sessions from the BBC archive such as the legendary 'Peel Sessions', and it also has studio sessions. 6 Music is the 'sister station' of Radio 2: they share the same studios and the same management team, which may seem strange given 6 Music's target audience of 25+, but Antony Bellekom the managing editor of both stations says:

When we talk about radio we tend to talk about it in demographic terms which I'm not sure actually works any more. I don't think that's how you would judge it. If that were purely the case how do Russell Brand and David Jacobs (both on Radio 2) co-exist? What is the demographic there? I think for 6 Music it's not a demographically led station although it has an identified target age range. I think it's much more about people's enthusiasms and their outlook and where 6 feels different from 2 is just how it treats the music. It's entirely music focused.

Having said that, Antony thinks there is a lot of symmetry between the two stations:

Radio 2 does have a long track record as a music station. It works very closely with the music industry, it records a lot of new artists and it puts on a lot of events and many of the things that Radio 2 does 6 Music does but in a different way. We need the relationship with the music industry and we need the relationship with the performers so there's an economy about having these relationships going on in the same building. The production team that came to us for 6 Music were really young, really savvy about digital. Some of them hadn't worked in radio, some had come from a web environment which was great. It was a melting pot. What Radio 2 gives them is the experience of older hands who can help shape programmes occasionally and what 6 Music does within the same building is the naughty young child teaching the older child some new tricks. It works very well together. They rub off on each other but they feel very different. You wouldn't mistake the two even when you have presenters shared. You'd say 'well that's Steve Lemacq doing his Radio 2 show. Here's Steve doing his 6 Music show'. There's a different feel to it.

As Mark Dennison of 96 Trent FM says 'Music is always going to be the biggest hot potato of all because everyone's a music expert just like everyone's a football manager.' But with digital stations in particular targeting niche audiences there is now a greater range of music available on radio, and as in the early days of broadcasting, a lot of it is live with 30 per cent of commercial radio stations playing live music at least once a month (RadioCentre 2008: 44). And despite so much music being available online, radio is still the main way for most people to hear new music. As the RadioCentre notes, 'Presenters remain a trusted musical guide. Consequently, radio continues to be the most vital driver for both discovering new music and stimulating music purchase' (ibid.).

Jingles and ads

Music also features heavily in jingles and commercials – either for products or other programmes – used on all radio stations, and just like recorded music they have to blend with the overall sound of the station and reinforce its image. Jingles in particular play a vital branding function: they are an aural encapsulation of the station's image. As Wilby and Conroy observe, 'Jingles are regarded as vital in fixing the station's role and identity within the consciousness of the listening community' (1994: 55).

Jingles are used to punctuate a programme or link from one item to another and they take various forms. A 'sting' can simply be a two-second burst of music used coming out of an ad break or as a pause between items. 'Lines' or 'station idents' that have music and use the station's name and how it can be heard (FM/ digital/ online) are used in a similar way. 'Sweepers' tend to be slightly longer and may have information about the show that is being broadcast.

As well as punctuating the programme, jingles teach listeners the name of the station, where it can be found, and what platform it is available on through constant repetition that embeds the information in listeners' consciousness. They also convey the style of the station instantly, and for this reason most stations have their jingles produced by specialist companies who work with the station's marketing department to produce jingles that encapsulate the ethos of the station.

'Trails' that are essentially adverts for other programmes are usually produced in-house because they are short-lived by definition, but careful consideration is given to the style and music used in these as well. The idea of a trail is to tempt people to listen perhaps at a time they would not normally do so, and a poorly produced advert would have the opposite effect.

Commercial radio also broadcasts paid-for advertisements and both the style of the advert and the scheduling have to be carefully considered to make sure the listener does not turn off. Advertisements essentially pay for commercial radio through the £600 million revenue they generate every year (Winter 2008: 30). As the commercial radio industry body the RadioCentre say in their *Introduction to Commercial Radio*, 'There are complex rules governing what products and services can be advertised on radio and what the advertiser can and cannot say in those advertisements' (2008: 15).[6] There are also certain categories of advertisements that have particular rules around them, for example, any adverts targeting children, as well as products like alcohol and medicines. These 'special categories' of adverts are approved by the Radio Advertising Clearance Centre which is now part of the RadioCentre:

> Once cleared centrally, a radio commercial can be transmitted on any station. However, each station's management still has the right to reject the advertisement or to impose scheduling restrictions and occasionally it can happen that a cleared commercial is still rejected by a station.
>
> (ibid.)

The biggest producer of radio adverts in the UK is the GCap Ideas Studio. They make 20,000 commercials a year and generate £3.75 million for the GCap group.[7] Phill Danks is head of the studio and he says getting the right ad for a station is vitally important:

> If a commercial turns listeners away from a station then we haven't got anybody to advertise to and the whole thing just spirals downwards, so we have to be sensitive to not only the simple 'that's annoying' but also be conscious of the brand of the station, how the station positions itself, who the station appeals to, and what their values are. All of this has to be borne in mind when we're creating a radio commercial.[8]

Phill explains that the ad writers are key in the production of advertisements. They usually meet with clients who want to advertise on radio to get an idea of what they want from their ad, and increasingly to consider other aspects like on-air promotional activity, sponsorship or online adverts. Phill explains how the process works:

> We have a centralised system for scripts and once it's been signed off it's just a case of flagging it up as something they now want to be produced. All of the producers pick up scripts for all over the group – it's not like any producer has responsibility for any particular station or region or writer. Upon picking up the scripts and seeing when it's due back the producer will have a read through to make sure they have in their heads an understanding of how it's going to sound before they even sit in the studio. The next thing is to ring the writer and talk

through in its entirety exactly what the writer's expecting. Clearly we ask for as much detail as possible written on the page but that can't replace a conversation. If the writer's lucky enough to have production on site – which in our case is only three of them – then more often than not they will be in with the producer on the process.

In normal circumstances the producer will then set about booking the voices. The first part of the process will normally be if there's any music involved and that gets laid down. If however it's a little more scene-based very often they'll lay down ambient background but not spot effects because the spot effect will normally depend on the voiceover's performance so that they fall at the correct places. So music and background ambience will be laid down ready for the voice because we like to give the voiceovers as much information as possible so they know what they're working with and so we can get the best performance from them.

Voiceovers pretty much exclusively these days work on ISDN, which means they can stay at home all day, which is a real boon for them. So we book in a time slot and arrange to link up with them.

During the link up the producer's role is to direct them, make sure it's good for time and the audio quality's correct. We always try to make sure we play the voiceovers the music because actually hearing the track is worth a thousand words of direction.

Once that's done it may be there's another voice that might have to interact with the first, in which case we play the first one down the line so they at least get a feeling of interaction. One of the drawbacks with ISDN, it must be said, is that realistically you can only have one line up at a time because there's about a third of a second delay, so if you have two lines you're not gaining much because the delay's quite off putting. Nonetheless we can play the first person with the spaces already built in for the interactions. We then get those interactions and shuffle it along the third of a second delay. The producer will listen to it and make sure it's meshing nicely, take the read and then start tidying up.

Then we're into mix down. Because of the way we've layered all the elements there's less to do than there otherwise would be because ideally you'd already have put everything in at around the right level, so it's now a case of being a balance engineer with the music against the voice against the sound effects being balanced.

At that point when it's mixed off we have systems whereby automatically the writer is emailed with a link through so they can listen to the audio immediately. If there's any subsequent changes they can ring the producer and say 'oh actually I had this in mind for the ending or the music to end this way'. About half the time there's a small tweak or revision made just to make sure the writer's completely happy and also to make sure that they're going to deliver to the client what they've promised. The writer is the pivotal point of contact.

When the writer's happy they'll then present to the client. Ideally they'd go and sit in front of them and play it and explain the process about why it sounds as it does. The worse case scenario is that we would send some kind of copy – but these days increasingly it's an emailed MP3. When the client is happy all the boxes are ticked and we can then load it to air and it's good to go.

Phill says a lot of thought is given to when ads are played, but it makes sense that the time of day a station has its peak of listeners is when the majority of ads will be used. That said, too many adverts in a row can put off listeners and in November 2005 the chief executive of GCap Ralph Bernard decided to limit adverts on Capital Radio to two in a row in an effort to gain more listeners and charge premium prices to advertisers. The policy cost the group £2.4 million in revenue (Milmo: 2006) and there was no clear evidence that it affected listening figures. The policy was reversed in February 2008. According to the Radio Advertising Bureau, radio has a very low rate of advertising avoidance compared to other media (www.rab.co.uk) perhaps because audiences in the UK have finally grown used to them and because they are highly produced they are less annoying. Phill Danks says the best ads are entertaining:

> What makes a good ad is engagement – and there are many ways of getting that engagement and I wouldn't say that one way is any better than another. Comedy is probably the most prevalent style, and a lot of commercials try to get that engagement by having an amusing situation, or they use celebrities and character voices and something that brings a smile and therefore feels like entertainment rather than a very dry selling message. Fundamentally they're all trying to do the same thing which is make people listen.

The visual side of radio

Although an aural medium, radio requires a visual identity to make its presence known and establish its identity, and increasingly stations advertise themselves in other media especially at the launch of a new station, as Phil Dixon explained earlier in this chapter. Stations also encourage their listeners to promote them with giveaway car and window stickers of the station's logo.

The purpose of a logo is to give the station a visual identity. Most give the station's name and frequency in the way that conveys the character of the station. For example, talkSPORT's logo makes it clear that although it is a talk station, the emphasis is on sport. The logo is also a way for stations within a group to be linked.

Figure 4.3 Logo for Siren FM

All BBC local stations, for example, have similar logos that give the brand BBC initials prominence, while the logos of stations in groups like GMG and Global only differ in the station name and frequency.

Another way stations give themselves a visual identity is through outside broadcasts (OBs). These can range from full-scale road shows where the station broadcasts live from shopping centres, factories, schools or special events, to the more low-key live links into programmes from a particular place. OBs are done using ISDN lines that produce broadcast quality audio simply. Many locations like council buildings, shopping centres and sports grounds already have ISDN points that can be plugged into using a shoebox-sized pack that is a codec – that converts analogue audio into digital form for transfer over ISDN – and a mixer combined. But Mark Dennison of 96 Trent FM says stations need to think through their reasons for going live:

> These days we go live for the right reasons. Years ago stations would do OBs just for the sake of it and I'd listen and think why are you doing the programme from a shop window? It was obvious the shop had paid to have the show but it was a presenter with a pair of headphones and a microphone and I couldn't see the point of it. If you're doing something like taking the radio station into the workplace it becomes interactive and that's more of a proposition. It makes the listener the focus instead of the presenter.

Most stations also have radio cars that are essentially mobile studios, but they are also a travelling advert for the station. 'When it comes to brand awareness using the radio car is really important,' says Sophie Stewart of BBC Radio Nottingham.

'One way we try to raise our profile is having the radio car out and about every morning for the breakfast show so we're seen and seen to be responsive.'

Station websites[9]

The most effective visual promotion that radio stations have is through their online presence. Surprisingly, most radio stations were slow to realise the value of their websites and it was only at the turn of this century that stations started to drive traffic through their websites as a way to promote their brand and offer listeners added extras. Now presenters regularly urge listeners to go to the website to take part in blogs and discussion groups, to email requests, enter competitions, and of course to listen online.

The importance of the internet to radio was underlined in February 2008 when GCap announced it was closing its digital radio stations The Jazz and Planet Rock and selling its stake in national digital radio operator Digital One to concentrate on FM and broadband platforms (Plunkett 2008a). Radio journalist Tim Humphrey[10] of Southern FM says a web presence for stations is vitally important. 'In many ways I think the actual station output will almost become an advert for the website,' he says.

Antony Bellekom, the managing editor of Radio 2 and 6 Music, agrees that the internet is important for all stations, but for digital only stations like 6 Music it is crucial:

> If there isn't a genuinely interesting online approach then the chances of getting the music out are not good because more people are going to listen through the internet than through digital radio certainly for the foreseeable future. For 6 Music its survival in a sense is largely predicated on how well it does online.

But while he thinks the situation is different for Radio 2 where the average age of listeners is around 50, and they may not be as comfortable with online as younger audiences, there is still a drive to get listeners to use the Radio 2 website:

> One comparison is how does a 50-year-old who uses Tesco now use Tesco online? Has it made their commitment to that retailer firmer as a consequence? Has it meant that they've bought there more often? Has it meant that they've been encouraged to buy things that they hadn't set out to buy? In a sense that's what you're trying to do with radio. You're trying to use it to encourage a bigger experience and to come regularly to it and to trust it and to bookmark it. So if you do your shopping through Tesco online and you buy your books from Amazon, if you want to hear some radio but you also want some information about music and events and a bit more insight, then we're trying to get people to bookmark Radio 2 in the same sort of way.

The website of a radio station provides an easy way for listeners to find out more about the station and its presenters. Local stations in particular can create a real bond with their audience by featuring photographs of listeners at local marathons or charity runs, school fetes or station sponsored events. It gives stations a dialogue with listeners through blogs and discussion boards, helping listeners to feel part of the station. 'We all like a good gossip and we've all got opinions on things so the website is a good forum for people to say what they think,' says Mark Dennison of 96 Trent FM.

On music stations in particular, the website is a way to provide more local information than could be easily delivered between tracks. Tim Humphrey from Southern FM says it is changing the way radio journalists work:

> One of the frustrations for a journalist, certainly on commercial radio, is that you'll do a fantastic three or four minute interview with someone and then you'll use two 10 second clips from it and you don't get it all on. How great it is now to be able to play that clip and say you'll be able to hear that interview in full online. That's very rewarding because you've done the interview and it's now being accessed in full. The figures prove that people do go to the bother of doing that.

As the section on emergency broadcasting shows (see Chapter 8), the website also comes into its own in keeping audiences informed about changing situations. Tim Humphrey cites the example of school strikes that took place in early 2008 when there were 100 schools in the area closed. 'There was absolutely no way we could read out a list of all 100 schools but we could put the list online and we had 60,000 hits in one day,' he says.

Concerts, campaigns and competitions

Another way for radio to connect with their audience and reinforce their brand is through promoting or sponsoring events. Music radio stations at both national and local level often sponsor concerts or festivals that reflect the music they play. The Proms, for example, are the highlight of BBC Radio 3's year and a prestigious way for the station to emphasise its commitment to classical music. Similarly stations that play mainstream chart music often sponsor summer music festivals featuring the acts they play year round. These events not only provide stations with live music that can be used in programmes, they also give them the chance to reach new listeners through the publicity given by other media.

Charity events and campaigns on radio also help stations to keep a high profile. Many local stations have running campaigns to support local charities, like Severn Sound's 'Money Mountain', and Radio 1's campaigns to tell their audience about

Figure 4.4 Hundreds of people turned out for BBC Radio Nottingham's campaign –
the Big Night Out

social issues like drug and alcohol abuse, sexual health and student finance are
justifiably renowned.

But campaigns need to be thought through carefully to make sure the cause is
one that is relevant to the audience and done in a style that is compatible with the
station's image. For example, BBC Radio Nottingham ran a campaign called the
'Big Night Out', which was in response to a text from a listener complaining that
they felt the city streets were not safe at night for older people. The station teamed
up with the City Council, restaurants and theatres and put on a special event to show
what was on offer. Editor Sophie Stewart says hundreds of listeners turned up on
the night and the event had a positive reaction from everyone involved. 'I think things
like that make people celebrate the city and make them think that their local radio
station helps them to celebrate the city,' she says. 'It makes people want to be part
of something.'

But judging from the profusion of high-profile competitions run by almost every
radio station in the country it seems that on-air contests are the most popular way
to hook listeners into the station. Virgin Radio (now Absolute Radio) created the
first 'radio millionaire' by giving away a million pounds on Christmas Eve 1999 as
the climax to a quiz held over the preceding months, and tickets for pop concerts
and film premieres are often used as prizes on music stations.

Competitions are a way for the station to interact with the audience and underpin
the values of their brand. Stations often use them to try to boost listening figures at

particular times of the day like early evening when listening traditionally drops off. That said, phone competitions became less popular with stations in 2008 following a series of irregularities uncovered by Ofcom. In June 2008 GCap (now Global), the owners of Capital Radio were fined a record £1.11 million regarding their 'Secret Sounds' competition, which ran on 30 of the group's stations in January 2007. An investigation by Ofcom found that entrants to the competition with the wrong answer were deliberately selected to go on air, prolonging the time the competition ran and encouraging more people to pay to enter (Plunkett 2008a: 27 June). A month later several BBC radio programmes were fined by Ofcom because of phone-in competitions where the winners were faked, including Liz Kershaw's 6 Music show, which faked winners on up to 17 occasions (Sweney and Holmwood 2008: 31 July).

As we have seen, branding a radio station is important to give a visual identity to an invisible service. But the most important part of any station is the people whose voices are heard by the audience – the presenters, newsreaders and reporters. Presenters in particular can inspire fierce loyalty in listeners and often take their audience with them when they change stations (Hargrave 2000: 15). They are literally the voice of the station, and the following chapter looks at the role of presenters on both talk- and music-based stations.

5 The voice of the station

....

W hether music- or speech-based, radio relies on the human voice to connect with its audience. As Andrew Crisell points out, 'radio is a "live" predominantly *personal* medium and unrelieved music with no visible human origination is dauntingly *im*personal' (1986: 65). In other words it is the voices of presenters and newsreaders that we most respond to on radio. They are the personification of radio providing a personality with which we identify and connect.

'All the best broadcasters are real,' says Trevor Dann[1] the director of the Radio Academy:

> The ones who generate a lot of adrenalin – who shout, who speak in a voice that's not quite their own – those are the ones who I think are not good at simple communication which is what a presenter should do. So don't worry about uhming and erring – don't worry about your accent – just be you because if you can't be you, you won't engage an audience because they'll know that you're a phoney.
>
> My general sense is that the broadcasters with longevity are the people you believe are real. Radio is still a one to one communication medium. It's not a shouty medium and it's not a heckling medium and it's not a medium for oratory – it's a medium for one-to-one conversation. If you're going to spend time in the company of a presenter or a DJ you're going to want to feel some warmth for them and that's going to come if they've developed some warmth for you.

From that description it is clear that the job of a presenter is much more than simply talking between the music. What they say and the way that they say it are important in reinforcing the station brand and establishing a relationship with the audience. There are various presentation styles and techniques but at root the role of the presenter is to be the station's representative to the audience and to represent the audience on air – to be 'just like us'. Obviously, different styles of radio require different skills from presenters, and this chapter examines the skills used by presenters on various stations.

Making the connection

One thing all experts agree on is that presenters have to connect with their audience and through that connection keep listeners coming back for more. 'We make a lot of fuss about being relatable to our audience,' says Mark Dennison[2] of 96 Trent FM:

> We try to appeal to 25–40-year-olds broadly who've got mortgages and kids and kids playing up. The more relatable you can be and the more local the better so we're reflecting real life. Even if you're not living that life, presenters have to understand it at least. I've heard presenters on other stations missing that trick and I think there's still a perception that the DJ has to be young and with-it and a little too cool for the room. From a commercial radio point of view we need to be as all-inclusive as we can and as real as we can.

Thankfully there is now a rich and varied range of regional accents on both local and national radio, but the advice of Elwyn Evans, a former head of the BBC's Radio Training Unit, is still pertinent. 'Don't put on any sort of act; your ordinary way of speaking is perfectly all right: if it weren't you wouldn't have been asked to broadcast' (1977: 20).

But being real and natural in front of a microphone in a studio is more difficult than it first seems and many stations spend a lot of time, especially with new staff, on voice training done either by senior staff or specialists brought in for training sessions.

Voices and scripts

The point of voice training is not to change the accent of presenters but to help them to use the full range of their voices so that what they say is clear and delivered in a relaxed and confident manner. Most voice trainers spend a lot of time teaching new broadcasters how to breathe deeply, using their diaphragm. This technique is useful for two reasons. The first is that deep breathing prevents any nervousness coming out in the voice, and the second is that it usually has the effect of lowering the voice to make it sound more resonant and authoritative. In order to breathe deeply more easily, many trainers recommend new broadcasters to stand in front of the microphone or at the very least to sit up straight. Sitting hunched over a microphone encourages shallow breathing that often makes the voice sound squeaky.

Figure 5.1 Broadcast voice coach Kate Lee

Another tip from voice trainers is to do a few mouth exercises before going on air to loosen the muscles and help prevent tripping over words. It is also useful to relax your shoulders so that there is no tension in your neck area that could constrict your breathing and so affect your voice.

Kate Lee[3] is a broadcast voice coach who works with radio stations across the country. She explains:

> Your voice is essentially breath, so how you breathe influences your voice. A natural sounding voice has no excess throat and muscle tension. The breath is supported by the lower breathing muscles in your abdomen, mainly your diaphragm. If your voice sounds thin, high pitched, harsh, nasal or shouty you probably have too much throat tension. If your voice sounds dull, flat, quiet, nervous or too deep you need to learn how to project using more breath.

Voice training can be very useful in helping broadcasters to realise the full potential of their voices but it is not a substitute for practice and an important part of practicing should be listening back to yourself. Only by listening to the way you sound to other people can you pick out when your voice has slipped into a monotone or when you sound inappropriately enthusiastic.

Voice training tips from Kate Lee

Exercise to strengthen your lower breathing muscles

- Put one hand on your upper chest and one hand on the base of your ribs.
- Breathe in slowly through your nose to the count of 3, at the same time push out your abdomen and don't allow your shoulders to rise. You should feel your rib cage swing out.
- Breathe out to the count of 6 through a controlled blow through your mouth.
- Eventually increase the out blow over 15 beats. This might take a week or so.
- You don't have to breathe like this all the time, but practising low breathing everyday (in bed, watching TV, on the train, at the computer) will improve your breathing equipment giving you better breath control.

Physicals and posture

Speaking is a physical activity and our voice is affected by how we use the rest of our body. To give our voice an open, relaxed quality we need to learn to be 'centred'. This means making your abdomen your power-house rather than forcing your upper chest and throat to do all the work. These exercises help.

Stand centred

Feet hip width apart. Feel the weight slightly on the balls of your feet. Take in a low-breath through your nose focusing on your lower abdomen. Hang your arms by your side and feel their weight pull your shoulders down. Head should feel gently balanced with chin parallel with the floor. Breathe out in a slow, controlled blow through the mouth.

Sit centred

Feet flat on the floor. Either sit half-way back on the chair or push the base of your spine into the back of the chair. In either position your back should be relaxed upright, head gently balanced with chin parallel with the floor.

Loosen-up

Devise yourself a daily routine to keep yourself loosened-up, particularly around your shoulders and neck area where tension likes to sit. Here's mine:

Shake out arms and hands, feet and legs
Stand centred

- With arms hanging loosely, swing to the right to look over your right shoulder then swing to the left. Allow arms to do their own thing.
- With arms dangling loosely hunch shoulders up to ears, hold for five beats then drop heavily.
- With arms hanging loosely circle shoulders slowly, forwards then back. Feel the tension being eased.

Voice range

An engaging speaker will use plenty of range in their voice. Here are a few simple exercises that will help you extend your range.

The three ranges

Very simply our voice uses three main areas for resonance – the head, throat and chest. Aim to speak through your 'magic triangle' range. Imagine drawing a triangle, the tip on your nose-bridge, the flat bit across the top of your chest. This is the range your voice should move through as you broadcast.

Here's an exercise that will help. Choose a note anywhere in your full range. Hum the note holding it on for 6 beats. Begin quietly, increase volume them back to quiet. Do half a dozen each session. Feel where the sound is made.

Voice glide

On an 'mmm' glide your voice through your range like a siren. Top to bottom, bottom to top. You may hear a croaky sound in the middle, this should eventually smooth. Do a few times a day (in the shower is a good time).

Relaxing a high pitch voice

We all have a different optimum (natural) pitch, but tension easily pushes the voice up a few notes. Raising the voice pitch is a quick fix to give the voice energy, but not a good one. If you think your voice is higher on air than your natural speaking voice you need to find and 'place' your voice before broadcasting. Say umm-hummm as if in agreement. This will indicate where your natural voice pitch sits. Then say 'Hello Harry' in the same voice pitch. Keep this note and speak on it to broadcast. You'll need to practise and it will require more breath power from your diaphragm muscle to replace the throat energy.

To brighten a flat, heavy voice

Again you need to learn to project with breath from your diaphragm. It will feel you are working much harder. It should! You'll get used to it.

To reduce jaw tension

As well as causing headaches, a tight jaw reduces mouth resonance, pushing the sound into the head. Three ways to relax the jaw are:
- Gently circle your chin three times one way then reverse. Feel the joint gently working. Then imagine you are chewing a toffee, again be gentle as the joint is delicate. Add appropriate mmmm sound as in delicious.
- Relax jaw by slightly gawping and massage the joint.
- Press your tongue tip against your hard palate – hard. Hold for five beats. Relax.

But as Elwyn Evans stresses, the most important aspect of broadcasting is to maintain the right attitude. 'The listener needs to feel that he is being spoken to personally. This can only happen if the broadcaster feels that he himself is talking personally, to a particular individual' (1977: 20). While this may be easier to achieve when presenters are not reading from a script, as on most music stations, it is also vital on speech-based programmes.

So why bother with scripts at all? Surely it would sound better if the presenter simply spoke about topics aided by a few key notes? In theory this might be better and some experienced broadcasters do just that, but in practice there are good reasons for scripting most speech-based programmes.

First of all a script takes some of the pressure off presenters doing live broadcasts. Presenters have enough pressure during a live programme – driving the desk, lining up inserts, dealing with studio guests or interviews down the line, watching the clock – without also having to speak coherently on a variety of topics off the top of their head. A script provides them with the reassurance that they know what they are going to say next so that they can concentrate on *how* they say it. Many broadcasters even write out their introduction to programmes: 'Good morning and welcome to the programme – I'm John Smith and today we're going to . . .' This is not because they do not know what their name is or what is in the programme, but because having it written down means they do not have to remember it so they can concentrate on their delivery of the words and make sure they flow well.

Scripts also ensure that an item is covered, fully, in a logical manner and to a set time. Just try to do a film review for exactly two minutes off the top of your head – the chances are you will either run out of time before you have covered all the points you want to make, or you will deal with the film for a minute and a half and have to waffle for thirty seconds. A script ensures the duration is accurate and that the review unfolds in an interesting way.

As will be dealt with in more detail below, writing for listeners is quite different to writing for readers. The tone of a broadcast script should be conversational and relaxed with verbs abbreviated to help the piece to flow. Sentences should be simple and short with the minimum amount of punctuation. Indeed some broadcasters prefer to write scripts as a series of phrases, arguing that very little conversation is in proper sentences and linked phrases give the script more 'life'. In any event the language used should be colloquial rather than formal with the facts spread evenly through the script. Most important of all, the presenter must be interested in what she or he is saying: without that there is no hope of engaging with listeners.

Take, for example, the following link into a live interview on BBC Radio 4's *Woman's Hour* presented by Jenni Murray on 8 August 2008:

Now at the beginning of 2006 the novelist Lia Mills went to see her dentist. She was worried about a painful lump in her cheek. Well – it turned out to be mouth cancer and she needed radical surgery and reconstruction of her jaw.

Throughout the experience she kept a journal which has been published as a book called 'In Your Face' and she joins us from Dublin . . . Lia – what symptoms did you first notice?

The tone of this link is conversational with short sentences that allow the listeners to take in the information easily. The use of linking words like 'now' and 'well' draws the listener into the piece, and help the introduction to sound less formal. Although this is only 25 seconds long, it gives enough information to interest listeners without overwhelming them, and the first question gets straight to the point. This is the sort of link that programmes like *Woman's Hour* do extremely well. There is no superfluous information and the style is relaxed and chatty as if the presenter is speaking directly to you.

Writing for radio[4]

The key principle of writing for radio is that it is not being written to be read but to be *spoken* – often by someone other than the writer – and *heard*. Putting this into practice is more difficult than it seems because writing as we speak involves abandoning many of the 'rules' of writing that have been taught to us from an early age. We need to concentrate on how the piece *sounds* rather than how it looks on the page.

As Robert McLeish points out, 'writing words on paper is a very crude form of storage' (1988: 48), because while written words convey information they do not convey the full meaning. What should be emphasised? Where do the pauses come? What speed should it be read at? What is the tone of the piece? For example, the simple statement, 'I am going out now' can convey different meanings depending on the way it is said. '*I* am going out now'; 'I *am* going out now'; 'I am going *out* now' and so on. If you read these statements aloud you will hear how each conveys a subtly different meaning.

As previously mentioned, one of the strengths of radio is that it speaks to individuals, and the way it does this is by *talking* to them, not *reading* to them. This means that whatever is said on the radio – whether it is a link in a magazine programme, a film review, or even a voice piece in the news – needs to sound as if it is coming from the mind of the speaker – almost like part of a conversation – rather than something that is being read. While underlining certain words and presentation skills can aid this process, the way the script is written is also important.

In order to make your scripting conversational a good starting place is to visualise the person you are talking to – a typical member of the station's audience. Although the audience may be older or younger than you, essentially they will be on the same level as you, so there is no need to change your normal language to try to impress them with your vocabulary, or to take a simplistic approach that might come over as patronising. In writing a film review for a BBC local radio audience, for example, think about how you would tell your mother about it. In reviewing a gig for an ILR station, think about how you would tell your friend about the band.

Visualising who you are speaking to also helps to remind you that although what you are saying is being heard by a mass audience, each member of the audience receives your words as an individual. As Guy Starkey points out, 'The relative intimacy of radio – which is often listened to by individuals working, travelling or otherwise occupied on their own – allows the broadcaster to communicate with each one as if addressing them personally' (2004: 69). One way to connect with the individual is to include them in what you are saying. This can be done by referring to 'us' and 'we' rather than the much more impersonal 'listeners' or 'the audience'. For example, you might start a film review by saying 'Most of us enjoy a night out at the pictures' or a report about Christmas shopping with the words, 'We all know Christmas is an expensive time'. This immediately includes the listeners and helps them to relate to the story.

Once you know who you are talking to, the next thing is to work out what you are going to say. Although writing for radio is conversational, unlike a conversation there is no chance for the person listening to you to ask you to repeat what you have just said, or ask questions about something they have not quite understood. For these reasons it is important that your script is logical and progresses at an even pace with the information spread throughout the script rather than bunched in the middle. Work out what points you want to make then see how they all connect together in a way that makes sense.

Your first sentence is vitally important. This is the 'hook' that will grab the attention of the listener. There is no need to ease into the topic gradually. The first sentence needs to be intriguing but relevant, and be backed by a second sentence that gives more detail about what you are talking about. Avoid packing too much information into one sentence: a rough rule of thumb is to have one idea per sentence, which logically links into the next sentence. Try to remember that you are not just giving information – you are telling a story and need to keep the audience with you every step of the way.

The best scripts allow listeners to visualise what you are describing. Too many facts bunched together will cause confusion rather than pictures, so space the information out and provide concrete images that explain facts. For example, instead of giving the physical dimensions describe it in relation to the size of a football pitch, which is something most people can visualise. BBC journalist Simon Ford has some useful comparisons to help (see page 93).

You also need to be careful with the use of abbreviations and acronyms. Only a few are well known enough to be understood straight away by most people. So, while it is fine to refer to the BBC or Aids without spelling them out, others should be explained the first time you use them. For example, the first time you refer to the National Union of Journalists you could say 'the journalists' union, the NUJ . . .' so

The height of Big Ben	320 feet
The length/width/area of a soccer pitch	Length : minimum 90m (100 yards) Maximum 120m (130 yards) Width: minimum 45m (50 yards) Maximum 90m (100 yards)
The area of a tennis court	2,808 square feet or 260,872 square metres
The distance round the globe	24,900.8 miles (40,074 kilometres)
The height of Mount Everest	29,035 feet (8,850 metres)
The age of the pyramids	5,200 years
	(Ford: 2007: 93)

that the next time you use NUJ everyone knows what it is. Similarly, the first time you mention a person in your script, you need to explain who they are or give their position. Never assume that just because *you* know who they are, everyone else will. For example, you might say 'film director Tim Burton' or 'Tim Fullbright, the leader of the City Council'.

The language you use in writing for radio can also help it to sound more conversational. Use everyday language and avoid literary or academic words. Keep the language simple and direct and make sure you translate jargon. For example, in describing a new sports complex it is better to say 'the complex was built on an old children's playground' rather than 'the complex was erected on a former recreation area for children'.

Your language needs to be colloquial – which is not the same as sloppy or slang. It needs to sound like ordinary speech. This means abbreviating verbs where you can, so 'it is' becomes 'it's' and 'would not' becomes 'wouldn't'. Should you need special emphasis you can revert to the full form: 'Gordon Brown says he will not back down' rather than 'Gordon Brown says he won't back down'.

Speech also tends to use shorter sentences that have a simple construction. Short sentences are both easier to understand and easier to read. For example, 'The dress previously owned by the pop star Madonna, and designed by Stella McCartney, was destroyed in the fire' is more difficult to take in than 'The dress destroyed in the fire used to belong to pop star Madonna. It was designed by Stella McCartney', and it also *sounds* more natural.

The best way to make sure you are writing as you talk is to speak the story out loud and write down what you say. You can always tidy your script up to make it more polished after you have finished it, and this is more effective than writing it then making changes to make it sound more conversational. Reading your script out loud also helps you to avoid tongue twisters or words you might find awkward to pronounce. It is not enough to read it to yourself: scripts read in your head always sound perfect.

Scripts should be set out as clearly as possible. Use a large typeface, double spaced, so that any small alterations can be made without rendering the piece unreadable. Sentences should not run over to the next page, and paragraphs should not be split between pages. Many stations now read scripts from the screen rather than using hard copy, and this advice is just as important for on-screen as for paper versions.

A lot of what you write will be read by someone else, so to help them get the exact sense of what you have written you need to use clear punctuation. Do not write scripts in upper case only. This makes it more difficult for the reader to see when a new sentence begins or when a 'proper' name is used. As a general rule, less punctuation is better. It is easier to interpret a dash than a semi-colon, and a sentence punctuated by a series of commas is usually better broken down into several shorter sentences.

Dealing with numbers in scripts can be tricky and the safest way is to write them out in full – especially those over six figures. It is very easy for the eye to miss a zero, so rather than 'more than £2,000,000' write 'more than two million pounds'. BBC journalist Simon Ford admits that one of the challenges of writing for radio is how to express large sums of money in terms the audience can visualise. 'An effective technique for communicating unusually large numbers is to compare them with commonplace ones: the price of a loaf of bread or a pint of beer' he says (Ford 2007: 94). It is also easier to understand if numbers are rounded up or down at the start of a script, and more detail given further down. For example, say 'Nearly half of us go abroad on holiday every year' rather than 'forty-eight point seven per cent of the population go abroad on holiday every year'.

If the piece you are writing is complex do not be afraid to repeat ideas but find a different way of expressing them. For example, you can use phrases like 'what that means is . . .' or 'in practice that means . . .' and then give a fuller explanation of the point.

Finally, a script should have a definite ending rather than just stop. Just as the first sentence needs to catch the listener's interest, the last sentence should give them food for thought. This can be in the form of a provocative question or a statement that concisely sums up the item. Ideally the end of a piece should refer back to the beginning in some way to remind listeners of all that has been said. What should be avoided are clichéd phrases like 'only time will tell' that leave the piece hanging in the air. The beginning and end of a script are the most important parts of it and also the parts most people remember.

The 'good' presenter

There are probably as many definitions of a 'good' presenter as there are radio stations. Each station wants presenters that reinforce its brand values: in other words, the personality they project should connect with that of the station's target audience. Piers Bradford,[5] an executive producer at Radio 1, says that connection is what keeps the audience coming back for more:

> People see presenters not only as massive stars but also as kind of their friend. And this massive star is telling them how they've got a leak in their floor and their central heating isn't working and actually their life's a nightmare and their flat mate's doing their head in . . . This stuff happens to Radio 1 presenters as well as our audience, and just having those sort of stories means people connect to what we're saying. I think that authentic voice that our presenters have is absolutely key and it's one of the things that distinguishes us from our competitors. The fact that we're relatively speech heavy kind of reflects that as well. We're not just a music station – it's hopefully entertainment.

And those skills are valued across all radio stations. Like all BBC local radio stations, Radio Nottingham targets an older audience and editor Sophie Stewart[6] says the audience has to identify with the presenters:

> The audience needs to feel that presenters have got life experience, that they're warm and they care and that they know the patch – even if they're not from the patch – they don't have to be but they need to have a knowledge of the patch – and that they embrace listeners and are interested and want to hear more, and that you can go to them and feel like you're in a safe pair of hands.

Although it may sound as if presenters simply open the microphone and chatter, in fact a lot of preparation goes into every radio show whether it is speech or music-based:

> I do my preparation in two ways – like having two bits of paper I suppose. On one is a list of timeless things that I've noticed or daft things the kids have said or things that have happened that I can use on air on any day. And then there's another sheet which is purely things for today – something in the news or something happening that's very time specific. Usually you end up with two long sheets of material that you've prepared and you use a fraction of that.
>
> (Mark Dennison, 96 Trent FM)

The preparation for a radio programme is vital and presenters spend a lot of time keeping up-to-date with what is going on not only in the news, but in the music

Figure 5.2 Mark Dennison on air at 96 Trent FM

industry, sport, and even on soaps and other popular television programmes. On commercial stations the presenters also have to fit in adverts and promotional messages at specific times, and quite often the format of the programme means there are only a couple of slots every hour where presenters can use their own material.

On national and larger commercial stations most key shows are made with the help of a producer. It is their job to structure the programme, to arrange guests, organise appropriate competitions, think of special features and make sure the whole thing flows together. The managing editor of BBC Radio 2 and 6 Music Antony Bellekom[7] says being a producer is the most creative place to be in radio and it is also the role with the most responsibility:

> In terms of the BBC, editorially it's not the presenter who's responsible for that programme, it's the producer. If something goes wrong on air, if there's an editorial error – it doesn't matter if it was said in a live programme by the presenter – it's the producer's responsibility. So there's a huge responsibility but with it comes a fantastic creative opportunity to take these raw ingredients and make something special.

So although the presenters are the front line of a radio station there is a whole team behind programmes. Usually the programme controller, producer or editor will have 'post-mortem' sessions after shows to see what worked well and what could be improved. As the public face of the station presenters are also expected to take part in station promotions, visiting schools or universities, opening fetes and meeting groups in the community. On smaller stations presenters are also expected to contribute to other programmes, preparing community news or making packages.

It is the team-work aspect of radio that appeals to many people, and as the following profile of Radio 1 shows, what comes out of the radio is only part of what makes a successful radio station.

Behind the mike at Radio 1

Although Radio 1 celebrated its fortieth birthday in September 2007 it is still the leading radio station in the UK for young people. As Ben Cooper,[8] Radio 1's head of programmes says, 'The target audience used to be 15- to 25-year-olds but I think more realistically it's 10- to 29-year-olds.' As we discussed earlier, this age group is notoriously difficult to engage with, not least because of competition from other media, as Ben Cooper explains:

> I don't think our main competition comes from other radio, I think it's things that young people do with their time – that's our main competitor. People talk about whether it's certain radio stations or TV channels – but it's everything. If you're a young person you've got a very busy life: do you play games, do you watch TV, do you surf the net, podcast, go on MySpace? A lot of them try to do quite a few of those things all at once and it's about making sure you're part of their lives and relevant to their lives. So you've got to produce your content in a way that they can consume it and in a way that they'll like it.

So it is no longer enough for the radio station to broadcast on FM and expect the audience to obediently tune in at a time set by broadcasters. 'Now we have to put content in front of them wherever they may be,' says James Wood,[9] head of marketing for Radio 1 and 1 Xtra. 'What we had to do was introduce Radio 1 as a visual brand. We had to look at where young people were engaging and playing with content, and then put ourselves in front of them.'

As Andy Puleston,[10] content producer for Radio 1 Interactive puts it, 'Sounding good isn't enough any more – we have to look how we sound and the website is the first point of contact in visualising Radio 1 as a brand.' As with most radio websites, the Radio 1 website carries information about the station, its programmes, the DJs, and the music. But for the Radio 1 the website is seen as vital in reaching their audience:

> The younger end of our 10–29 audience have grown up knowing fast internet access. They've grown up knowing how to use and share media when they

want it. You look at things like MSN messaging, YouTube and MySpace and they're pretty much the passwords into that world and they're what they're used to using all the time, and use probably in a different way to the majority of people over the age of 21 or 22 and we have to make sure that our content lives in that world.

(Ben Cooper, Radio 1 head of programmes)

So the website provides added extras to the Radio 1 audience, but it also helps to shape programming by showing what is popular in a far more exact way than FM's RAJAR figures can do by counting the number of people accessing particular pages and how long they stay on that page. As Andy Puleston explains, the starting point for someone accessing the Radio 1 website may be music, but they have to offer a lot more than new music to keep up with the competition:

The content that sits around the music is what makes us broadcasters. Radio 1 is not a jukebox service – we don't just play music. Radio 1 is the bits between the music – that's what gives us our strength in the market place. We're lucky enough to have a legacy which means we attract the biggest talent. In radio terms we're very strong when it comes to supplying music. But we've got a competitive environment that's beyond belief sometimes. The Radio 1 website is in competition with things like My Space, Last FM, iTunes, Limewire – this huge brand soup of music providers and content suppliers.

You've got young people who use music to define who they are in a way. I think up until the age of about 24 or 25 you don't have a career to speak of, you don't really have any assets, you don't tend to have a lot of money and you tend to identify who you are through the music you listen to and that tends to dictate the way you dress, who you hang out with, where you go, what you say . . . so the conversation around music is almost as important as the music itself sometimes. It's about facilitating a dialogue between the audience and the talent at the station and if it's done properly the whole thing becomes a seamless conversation. We use the technology to get listener interaction and feedback and steer, that then affects the broadcast and goes back into the conversation to find out what the next move should be.

We learn how to cover events and what people like by looking at the stats from previous events and looking at what was looked at most, or we look at what was looked at least and drop stuff, so we tend to shape how we cover events by basing it on the figures.

And Radio 1 is also aware that it is important to reach the audience on as many different platforms as possible, so as well as having video clips on their own site, they regularly post clips on social network sites like YouTube, MySpace, Facebook, iTunes.

The term being bandied around at the moment is atomisation. It's about chunking stuff up into 5 to 20 minute or half hour bits and just pushing that out as far as possible using all these websites we've spoken about (MySpace, Beebo, iTunes, Facebook) to pump our stuff out that way and not just through the transmitters.

If you can get someone to consume five or ten minutes of your content away from bbc.co.uk and away from FM you've still got them. It doesn't matter where you are and how you've arrived in front of them you've still done it. Just because something's not being consumed on our site and we don't get the click on bbc.co.uk shouldn't matter. When we do anything that's content produced for third party sites that's artist specific it always carries the logo and a track back to our site if people want the parent content, as it were.

The biggest currency is attention – that's all people in the media are after – people's attention. Keeping and maintaining the attention of their audience and not letting them go once they get it.

(Andy Puleston, content producer,
Radio 1 Interactive)

Reaching the audience

But the bottom line for Radio 1, as for all radio stations, is knowing the audience – and that is something the station spends a lot of time and effort trying to get right. Piers Bradford is an executive producer for Radio 1 Creative Projects, which are the features the station uses throughout the year. Some of these are big events that they know will instantly be of interest to their audience like the 2006 World Cup or festivals like Glastonbury. Others might be Radio 1 events like the Big Weekend. But some of the most successful projects come from ideas thought up and developed by producers, like the Big Movie Weekend that ran on the eve of the Oscars in 2007. For that day the schedules were scrapped and instead six Radio 1 DJs did an hour-long session dedicated to their favourite movie live from the National Media Museum in Bradford, which ran the films to an audience of Radio 1 listeners. Piers explains how the Radio 1 creative process works:[11]

Each of our ten or twelve events across the year will be given to a project champion. They're a producer who works on that project in conjunction with their everyday working life. That means they have to be motivated to put in the hours over and above what is a very demanding job anyway.

With the responsibility of championing a project I will give them a set process to follow. The starting point for all these projects is audience insight. This comes from various sources which primarily could be just going and talking to young listeners and non-listeners in their own environment. So getting out of London anywhere in the country and going to a place where young people are – usually a shopping centre – and sitting down and chatting to them about whatever the subject may be. So if it's film, finding out a broad picture of how they consume film, what experiences of film are, what their favourite movies are and trying to drill down and see what's really going on and see if there's a universal truth that we can call an insight, where you go 'oh yes – that makes sense!'.

The big insight we had for movies is – 'mates recommendations not media manipulation'. So after speaking to those people we thought 'where do they find out about films?' They don't listen to it on radio, they certainly don't watch Jonathan Ross on telly, they don't read Empire magazine, and actually people seem to be a bit sick of 'a big blockbuster's coming out this week and we need to see it this week'. What they were telling us is that they might see it two or three weeks after the release because by then enough of their mates had been to see it and tell them if it was worth going to see, or they might wait for it to come out on DVD because their mates said it's not bad but wait for it on DVD – and no-one in the media will ever tell you that – that's what we were starting to find out.

Once we have that insight then we take it to a brain storming session. Brain storming sessions vary hugely but the one thing I encourage the producers to do is be really bold with them – get guest speakers, do them in weird places . . . throw people off their normal way of thinking and get out of the way of thinking how did we do this last time.

That movie weekend would never have happened if we'd just thought – what can we do – let's give away tickets to a premier. But that's media manipulation so we were trying to think from another angle.

The process is – gather audience insight – brainstorm – then condense some of those thoughts, distil the best so you're taking some bits and rejecting others then at the creative calendar meeting they (the project champions) get a steer from the executive producers. Sometimes it might be a bit of a reality check and someone might say that's brilliant but we could never afford it, or someone might say that's brilliant because I happen to know we could tie in with BBC 2's film season or whatever. Then we take it to what we call the watering hole, which is where we finesse the idea and see how it would work on air. What are the practicalities, what's the visual offering, what can we do on-line? We try to give everything a multi-platform approach.

In the watering hole we hammer out the practicalities – what works what doesn't work – and build it into a workable proposition. At that point we go back to a meeting and I try to encourage the project champions to use what's called an elevator pitch. This is an idea from American film studios – you're stuck in a lift with the head of the studio and you've got the time it takes to get to the 16th floor to say 'I've got a great idea and it's going to rock your world.' There's a set format for doing this, which is to kick off with a hook that will grab their interest, then explain what the audience need is, then explain your idea, then close with something really exciting that's a call to action. So the champion gives their pitch and we go round the room and say what we liked and what we didn't like and how it could be made better. Other times we'll split people into pairs and get them to discuss the pros and cons and report back the headlines. We have to keep these meetings fresh. That's a big watch-word with creative meetings because as soon as they become routine then people get creative fatigue so we need to keep the creative process as fresh as possible.

Audience insight – brainstorm – feedback – watering hole – more feedback – then deliver it on air – then review. The review is important and we make sure all our thoughts and actions are written up and stored so they can be acted on in the future.

The Big Movie Weekend is a classic example of a Radio 1 creative project that went very well in my opinion. The end result was that we came up with something innovative – a radio station promoting a visual medium – but it worked!

The level of research Radio 1 does into its audience and their taste is impressive. Producers are taken off their normal shows for a week and sent around the UK to find out first-hand what the audience wants:

We work very hard to ensure that we're not London centric. We try to reflect young people in the UK in the broadest of brushstrokes, rather than people who live in Camden and read NME every week.

The producers spend all day meeting people in the street, then in the evening we set up interviews with three people who're in our target audience, and they just explore aspects of their lives, chat to them and get an insight into what they think of Radio 1, how they consume Radio 1, what they know about Radio 1. Some of them don't even listen to Radio 1 – so how do they find out about new music?

So the producers are just finding out about their listening habits, then they come back and have three days to absorb that information, come up with insights, brainstorm them, pitch their ideas and refine them.

It's not just the producers who do audience research. A lot of the presenters DJ in various forms. Not just our specialist dance DJs who do club nights and things. Scott Mills and Edith Bowman do things like uni gigs and they take the time to talk to people and find out what's going on in their lives and that grounds them.

We also get 2–3,000 text messages on every day time show and emails as well. They're a good insight.

(Piers Bradford, executive producer, Creative Projects)

Radio 1 and the BBC

Of course, Radio 1 is part of the biggest broadcasting organisation in the UK – the BBC – and as such could be regarded as part of the establishment. But its combination of irreverent presenters, cutting-edge music and innovative use of different platforms for its content keeps its image slightly apart from the rest of the Corporation. 'I think Radio 1 is often seen by its audience as not being part of the BBC,' says Andy Puleston. 'I think its brand is quite distinctive and people think it's different to the rest of the BBC. We're like the naughty teenagers of the Corporation which is how it should be because we're for young people.'

However, not being seen as part of the BBC also has its down side, and the BBC Annual Report for 2006–7 noted that 63 per cent of 15–29-year-olds who listen to Radio 1 do not tune in to any other BBC radio service (2006–7: 20).

Nonetheless, Radio 1 still conforms to the Reithian tenet to 'inform, educate and entertain' not least through its news service – Newsbeat – as Ben Cooper explains:

> Newsbeat is very important to Radio 1 in the sense that it gives the young the news in a way that they feel comfortable with. They can trust it and it's not talking down to them. It's presented in a way that they get and understand. It's very important to the BBC that Newsbeat exists on Radio 1 because if you look at the way that young people consume news, it's probably one of the only areas that they get in-depth news to a certain level of understanding.

The station is also well known for the various campaigns they run on everything from sexually transmitted diseases to dealing with exam stress.

> If you look at some of the campaigns we've done they're about getting important messages across about very sensitive and sometimes difficult subjects and that's massively important. It's part of our role as a public service broadcaster that we should do that and work with health authorities or charity bodies and get important messages across to young people but do it in a way that's credible and that's what I think Radio 1 can do brilliantly. It's not a vicar in trainers – it's able to do it in a unique way that means people trust us and we're not going to patronise them. If people want to take drugs then they're going to take drugs, but we'll tell them what affects those drugs will have on them and what sort of side effects they could have, and how it might affect their lives and their social relationships with friends and things like that. We give them advice so that they can make informed decisions.
>
> (Ben Cooper, Radio 1 head of programmes)

But because Radio 1 is essentially a music station it is music that takes centre stage and to that end the station makes sure it covers big live events and brings them to people who might not be able to get there to experience it for themselves. 'Live events are important to us because they help us to connect with our audience,' says Ben Cooper:

> There was some research done recently that showed that people love to hear a crowd cheer. For some reason you connect with that feeling of being at gig, being in a tent at a festival or in a field and seeing a band perform or DJs play and that feeling of euphoria that people relate to quickly. So live music and new music is core to what Radio 1 does: that's our core brand essence, so being out and about where our audience is going to consume music in a live environment is very important to us. We meet our audience that way and see what they like and get to broadcast music that bands and DJs are creating.
>
> (Ben Cooper, Radio 1 head of programmes)

Andy Puleston agrees, and he says the station aims to make its live coverage of events as close to the real experience as possible, whether it is Live from Ibiza or the Big Weekend:

> One of the rules of thumb we have for covering events is that you should be able to go to the website, absorb it, and have a conversation with someone who was actually there and be able to talk about it like you were there and feel as if you had a similar experience.
>
> That's the other thing about providing that sort of service. It's about giving people who can't go to Ibiza access to what we do there so that at least they can feel they were part of it. They heard the show, they saw the pictures they saw the films they heard the music.
>
> (Andy Puleston, content producer, Radio 1 Interactive)

The future

In 1967 when Radio 1 was launched the only way to get the programmes was through a traditional radio set on the crackly AM frequency. Now what is produced by Radio 1 can be accessed from numerous platforms. 'I suppose it's a mind set,' says James Wood. 'We're still radio and they're still consuming us but it's on different platforms. We're repackaging the content and not calling it just radio.' Ben Cooper thinks this kind of broadcasting is still evolving, but there will always be a place for 'traditional' broadcasting.

> Breakfast and Drive will still be important but there will be a split between mood FM broadcasting for your big audiences and that could be daytime versus night time or it could be early morning shows and going to bed shows. But you'll

have your big personality shows – giving entertainment and new music – and then you'll have your genre specific shows which you could say – 'well why do they have to be two hour shows or three hour shows'. If they're a certain genre and you just want to play the best music from that genre for that week well maybe it's 20 minutes or 45 minutes, or maybe we need to vary it from week to week. With those shows it won't matter because most of the listeners will be on listen again, or podcasting if we get the rights, or chopping them up and chucking them on the web. You maybe even take one interview or one track from a show and make what people would consider a traditional radio trail but put it on the web so people can exchange it on their MP3 players or phones or what have you. Big event programmes during times when people are able to listen to the radio will not change that much but the genre specific programmes and niche programmes will change dramatically and going alongside that will be the idea that you bring in a visual element that will live online and will enhance some of the FM broadcasting.

(Ben Cooper, Radio 1 head of programmes)

And just as in 1967, when one of the main functions of the new radio station was to engage with young people and make them feel that the BBC was relevant to them, that is still the job of Radio 1 today whether it is through a traditional radio set, mobile phone, the internet or even a virtual world environment, as James Wood explains:

Radio 1's job is to bring young people into the BBC – I think we're a conduit – the thin red line if you like. They're disconnecting more and more with TV and other platforms so I think the job of Radio 1 is to re-engage young Britain with the BBC by giving them Chris Moyles, by giving them Radio 1's Big Weekend, by giving them Live from Ibiza. Then they come to us and we tell them about other things the BBC does – BBC 3 – 1 Xtra – the Asian network – great drama on BBC1 and stuff that's relevant to them. I suppose we're the hook – we're the ones out fishing for young people – we get them in and tell them what else we've got.

(James Wood, head of marketing,
Radio 1 and 1 Extra)

6 The role of news

....

Living in a multi-media world means the news is more accessible than ever before through the internet and 24 hour rolling news channels, but it can still be argued that the immediacy of radio means it is eminently suited to delivering news to its audience whether in the form of a newsflash about a breaking story, through presenters chatting about the latest celebrity news, as topics for phone-ins or discussion programmes, or in regularly scheduled news bulletins or magazine programmes. News in all its varied guises – from serious economic analysis to celebrity gossip – is an important part of the voice of a station, and the way it is used says a lot about a station's brand values. This chapter examines the way news is used by different radio stations, how it is selected, and what components make up news programmes and bulletins. It ends with a brief analysis of two radio news bulletins to demonstrate how different stations provide a different 'world' to match their target audience.

When we talk about the news on radio most people think about the traditional news bulletin at the top or bottom of the hour that lasts from between 60 seconds to 5 minutes. On top of this there are well established news magazine programmes like BBC Radio 4's *Today*, *The World at One*, and *PM*. But whether a station is speech-based or music-based the news – in its widest definition – plays an important role in the output of all radio stations. Music station presenters need to keep abreast of what's happening in the world that might affect their listeners, whether it is the latest music industry gossip or a local event that people are talking about. Thanks to texts, emails and blogs, the news is a way presenters on all stations can interact with their audience and make them feel part of the station with contributions read out on air stimulating even more responses.

Of course, stations still have to select the news that is appropriate to their audience, and critics of radio news say this reduces it to the level of entertainment. But matching news to a specific audience is a practice long established in newspapers, and most people select what news they want to know about by choosing a particular

Figure 6.1 Lewis Skrimshaw, news editor at 96 Trent FM

news product. Those who want in-depth information and analysis of national and international news would go to BBC Radio 4 or 5 Live, while those who prefer brief but pertinent headlines about events in their area would most likely choose their local or regional commercial station as Lewis Skrimshaw,[1] news editor at Nottingham's 96 Trent FM explains:

> Our news is what gives us the advantage over our main competitors – that's not Radio Nottingham or Heart FM – in a straight fight for listeners it's BBC Radio 1 and Radio 2. By doing bulletins that are heavily slanted to local news we're giving listeners something those stations can't. We like to get the sort of news stories that have a big local interest and that are going to affect a large part of our audience.

Most people agree that radio news is at its best delivering breaking news stories. Radio programmes are more easily interrupted for a news flash than those of television, and newspapers report what has already happened rather than what is happening now.

However, as a news medium radio has limitations. As Robert McLeish points out, a ten-minute news bulletin is the equivalent to one and a half columns of news print and most papers carry 30–40 columns of news copy (1994: 5) so the amount of information in a news bulletin is considerably less than can be delivered by newspapers. For this reason radio is often regarded as a summariser of the news, particularly on music-based stations where formal news output is confined to a couple of minutes at the top of the hour. As Stephen Barnard comments, 'all too often the analytical ground, the sense of context, is conceded to other media' (2000:148).

But even stations with very short news bulletins can counteract this limitation by giving more information or analysis on their website, as Lewis Skrimshaw of 96 Trent FM recognises:

> The website is massively important and becoming more important. The growth of on-line news is well documented and people are turning to the internet for news because they can get it when they want it, and particularly if they're in an office – that's where they'll turn to for news. It's great for getting our material on and it lets you give more depth or detail than you can give in a three minute bulletin.

And radio news gives us what Andrew Crisell calls an 'indexical' sense of the news through the use of actuality: background noises like sirens or birdsong, or the way the report is delivered, that allow listeners to create the scene for themselves:

> On the radio we hear the noises of the news, or at least the informed view or the eyewitness account 'straight form the horse's mouth' and often on location – outdoors, over the telephone – that newspapers can only report in the bland medium of print, a medium bereft of inflections, hesitations and emphases of the living voice which contribute so largely to meaning, and also less able to evoke the location in which the account was given.
>
> (1986: 121)

The news is an important way for stations to connect with their audience, particularly regional and local stations. Through story selection and a particular style of delivery, news bulletins can reinforce the bond between a station and the community where they broadcast. Nick Wilson,[2] news editor at *Heart 106 FM* in the East Midlands recognises this:

> News is important because it's the way we provide a service for the community. A commercial radio station is there for the music and people listen to the station for the music. The news is where we become local and that's absolutely crucial – we touch the community through the news. We have the responsibility for providing what we think everyone needs to know not just in their community but for the whole world. I see the newsroom here at Heart as an international newsroom based in the East Midlands because the news we provide is local, regional, national and international.

Speech-based stations like local BBC stations use news even more in programming: day-time shows and phone-ins are often based around events and issues of importance to the local community. Most BBC local radio stations have a speech-based breakfast show, and many like *Radio Nottingham*'s are news-based, as Aeneas Rotsos[3] the news editor explains.

I think news is very important to a station like Radio Nottingham. It's obviously one part of what we do but people do tune in to the BBC both locally, regionally and nationally, for a fair and accurate report of what the day's events are so as a result of that news is integral to what Radio Nottingham does and the news team is one of the largest teams on the station.

Radio Nottingham has a news team of about 12 journalists who provide material for the news-based breakfast and drive-time shows, as well as bulletins throughout the day. But because the station is speech-based reporters also feed into shows:

It's not unusual if there's a big breaking story for a reporter to do a two-way into day-time shows. We did a very joined-up day for the budget where the breakfast, mid-morning, lunch and drive time all looked at the budget in a different way and in a way that reflected the sound of those programmes but also gave information as soon as it came out.

(Aeneas Rotsos, *BBC Radio Nottingham*)

But while stations use news throughout their programming on an everyday basis, most local or regional stations do not provide 24 hour news bulletins, mainly because news is expensive to run. Most BBC stations provide hourly bulletins from 6 am to 6 pm, then provide news on a regional basis until midnight when they switch to 5 Live output. Most commercial stations follow the same pattern of locally provided news until early evening when news from Sky or IRN is taken overnight.

Selecting the news

One of the most important factors in deciding what news to use in a radio bulletin is the target audience of the station. This is not to say that some news stories will be ignored altogether, but it might mean that they will be given less prominence on one station compared to another. 'You have to constantly have the audience in mind,' says 96 Trent FM's Lewis Skrimshaw. 'We want to keep the audience informed, but not in massive depth, so they know what's going on and don't feel stupid if someone at work's talking about something.' No matter what size the station, most radio bulletins are a combination of local, regional, national and international news and covering that amount of news from a local radio newsroom can be a challenge. GCap stations (now Global) try to get around this by operating on a group level. They take their international and most national news from Independent Radio News (IRN), but they also have a team of journalists in London based at Capital Radio who tailor national news stories to specific GCap stations. For example, when the new Eurostar terminal opened at the revamped St Pancras station in London in November 2007, GCap journalist Tim John did a series of voice pieces for stations across the group so that audiences were getting an individual version of the event. The result of this sort of service means that local newsrooms can concentrate on local stories rather than spending time re-working national stories with a local angle.

The challenge of making stories relevant to the audience is even greater for regional radio stations. 'Every time we look at a local story – and 'local' can be anywhere in the East Midlands – we have to consider how to write it to make it appeal to the rest of the region, which is why we don't cover a lot of stories that more local radio would do – they're just too local,' explains news editor Nick Wilson at Heart 106 in the East Midlands. And Nick also believes that stories should be judged on their importance to the audience rather than where they originate from:

> I've listened to stations that have a policy of always putting a local story first but I think that just upsets the balance of the news. If you listen to a bulletin then you have to believe that the top story is the most important story in the bulletin. We have a philosophy that it's not the be-all-and-end-all to get a local angle on every single story – it's about getting the story across. If the story has no local angle but it's hard-hitting and relevant to our audience then that's not a problem and we'll run it as it stands. If it's a story that can be enhanced by a local angle then we'll do that.
>
> (Nick Wilson, Heart 106)

BBC local radio has an older target audience than commercial stations. In the main they target people over the age of 45. And while the news editor of BBC Radio Nottingham, Aeneas Rotsos, acknowledges that his station keeps the age of their audience in mind in the selection and treatment of the stories they do, he does not see this as limiting their output:

> At Radio Nottingham we try to get a mix of light and shade stories on air – things you'd want to tell your friends down the pub, things you'd want to know about your local area. I think one of the strengths of BBC local radio is providing local news which you might not hear or see or read elsewhere.

News sources

News comes from a variety of sources depending on how it is being used but for journalists one of the most important sources of news is their own contacts built up over time. What radio does is give listeners the voice of the news so that they can hear from people directly involved in a story whether as the main character or as an expert commenting on the situation. So almost everyone a journalist meets is a contact who might be able to comment on a story or put them in touch with someone who can. For that reason one of the most precious possessions a journalist has is their contacts book, which should be backed up regularly to avoid disaster if it gets lost.

But news is not as random and unpredictable as journalistic myth would have us believe. Many events are known about in advance and a note kept on them in the newsroom diary. This will include a note of standard events like the Christmas lights switch-on or St Patrick's Day parades, as well as reminders about the start or end of important court cases, or public inquiries, and events like royal visits or MPs opening new schools.

Newsrooms are also fed information through news releases sent to them – most often by email – from a wide variety of people and organisations. While the majority of these are either already known about or not of interest, it is often worth noting the contact name, telephone number and email address of the organisation for future reference. It is much easier to access information through a named individual than trying to get it by asking for an anonymous press officer.

As well as the station's own news diary, the Press Association publishes a daily prospects list showing all the major stories they are covering that day, and on local stations this is supplemented with a prospects list from national news suppliers like IRN and Sky for commercial radio stations, or RNS (Regional News Service) at the BBC.

Throughout the day local stations are fed audio and text from their national providers. In most cases national and international news on local radio is provided by either RNS, IRN or Sky. The BBC's RNS is serviced by correspondents all over the world as well as through the BBC network of local stations throughout Britain who keep it supplied with audio and text, which is then sent on a 'circuit' to BBC regional and local stations through the system known as ENPS (Electronic News Provision Service).

Commercial radio news providers work in a similar way. IRN is owned by Global Radio and Bauer with ITN having a minority share. Until October 2008 IRN had access to all ITN material, and ITN reporters supplied audio versions of their stories. These were then sent in the same way as at the BBC, via satellite or sometimes the internet to newsroom computer systems or other automatic recording points. But in 2008 IRN dropped ITN in favour of being supplied by Sky News giving Sky a 'virtual monopoly in the commercial radio news market' (Plunkett 2008i) because any stations that do not take IRN are supplied by Sky News.

Another important source of news is the emergency services. Police, fire and ambulance services are usually contacted every couple of hours to make sure any incidents are found out about as soon as possible. In larger towns and cities these services usually have a 'voice bank', which is a taped version of what is happening, updated throughout the day, although not as often as journalists would like it to be. The ubiquity of email means that where there is a big story the emergency services can instantly inform all relevant news outlets at once.

Similarly, the courts and councils are a regular source of news, although it is not common for radio reporters to attend their proceedings. Recording for broadcast in courts and at council meetings is forbidden, although under section nine of the 1981 Contempt of Court Act some courts will allow a recording to be made as long as it is surrendered to the court at the end of the day's business. Generally the actual sittings are covered by freelance 'stringers' who send their copy to the station where it is turned in to copy or a voice piece to be included in bulletins. However, if the council is making an important decision, for example, pushing through plans for housing development against the wishes of the community, a reporter may be sent to the meeting to hear the decision, then get interviews with councillors and protestors. Similarly, if there is a major court case involving a particularly high profile murder, or a case involving major fraud, reporters can be sent to hear the sentence and then try to interview the victim's family or those who were affected by the fraud about how they feel about the verdict. These interviews should be done outside the court buildings.

Like all journalists, radio news reporters also use other media to keep track of what is going on both locally and nationally. Most stations monitor the output of other radio stations in their area, as well as local television and the press. But no matter where a story comes from it is important for reporters to check the facts for themselves before broadcasting it.

The internet is another valuable tool for any journalist, but like any tool it has to be used carefully. It can be used to check breaking news stories but because it is constantly updated the 'facts' sometimes change as more becomes known about events, so ideally anything from the internet should be cross checked before it is broadcast. Where the internet is of most use is as an archive to give background to running stories or provide information about someone a reporter is going to interview. That said, not all sites are equal and reporters need to use reputable sites to do background searches.

But as radio stations across the country invest more in their internet sites they can be a source of original news. Many stations have sections for users to comment on stories or even give their own stories for consideration, as Lewis Skrimshaw from 96 Trent FM explains:

We have a 'your news' section and a 'comment on this story' section so we can actually generate content through it. It might be, for example, a story about raising the tax on alcohol to stop binge drinking – 'what do you think about this' – and we can use that feedback, for example, in voice pieces 'this is what you've been telling us through our website today'. It's listener interaction. We also get story tip offs this way which when you've only got one or two reporters in the field is priceless for your listeners. The easier you can make it for your listeners to tell you stuff the better.

Provided information from the internet is cross checked it can be very useful to reporters, but because it is so vast there is also the danger that reporters spend too much time trawling for information and not enough time actually getting on with producing news. The key is to get to know a few search engines well and use them discriminately.

The bulletin

Radio news bulletins vary from 60 seconds on some commercial stations to ten minutes on some BBC stations. Unlike longer news magazine programmes, their function is to summarise events and bring the audience up to date with the latest stories, and that means any analysis pieces or longer interviews are generally not included. Most feature a mixture of local, national and international news covering politics, crime, social issues, entertainment and sport.

On most stations the news is compiled and put into a running order by the newsreader, usually to an agreed format. Some stations, for example, like to end their bulletins on a lighter note with showbiz news or an 'and finally' story. Others insist that the lead story should always have audio – either a voice piece or actuality – to stress its importance.

As Crisell points out, while newspaper readers can select the order they want to read items of news, 'on radio, order is both a more and a less rigid matter' (1986: 85). It is more rigid because the listener has no choice about the order of items in a bulletin, and less rigid because it does not always follow that stories are read in order of importance. Generally the item deemed to be of most importance to the audience of a particular station is read first, but there-after other factors influence the order. These include the need for a variety of topics with a mix of local, national and international items; a variety of sounds with a mix of voice pieces and actuality along with the newsreader's voice; and whether the duration of an item fits into the rest of the bulletin.

However, all radio news bulletins are constructed from the same basic components described below.

Copy

Copy is a news story written for broadcast. Copy lines vary in duration from 8 seconds to around 35 seconds but in every case they have to tell the whole story in more or less detail. Obviously a short copy line will be no more than an extended headline but it still needs to be able to tell the basic story of what has happened. Short copy lines are often used in 60 second round-ups used by some stations on the half-hour during breakfast and drive time shows. The important thing is that the story is clear and interesting, as Aeneas Rotsos of Radio Nottingham explains:

I think there's a danger that sometimes you can tell a story in too few words and it almost makes no sense and if you tell it in too many words it becomes uninteresting to listen to. We try to go for a middle way that means we can tell the story, be accurate, provide the information we need to provide but make the bulletin sound lively.

Regardless of its duration copy should be written in a direct style, abbreviating the verbs wherever possible to help the piece to flow and sound more natural when read aloud. So write 'it's' not 'it is' and 'they'll' not 'they will'. There is an argument that readers will abbreviate verbs as they read, but it makes the newsreader's job easier if verbs are already abbreviated where they should be and left whole when emphasis is needed, for example, to confirm an event, as in 'Prince Harry *is* being flown back from Afghanistan.'

You only get one chance to get the story across so it needs to be written as we speak. 'We write in a way that people can understand, using easy to understand words and phrases, not being too fancy about it and not trying to be too clever,' explains Nick Wilson of *Heart 106FM*. 'We just keep it down-to-earth. We like to think that we deliver the news in the way that people talk about it in their daily lives.'

The first line of a copy story – also known as the top line – needs to get the main point of the story across and hook listeners into it. There is no time for a preamble leading into the story, but at the same time you do not want to cram the top line with details. The best written copy stories start with a statement that encapsulates the story then adds detail as it progresses. So if you are writing for a Newcastle-based station it would be better to start with 'A Newcastle hairdresser's celebrating winning £3 million on the national lottery' then later add what particular area of Newcastle the hairdresser comes from, rather than start with 'A Heaton hairdresser's celebrating . . .' By putting Heaton in the top line there's a danger that anyone from other areas might mentally switch off, but keeping the top line open by using Newcastle keeps listeners more interested. In the same way, it is best to avoid starting stories with the names of official organisations like county or city councils, health authorities or police forces. Apart from the fact that these official bodies are a turn-off for most of the audience, the point of the story should be how it affects your audience rather than who is behind the story.

Keep punctuation to a minimum. It's very difficult to vocally interpret just about any punctuation beyond a full stop. We don't talk in carefully constructed sentences with multiple clauses – we tend to talk in phrases – so write that way. Use dashes or dots rather than commas – they're easier to see for the newsreader and easier to interpret with your voice. It is also easier for newsreaders if numbers under 10 and over a thousand are written out in full – it's very easy to stumble when faced with a row of endless zeros.

Radio is an immediate medium, so wherever possible use the present tense and the active form of the verb to make copy lively and happening. So it would be

'Gordon Brown says he's planning to withdraw troops from Iraq' not 'Gordon Brown said he planned to withdraw troops from Iraq.' It's also less confusing for the audience if you round numbers up or down rather than making them exact, especially in top lines. So it would be 'nearly 40 per cent' rather than 38.5 per cent' or 'just over 80 per cent' rather than '81.6 per cent'.

But perhaps the most important piece of advice is to read your writing out loud before it is broadcast. It's well known that copy read in your head is always perfect – only by reading the words out loud can you spot any awkward words, or phrases that jar or simply don't make sense. And although your language should be colloquial that is not the same as slang, as Lewis Skrimshaw from *96 Trent FM* explains:

> We keep our language as accessible as possible. If you can use fewer words – do. If you can use simpler words – do. If you can tell something clearly without the audience reaching for a dictionary – then do. There are certain banned words that we feel take us towards dumbing down and damage our credibility – words that give the listener the idea that you're not credible or authoritative. If you're using slang that's the impression you can give.

Most stations have an on-screen proforma for writing copy, cues and scripts. This will contain information about who has written the story, what bulletin it was prepared for, and a 'slug' or 'catchline' to identify the story. All this information is important to whoever is compiling the bulletin. They need to know who has written it in case there is a query, and when it was written in case it needs to be updated. Ideally copy should be rewritten for every bulletin, even if nothing has changed, to make it sound fresh for listeners, but in practice this often slips. Another important detail that needs to be included on all copy, cues and scripts, is the duration of the piece so that the total duration of the bulletin can be worked out. On most systems this is done automatically, but where it is not, it can be worked out on the basis of three words per second and included at the end of the copy.

Cues

Every piece of audio played on radio must have a cue. The cue introduces the audio, whether it is the voice of an interviewee or a report from a journalist. It is important for cues not to repeat what is going to be heard in the audio. Instead a cue needs to explain the story and set it up selling the story to listeners so that they want to hear what comes next. To make cues effective and relevant to their audience journalists at Heart 106 in the East Midlands routinely rewrite cues sent up from their national news provider, Sky, as news editor Nick Wilson explains:

When you're selling a story the first two or three words are the most important. For example – Home Secretary Jackie Smith defending her department when it was revealed that illegal immigrants were working in the security industry. Sky's version started with 'Home Secretary Jackie Smith' . . . well immediately that's politics and in someone's head they've gone 'politics – not interested in that'. If you've got a clip of Jackie Smith then you use those words going into the clip of her – she's not the story – the story's about illegal immigrants which is a big story. A lot of people get emotional about immigrants and migrant workers in this region so it's a relevant story, but to start it with Jackie Smith doesn't work. It's a matter of looking at scripts and saying 'where's the story and how does this affect us' and then write it that way. In the top line you say this is how this affects you, in the middle you give the thrust of the story and then you lead into the clip.

There is no strict rule about the duration of cues: they need to be long enough to explain the story but short enough to keep the listeners' interest. As with copy, they need to be headed with the author's name, bulletin time and a slug that is the same as the one used to label the audio. Along with these details there should be a duration for the cue, duration for the audio, the total duration of the piece (that is, cue plus audio) and the 'out words' – that is the last couple of words of the audio.

Clips

Clips – which are also called cuts or soundbites – are the simplest form of news presentation. These are short bursts of an interview that best illustrate the story and they can be as short as 5 seconds. Commercial radio tends to keep clips under 15 seconds, while the BBC tend to prefer slightly longer clips of up to 25 seconds, but there is no hard rule. The length of a clip should be determined by what is being said in it. For example, the mother of an abducted child might not add any new information to the story through a clip, but the emotion she displays will convey her distress more effectively than any number of words spoken by a journalist. As Lewis Skrimshaw from 96 Trent FM explains, 'For run-of-the-mill stories audio should be about 16 seconds, but if the audio is powerful it doesn't matter – if it's going to keep people hooked it could be 40 seconds.'

Clips can also be used in a 'wrap' when the reporter literally wraps their explanation of the story around a clip of someone directly involved in the story. This is often done on reports from Parliament that need more explanation than a simple cue could provide. Including the actuality of the politician speaking adds weight to the report and can also convey the atmosphere of the political debate. The best clips move the story along either by providing new information, or through conveying emotion or atmosphere.

Voice pieces

A voice piece is a report voiced by a reporter either live or pre-recorded. They consist of two parts: the cue, which is read by the newsreader, which sets up the report and introduces the reporter, and the script, which is the actual report voiced by the reporter. Generally they are used when the story requires more explanation than a copy line could convey, for example, at the end of a long court case when it is necessary to remind listeners about the background of the case. They are at their most effective when they are voiced at the scene of the story when background noise adds atmosphere to the report, as Lewis Skrimshaw, the news editor at 96 Trent FM, explains:

> We've moved to a position where we have more people out and about so some of our voice pieces are live from the scene and I think that adds to our output because we're making a statement – 'we're here, we're live on the scene at the heart of the story'. Studio based voice pieces also work because they add colour to the bulletin – it's not the same voice reading what might end up becoming a long piece of copy. A straight read from the newsreader that might take 30–40 seconds may have the listener losing interest. A voice piece can liven the story up with the use of a second voice that aids explanation and adds colour.

But while a report from the scene of a story can bring it alive for listeners, news editors tend to agree that you should only say a report is live if it is actually live:

> We do pre-record things that we broadcast as if they're live but it's about what you're not telling the audience rather than what you are telling them. If we can only get the Chief Constable on the ISDN at 12.30 pm and we want to run it in the 1 pm as a two minute interview in a conversational style we would go into it by saying 'I'm joined now by Chief Constable Steve Green'. I'm not saying I'm being joined live. We're not conning people – we just want things to knit in together.
>
> (Nick Wilson, news editor, Heart 106 FM)

The use of voice pieces varies from station to station. Some stations never use them arguing that a tightly written copy line is more effective than a voice piece, while others, like *96 Trent FM*, like them because they add a variety of voices to the bulletin. Similarly, some stations like their reporters to use a standard out cue (SOC) at the end of a report, such as 'John Smith, IRN, Central London' while others feel the reporter being introduced at the beginning of the report is enough.

Vox pops

Vox pops, from the Latin *vox populi* – 'voice of the people' – are created by a reporter going out on the street and recording the opinions of people on a particular issue. The reporter then edits the best replies together in a continuous anonymous stream. Vox pops can be an effective way to convey the general feeling about an issue, but they should not be presented as a representative sample. The reporter needs to select the most lively or best-expressed comments without distorting the general trend, and should aim for a mix of male and female voice unless the topic dictates otherwise.

Getting the right question for a vox pop is crucial to its success. It needs to be brief and easy to understand, and phrased so that a simple yes or no is not possible for a reply. So if the topic is about government plans to raise taxes on alcohol to stop teenage binge drinking, the question should be 'what do you think about government plans to raise taxes on alcohol to stop binge drinking?' rather than 'do you think the government should raise taxes on alcohol to stop binge drinking?', which could simply be answered in one word.

It is important that the topic is one that everyone knows about and has a ready response to. If people have to have the issue explained to them, or have to think too deeply before responding, it is likely they will not bother. Vox pops can be a good way to make a national issue more local by getting local responses to it, but they can be over used.

The best vox pops feature a series of very short responses, rather than a few ponderous replies, and that takes careful editing. Unlike straightforward interviews when the pauses and stammers in a reply can reveal as much as the actual words being said, vox pops need to be tightly edited with the best response used first and the second best one used last so that listeners hook into the responses and are left with a positive image of it. The reporter's voice should not feature in the finished product at all, so the question that has been asked needs to be worked into the cue.

Reporters need to be careful where they chose to record their vox pops. Interviewing people next to a busy road might add colour to the piece if it is about traffic congestion, but you need to be careful that the sound of the traffic does not drown out what is being said. It is also important to get permission to record on private property. This includes bus and train stations, shopping centres and pubs. If it is difficult to get permission to record inside these places, it is often easier to stand on the street outside and stop people coming and going.

Packages

Most news stories have at least two sides to them; a package is a way to present more than one side of a story in a concise way. Generally a package will have clips from two or more interviews linked by a script that is voiced by the reporter.

The best packages use sound effects and music to bring the piece alive but care needs to be taken not to overuse them: music randomly stuck behind links and interviews is meaningless, and if the track chosen has lyrics the words of the song can end up in competition with what is being said in the report. But well chosen music can evoke atmosphere, and sound effects are a good way to provide a sense of location in a package, as the example opposite shows.

The entire package, including the cue, was just over a minute and a half long and it is a good example of the kind of tightly-written and well-produced packages that Newsbeat does so well. On the face of it, a story about traffic congestion might seem very dry, but because the reporter did it from the point of view of people that congestion affects, and aurally took the listener on a journey to hear from those people, the package was engaging and effective. Using short clips and short links ensured that the package had a lively pace, with voices changing every few seconds. The traffic sound that ran throughout the package effectively established the location, and hearing Simon and Ket chatting as they loaded their van finished off the picture: we all instantly saw the industrial estate, the van being loaded and the motorway running in the distance.

The links are all very direct – there is no preamble. Right from the start we are transported to that industrial estate and by using actuality of Simon and Ket chatting as they load the van, within the first seven seconds we have been introduced to the main interviewees without the reporter having to do so in a link. The longest link explains how the new road system works, which the reporter does in 12 seconds by being direct and keeping it simple. No doubt the explanation could have included a lot of technical information but it was not needed for the purpose of this story so it was left out. Then the other side of the story was given in a telephone clip from the spokesman from the RSPA, before going back to Simon and Ket for the final word. 'The ingredients of a good package are the ingredients of any news story,' says Aeneas Rotsos of BBC Radio Nottingham. 'That the story's told well, that it's brought to life and it takes people on a journey through sound.'

Of course not every story can be told in short links and clips, and not all stations have that sort of style. But a common mistake is for reporters to try to include too much information. It is better to strip the story down to its essence then add any extra information you think is needed to tell the story effectively, rather than get bogged down with too much detail.

Telephone clips

Many public service providers, like the police, fire service and local councils, now have ISDN lines in their headquarters so that interviews can be done on the telephone in digital quality so that the listener is not aware that it is a telephone interview, but telephone quality interviews are still very common in radio. The chief advantage of a telephone interview is that they get the story 'from the horse's mouth' on air

Cue for package from BBC Radio 1 Newsbeat, read by newsreader

We'll soon be able to drive on the hard shoulder on some motorways. The government hopes it'll help ease rush hour jams following a successful trial on the M42 in the West Midlands. Newsbeat's Dan Whitworth is there . . .

Reporter Dan Whitworth with sound of traffic and men loading a van in the background	Courier drivers Simon and Ket work on an industrial estate just two minutes drive from the M42 . . .
Fade up actuality of men loading the van	All right Ket. These are the boxes from Oxford.
Reporter	. . . and they spend hours on it every week
Actuality of van loading And Simon and Ket chatting	Brilliant! How many is there mate? 'Ehm – about 10 altogether.'
Into Ket on his own – sound of traffic still in the background	It used to be a complete nightmare. You'd pull onto the motorway or come up to this area and you'd just come to a complete halt – it was stop-start – it was like typical motorway congestion.
Reporter	That was before the hard shoulder opened up to traffic a year ago.
Back to Ket	It's a lot better now – the traffic continually moves – we don't have so many hold-ups. Because our work is so time-sensitive with ETAs (estimated time of arrival) we're getting to our jobs a lot earlier so the customers are a lot happier.
Reporter	It works like this: CCTV cameras and sensors on the motorway detect when traffic's building up, then electronic signs above each lane bring the speed limit down to 50 and directs drivers onto the hard shoulder.
Simon	I haven't seen any breakdowns. There are lay-bys every 500 yards or so, so if there are any problems they can be quickly rectified but I've never seen a breakdown myself. It seems to run quite well.
Reporter	Not everyone thinks it's a good idea though. Kevin Clinton is from the Royal Society for the Prevention of Accidents.
Kevin Clinton – telephone clip	If the hard shoulder is used as a running lane, if there's a major crash it may take the emergency services longer to get there, or when someone breaks down they may not be able to get their vehicle out of the running lane.
Reporter Simon Ket Simon	The scheme's being rolled out elsewhere over the next two years including on the M25, M4, M20, M1 and M6. I definitely think it's a good thing . . . Yeah – it's a good thing. It's definitely improved the state of the road so it makes things a lot easier – a lot smoother. It keep the traffic running smoothly and it seems to be controlled well and with the speed limits it keeps it still safe.

quickly, and they are particularly useful if the subject of the story is in a remote place, or when a story is just breaking. A lot of the first eye-witness accounts of the London bombing in July 2005 were from people on the scene, and the fact they were telephone quality added to the immediacy of the accounts.

Most studios have a facility for telephone interviews to be recorded directly onto a computer and edited from there, which not only diminishes the amount of sound degradation but also speeds up the turn-around time for getting the clip to air. Both the BBC and Ofcom guidelines stress that reporters must tell interviewees in advance that they are about to record the interview and get permission to do so before recording begins. Ideally, phone clips should be used as a holding position until better quality audio can be obtained, but in practice under-staffed newsrooms often end up relying on the telephone to get audio in preference to sending a reporter out, especially on regional stations that have a large area to cover, as Nick Wilson from Heart 106 explains. 'You could drive for an hour and a half in one direction and still be in our TSA (Transmission Service Area) – that's how big it is – so we have to sacrifice quality and do a phone interview every now and then.'

Two-ways

Two-ways or 'Q&As' (question and answers) are popular within news programmes because they allow complicated stories to be explained and they stress the immediacy of the medium. Often they are used where the reporter is at the scene of an incident telling the story in response to questions from the newsreader or presenter, but they can also be effective as a way to summarise and explain events like the budget or complex government reports. Because they have more than one voice they are more likely to keep the interest of listeners, and the questions help the story to develop in a natural way.

Two-ways need to sound spontaneous to be effective – the listener should feel as if they are overhearing an informed conversation – and that takes careful planning. Ideally the reporter, whether at the scene or in the newsroom, should write a cue for the presenter and suggest some questions to be asked. Although it is possible to script a response to the questions, it usually sounds better if a reporter has a note of key facts in front of them and answers the questions in a more conversational style. The key is to trust that you know the story well enough to respond off the top of your head, and this is made easier because you know in advance what questions you will be asked. One way to make two-ways sound more natural is to avoid a straight question and answer format and instead let the presenter add comments before asking the next question. For example, if the two-way is between a presenter in the studio and a reporter live at an anti-war demonstration, the presenter might start by saying 'it sounds pretty noisy there – how's the demonstration going?' and after hearing from the reporter the next question might begin with 'that's a huge number of people

– so how are the police coping?'. This makes the piece sound more like a conversation than stark questions, and that makes more interesting listening.

Interviews

The actual mechanics of interviewing – equipment, setting levels, locations – are dealt with in Chapter 7 but it is worth looking at the approach to interviews at this stage. Longer interviews are seldom used in news bulletins, where a cue and clip is preferred, but they do feature in news programmes. The strength of a radio interview is that it demonstrates *how* questions are answered – whether there is hesitation or aggression – which conveys as much as the actual words being spoken.

The key to a good interview is preparation. Where time allows, reporters should get as much information as possible about the story and check the internet for background facts. In any event it is important that the *aim* of the interview is clear. Is this a fact finding interview, for example, following a major accident where you need to find out how many people were killed or injured, where the injured have been taken to, how the accident happened, and so on? Or is it an interview where you need the opinion of the interviewee, for example, when interviewing protestors to a proposed ex-offenders unit when you need to find out why they object and what they plan to do about it? Or is it a personality interview with an actor or musician? Once you know the aim of the interview you can then plan your approach.

It is also useful to know how the interview is going to be used. If all you want from the interview is a 15 second clip, or if it is going to be clipped up for use in a package, there is no need to record half an hour of questions and answers. Instead work out two or three questions that get to the heart of the story and confine yourself to those. But although you may have a good idea of what you want to ask in the interview, it is not a good idea to write down a list of questions. If you have a list there is a tendency to follow it, rather than listening to the responses being given and reacting accordingly. Experienced interviewers all agree that listening is vitally important in an interview because the interviewee may say something that takes the story in a different direction and opens up a new angle on the story. That said it can be useful to have a note of key points that you want a response to, so that towards the end of the interview you can quickly check you have everything you need.

Questions need to be quite brief and direct: a long complicated question can lose the interviewee and they may end up not answering a key point. You should also avoid asking about more than one point in the same question because usually only one point will get a response – and it may not be the point you most wanted them to answer. Try to avoid asking questions that can be answered by a simple yes or no – keeping questions open allows people to respond more fully – and try to remember the basic 'who, where, what, when, why and how' that good interviews should cover.

Whether the interview is live or recorded, and where time allows, the opening question should be quite general to put the interviewee at ease: a relaxed interviewee will open up much more than one who feels they are being put on the spot. For the same reason you need to try to maintain eye contact with the person you are talking to: set your levels, get the microphone in position, then only occasionally glance at your recorder to check the recording so that the interviewee feels you are listening to them and are interested in what they are saying, rather than fussing with the equipment. Any 'hard' or probing questions should be used towards the end of the interview when you already have something recorded. If you start with a probing question the interviewee may refuse to answer or even back out of the interview and you would be left with nothing, whereas if you leave the 'killer question' until later you will have established a rapport with them and, even if they are uncomfortable with the question, they may give you some kind of response. In any event, no matter what the attitude of the interviewee is towards you, you must remain polite at all times: losing your temper or making snide remarks will get you nowhere and could result in your station being blacklisted in the future.

However, courteous behaviour does not mean total compliance. Your job is to ask questions that the audience would want to ask, and at times that will include awkward questions. Sometimes interviewees will ask for a list of questions in advance, and this should be avoided. Instead explain that they will come across much better if their responses are spontaneous, and tell them the broad area that you will be discussing so that they can prepare themselves.

Where possible, the location of the interview should be thought through (see Chapter 7 for more details on locations). For example, an interview about healthy school meals will sound much better if it is recorded in a school kitchen with the sound of pots and pans in the background rather than in a quiet office. This means you need to set your levels to make sure the background noise is not overwhelming, but the end result is worth the effort. You also need to be careful not to record near computers, air conditioning units or other electrical appliances because they get picked up by the recorder and your interview will end up with an annoying hum on it. Similarly, recording an interview in a high-ceilinged sparsely furnished room will make the recording sound echoey. If this is the only place available for the interview, make sure you stand quite close to the interviewee to shield the microphone and avoid the sound bouncing off the walls.

Wherever the interview takes place you need to make sure that you are in a comfortable position so that you do not need to change half way through. If you are sitting down, try to be side-by-side so that the microphone is less intrusive. If you are standing, put yourself to one side rather than directly in front of the interviewee as this is a less confrontational position. Never interview someone across a desk. You will not be close enough to get a crisp recording and after a few minutes your arm will ache. If the interview is to be used in its entirety you will need to make sure your questions are recorded at the same level as the responses, so position the microphone so that you can tilt it towards yourself when you ask a question. It is important to get the microphone in the correct position because you need to avoid too much movement, which can cause microphone rattle on the recording. You also need to be aware that anything you say will be picked up by the microphone so avoid making noises of agreement or encouragement while the interviewee is talking. Instead give encouragement by nodding and smiling.

Before the interview begins you need to establish basic facts like the person's full name and title and any relevant dates or hard facts you might need for the cue. It is a good idea to have this recorded because it allows you to set your levels, to identify the interview later, and it also means that if you want the person to introduce themselves within a package you have them doing so. At the end of the interview make a quick check to make sure that it has recorded, but avoid allowing the interviewee to listen back to it – he or she will nearly always find something they want to change.

News presentation

The style of news presentation varies according to the station's target audience and programme style. On music-based stations the news is generally only two or three minutes long, so copy and clips are quite short and it has a faster pace. In contrast, BBC local radio and speech-based stations like *Radio 4* tend to have longer bulletins, so more time is spent on each story and the style of delivery is more formal and evenly-paced. That said some BBC local radio stations are changing their style. 'I think there's this image that the BBC has to be very staid,' says Aeneas Rotsos from BBC Radio Nottingham. 'But actually a lot of stations are experimenting with using music beds and audiences are responding very well.'

Most news bulletins start with the newsreader announcing the time and their name, and often short bulletins begin with a headline or 'top story' to grab listeners' attention. On music stations the news is often read over a music bed to integrate the bulletin into programming and give it the same overall sound as the rest of the station output. 'The presentation style is really important,' explains Nick Wilson from Heart 106:

> On a music station they're listening for the music and the radio is inevitably on in the background. To grab their attention you've got to sell the story so much more than just reading words blandly off a piece of paper and you do that with the pace of your voice and the style of the words you use.

Aeneas Rotsos agrees that the writing in a bulletin is very important and he has created a style guide for *BBC Radio Nottingham* to give the bulletins a uniform style that the audience would recognise as being the BBC but would keep bulletins and programmes lively and interesting. 'One of the things we looked at for the style guide was our story count and we now try to increase the number of stories we have in our bulletins by tightening up the writing,' he explains.

Below are the transcripts from a Radio 1 bulletin and one from BBC Radio 4 that illustrate the style and different content used by each station. Even without knowing that music-based Radio 1 targets 15–25-year-olds and speech-based Radio 4 is aimed at over 45-year-olds, it is clear the bulletins are designed for different audiences.

Radio 1, 26 March: 11.30 am

Reader introduced by Jo Whilley
Duration: 2 minutes plus 20 second promo

Jingle	Digital . . . FM . . . Online . . . This is Radio 1	3″
Headline	Mums-to-be are told not to drink at all	3″
Sting	Newsbeat	2″
	There's new advice for pregnant women. In the past the health watchdog NICE said a daily glass of wine was ok after 12 weeks but now they think mums-to-be should avoid booze completely. Gillian Laing speaks for them.	13″
Clip from Gillian Laing	If you want to be completely safe then avoid alcohol intake when you're trying to get pregnant and throughout pregnancy. The risks are particularly great during the first three months of pregnancy – there's a risk of miscarriage.	12″
	The watchdog that's meant to keep Britain's banks in order has admitted it messed up over Northern Rock. The FSA says it didn't keep a proper eye on the bank, which nearly sank when it lent more money than it could afford.	12″
	In Iraq government troops are involved in a second day of fighting against militia groups. It's thought 40 people have been killed in Basra. Four thousand British troops remain on standby just outside the city. Major Tom Holloway is with them . . .	13″
Telephone clip of Tom Holloway	There's a curfew downtown, there's restrictions on vehicle movement, the conditions are not good. People are holed up inside their houses fearful of going on the streets while the fighting's ongoing.	10″

Sting	Radio 1 – Newsbeat	2"
	It's claimed you could get up to £20 a month slapped on your broadband bill if you download TV shows and films. Lots of users are now said to be going over their monthly download limit.	10"
	Rio Ferdinand says captaining England tonight will fulfil a childhood dream. The side take on France in a friendly in Paris.	7"
	And George Burley manages Scotland for the first time as they face Croatia at Hampden Park.	5"
	Millions of viewers – 16 contestants – one TV show . . .	5"
Clip Sir Alan Sugar	Some of the nutters that turn up – I mean they're just thrown straight out the door . . .	4"
	The Apprentice is back tonight. The hopefuls include a woman who says she's related to royalty. Sir Alan's admitted that some are only in it for the fame . . .	9"
Clip Sir Alan Sugar	It doesn't concern me anymore because nothing ever comes of them. Some are there for the wrong reasons. They get a bit carried away with themselves afterwards when they're seen on screen.	9"
	And you can hear more from him in the entertainment news with Nat at midday . . .	3"
Music sting	And coming up on the lunchtime newsbeat why this comment . . .	4"
Hilary Clinton clip	I remember landing under sniper fire and we basically were told to run to our cars . . .	5"
	. . . has got presidential hopeful Hilary Clinton in trouble . . . and we're talking about the two British brands of car being sold to India – That's Newsbeat at 12.45	9"
Radio 1 jingle mixed in with start of next music track.		

BBC Radio 4 News, 26 March 2008: 12 pm

Newsreader not introduced

Duration: 4 minutes

	Greenwich time signal	
	BBC News at midday	2"
	The Financial Services Authority has admitted making a series of mistakes in its handling of Northern Rock before its collapse in November. A report by the City watchdog says its supervision of the bank was unacceptable and no senior FSA staff had met anyone from Northern Rock since January 2005. The authority's chief executive Hector Sants says he was making changes to ensure that in future proper standards were upheld. Robin Ashley of the Northern Rock Small Shareholders group said it was all too little too late.	33"
Robin Ashley clip	It's all very well them holding their hands up and saying it made a mistake – the shareholders rely on people like the FSA to exercise some kind of supervision, which they failed to do. And it's not just about words – it's about actions as well – and shareholders feel very aggrieved that the company's been taken away from them now so they have no redress of any sort except through the courts.	22"
	President Sarkozy of France has arrived in Britain for a state visit. He flew into Heathrow airport and is now meeting the Queen at Windsor. Our diplomatic correspondent Bridget Kendal is there.	12"
Voice piece from Bridget Kendal	President Sarkozy and his wife Carla stepped onto the red carpet on the tarmac at Heathrow airport to be greeted by the Prince of Wales and the Duchess of Cornwall. Madame Sarkozy, the former Italian supermodel Carla Bruni, was dressed in a sombre grey outfit and pillbox hat. President Sarkozy in a dark suit and tie was within minutes in animated conversation with Prince Charles. It is the first full state visit by a French president in 12 years and is being seen as a chance for President Sarkozy to relaunch his battered image in France and reach out to strengthen ties with the UK by expressing his personal enthusiasm for Britain. Unusually his party includes, among others, his new mother-in-law, but his own mother – who was originally also due to come – has cancelled for family reasons.	47"

	Unions in the motor industry say the new owners of Jaguar and Land Rover have given a commitment that they'll continue to make the vehicles in British factories. The Indian firm Tata has just confirmed that it's buying the two brands for more than a billion pounds from Ford. Sixteen thousand jobs will be guaranteed.	19"
	The Iraqi Prime Minister has given Shia gunmen in Basra a deadline of 72 hours to lay down their weapons. Iraqi government troops are involved in a second day of operations against the militias including the supporters of the powerful Mahdi army of the radical cleric Moqtda al-Sadr. There's also been fighting in Baghdad. Police say 20 people were killed in clashes between the Mahdi army and Iraq and American troops.	27"
	The RSPB is warning that the number of birds in people's gardens is falling. The claim is based on a survey carried out by almost four hundred thousand amateur ornithologists throughout the UK. There was some good news about finches – they've increased in number. Chris Packham is a BBC wildlife reporter. He says people should do more to encourage birds in their gardens.	24"
Chris Packham clip	The general message is the trend is not good but we can do something about it and I'd like to see lots of these people who've seen the number of birds going down in their garden getting hold of information like this, getting hold of some feeders and getting them back in, because we can't be complacent in the world of conservation. We've got to redouble our efforts to make sure things are good for birds.	19"
	Marriage rates in England and Wales have fallen to their lowest levels since records began nearly 150 years ago. Provisional figures from the Office for National Statistics show that in 2006 only 23 in every thousand men got married and only 21 in every thousand women.	19"
	The holder of the winning Euro-millions lottery ticket has until five thirty this evening to claim a jackpot of six point nine million pounds. If they don't the money will go to good causes. The ticket was bought in Devon for a draw last September.	15"
	BBC News.	1"

As well as the content of the bulletins being different, the presentation style is also different. The Radio 1 bulletin is read over a music bed with lots of stings, short stories and clips, and no gap at all between the end of one story and the start of the next. The Radio 4 bulletin in contrast is calm and measured, the only introduction being the Greenwich Time Signal, and the stories are given more time. If you take out the 20 second promo for the 12.45 pm programme, the Radio 1 bulletin was two minutes long, while the *Radio 4* one was double that at 4 minutes duration, but both bulletins covered seven stories each, and three of the stories in each bulletin contained audio. As Nick Wilson from Heart 106 explains, the duration of your news bulletin should not necessarily dictate the number of stories you cover, but it will affect the way you cover them:

> With a three minute bulletin you can get through eight stories – in a five minute bulletin you can get through 13 or 14 stories which is far too many. If you're talking about sound bite news you can get through an awful lot in 15 minutes[4] and that would just send people's head into a spin. What we try to do in each bulletin and show is run with the same number of stories. If we're running eight stories in three minutes we're probably going to run just eight stories in 15 minutes but do a lot more on these stories. It's an opportunity to go a bit deeper and get under the skin of it a bit more.
>
> (Nick Wilson, Heart 106FM)

Radio 1's top story is perfect for its target audience of young people, many of whom may be considering having children, or already be pregnant. Similarly, the lead story on Radio 4, which dealt with the crash of the Northern Rock bank would suit its target audience, many of whom may have been shareholders or at least have an interest in the financial market. The Northern Rock story was also done by Radio 1 because although it is unlikely that their audience would be directly affected by the bank's crash, the event had wide implications for the economy so it is important for everyone to be kept up-to-date with the latest developments. The other story that both bulletins shared was about the war in Iraq. This is important for everyone in the country regardless of their age, and it could also be argued that because so many service people are serving in Iraq both audiences may well have a more direct connection to the story through friends and family in the forces.

Radio 1's inclusion of a rise in broadband charges for downloads again fits in with their target audience because more young people download films and television programmes than older ones. The two sports stories that followed were little more than a reminder that the games were taking place that night, but it is the sort of information that is socially useful. The most time devoted to a story was the 27 seconds spent on a new series of the BBC television programme *The Apprentice* – that is nearly a quarter of the total bulletin. While some might regard this as blatant cross-promotion by the BBC, it can also be argued that because of the popularity of the programme this is just the sort of story younger people would be talking about so including some irreverent quotes from Sir Alan Sugar reinforces the connection between the audience and the station. It was also used as a bridge between the bulletin and a promo for the lunchtime Newsbeat programme.

In the Radio 4 bulletin the story about the state visit of President Sarkozy to the UK was given the most time at 59 seconds duration – almost a quarter of the total bulletin time. Because it was an official state visit it might be expected to be included, but given the strained relations between the UK and France over many decades it would have added interest to older people who would be aware of that history. This was followed by news of Jaguar and Land Rover being bought by an Indian firm, an event that could have repercussions on British industry in general and so affect the stock market. Although Radio 1 did not include this story at 11.30 am they did tease it for their longer programme most likely because of its potential to affect jobs that would be of interest to their listeners. The story about garden birds, fairly obviously, has more appeal to older people than 15–25-year-olds, but another reason for its inclusion may be that Radio 4 actively promotes the annual survey through programmes like the *Today* programme, so it is likely a lot of listeners actually took part in it. The final two stories in the bulletin are interesting but quite light, giving a more up-beat end to the bulletin.

Predictably the language used in the Radio 4 bulletin is quite formal, but in line with good broadcast writing it is simple and direct with quite short sentences that are easy to take in. The Radio 1 bulletin is less formal with phrases like 'mums-to-be should avoid booze' and '£20 a month slapped on your broadband bill' but it avoids slang. As *Newsbeat* say on their website:

> We aim to give clear explanations of complex issues, in modern English. We don't like tabloid language or clichés. We avoid jargon and use slang sparingly. Our extensive research shows listeners appreciate this approach and style.

But for all the differences between the bulletins there are also a lot of similarities. Both have a mix of copy and audio, both start with the story deemed most interesting for their audience, and both end on a lighter item. So like so much in radio, the key difference between the two is the target audience, and whether it is a news bulletin or a two-hour show it is vital to connect with that audience in everything that is broadcast.

7 The tools of broadcasting

·····································

T he simplicity of radio is one of its greatest assets. At its most basic all it
requires is a microphone and a transmitter to take to the airwaves, although
even the smallest stations have considerably more equipment than that. The
purpose of this chapter is not to provide a comprehensive list of equipment used in
radio, but to explain how certain key pieces are used to produce the sophisticated
sound we all take for granted on the radio.

The studio

·····································

The obvious starting place for any explanation of the equipment used in a radio
station is the studio. This is the hub of the station and it is from here that we hear
what is broadcast. Generally, these are self-operating studios driven by the presenter,
but sometimes there is also a facility for the output to be driven by a technical operator
who works the desk in a section sealed off from the studio with sound-proofed glass,
linked to the presenter by a talk-back system. Stations usually also have at least one
other studio that can be used for production work, and a news studio used for
broadcasting the news and recording items like voice pieces and links for packages.

The key piece of equipment in the studio is the desk. This is the control panel
that links various pieces of play-out equipment to the transmitter for broadcast. The
design of the desk is important especially in self-drive studios where one person has
to have easy access to all the studio facilities. As well as the desk controls there are
usually two or three computer screens to let presenters access music, jingles, adverts
and packages and clips for news programmes, as well as texts and emails. In a news
studio, for example, there will be a screen to access news feeds and another one for
playing out the bulletin. Most studios also have a telephone balance unit that allows
callers to be put directly on air, or that records the interview to a computer for editing
and later play-out. News studios are usually very small – often no bigger than a large

Figure 7.1 A typical radio studio

cupboard – while programme studios tend to be slightly bigger to accommodate guests.

Although a studio desk can look intimidating with rows of sliding faders, knobs and buttons and various flickering meters, it is essentially very simple. Each vertical column of controls links to a particular sound source like a microphone, CD player, telephone or ISDN line, and so on, and usually these are marked to show what they connect to. On some desks channels have dual purposes and can switch between two different sources, but these are usually marked as such and show how to switch between the two. There are also equalisation buttons that adjust the tone of the audio, and a pan button that switches the sound from one side to the other in stereo output, but unless you are involved in creating specialist sounds for dramatic effect these are usually pre-set and do not need to be adjusted.

Probably the most important part of each channel is the gain control, which adjusts the level of sound passing through it. The sound is measured by meters that give a visual indicator of the sound level. There are two systems of measuring sound levels: VU (volume unit) and PPM (peak programme meter). The VU scale indicates the average recording or playback levels, while the PPM measures the peaks of sound. One way to understand the difference between VU and PPM is to think that the average height of the Himalayas is 18,000 feet, while the highest peak is Mount

Everest at 29,035 feet. A VU reading of the mountain range would give you a read out of 18,000 feet – the average height – while the PPM reading would be 29,035 feet – the highest peak. That said VU meters are more common on portable recorders, and most desks use PPM.

Radio stations have pre-determined levels where output should peak to ensure an even level of sound. If levels fluctuate too much listeners constantly have to adjust the volume on their radios, but there are also technical reasons for maintaining consistent levels. If the levels are too low the transmitter will attempt to boost it artificially and this can cause a 'hiss' on the output; if levels are too high the sound will distort and become difficult to understand. Although each studio may have a different standard, generally it is accepted that the gain button should be adjusted to that music peaks at around four and speech at around five: the difference is to take account of recorded music having been compressed when it was recorded. By playing speech and music out at these levels they will both sound the same coming out of the radio. Similarly, recorded telephone clips sometimes need to be set slightly higher than five so that on play out they sound as loud as other audio.

In order to allow the level of any output to be adjusted before it is played out, each channel has a 'pre-fade' facility that allows the presenter to hear the source through headphones on a different listening circuit so that the level can be set while

Figure 7.2 Close up of a radio studio desk

another item is being played out. Before doing a live studio interview, for example, the presenter will usually use the time when a piece of music or a pre-recorded item is playing out to adjust the level of the guest microphone on pre-fade to take account of the interviewee's voice and make sure both microphones will be heard at the same volume. In theory anything played through the studio computer should not need to be adjusted on pre-fade because it should all have been loaded at the prescribed level. In practice, however, this is not always the case, and wherever possible everything should be checked before being broadcast.

Headphones or 'cans' are part of the uniform of all radio broadcasters. It can take a little time for new broadcasters to get used to using headphones because they feed your own voice via the microphone back into your ears and the fraction of a second delay this gives can be disconcerting until you get used to it. But headphones are a vital piece of equipment. They are needed not only to set levels on pre-fade but also to keep the presenter in touch with other people and hear the station output. Most studios have speakers that play the studio output but as soon as the microphone fader is opened the speakers cut out to prevent feedback, and the output can only be heard through the headphones. Headphones also allow presenters to talk off-air to producers or technical operators through a talk-back system, and they link to external sources like telephone callers and traffic-news centres connected by an ISDN line.

Traffic and travel news

These are an important part of radio output particularly on local stations. They provide a service to listeners and at the same time reinforce the station's links with the community by referring to local routes and public transport operations. Many stations feature traffic and travel slots every 15 minutes during breakfast and drive-time programmes, and hourly at other times of the day.

Stations draw on a wide range of sources for their traffic information. Most have an agreement with commercial services like AA Roadwatch or Metro Networks that link their own announcers to the station via ISDN lines. Some stations work with local authorities that use their network of traffic cameras to report on traffic congestion, and utility companies provide advanced warning of any road works they are planning in the area. On top of this stations often encourage listeners to phone in with information about any delays they are experiencing, and some even employ helicopter reporters or motor-bike riders to cruise the area on the look-out for hold-ups.

The newsroom

Most radio stations have an open-plan design with a certain area designated for journalists working on news programmes. At most BBC local radio stations, for example, radio journalists work alongside those working for BBC television and BBC online. In commercial stations the journalists have a section alongside presenters and commercial activities. While this sometimes means that news rooms now look like any other office, it also means all of the station's staff are integrated so there is more awareness of the total output of the station and this creates a stronger station identity.

The news editor is in charge of the station's journalists. They decide what stories will be covered and how they should be done (see Chapter 6 for the role of news on radio). Reporters are delegated stories and when they have done them they send them to a central computer to be used in programmes or bulletins. Each reporter has a workstation where they download their audio and edit it, write cues, and often record voice pieces and telephone interviews using a headset microphone. In the past a lot of this work had to be done in a studio, which made producing news a more time consuming affair.

Editing

Very little pre-recorded material goes on air without at least some editing. The most basic edit is a 'top and tail' when an interview runs unedited except for its beginning and end to ensure it starts and finishes cleanly when it plays out. But generally material needs more work than this either to get rid of material that is irrelevant, or when there is not enough time to use it all, or when it is just plain boring. Editing is also useful in re-arranging material to make sure it has the most impact with an interview starting with the response to the third question that was recorded then bringing in the responses to questions one and two, or to make sure the best clip is used first in a vox pop even though it was the last to be recorded.

But whatever the reason, editing should not be used to change the sense of what has been said or put it in a different context by, for example, editing a response to one question onto another completely different question. Not only is this unethical but in some cases it can lead to legal action if the interviewee feels they have been misrepresented.

Both the BBC Editorial Guidelines and Ofcom's Broadcasting Code have sections on 'fairness to contributors' that give advice on dealing with contributors to programmes, including news. The Ofcom Broadcasting Code (2005) says:

> Where a person is invited to make a contribution to a programme (except when the subject matter is trivial or their participation minor) they should normally, at an appropriate stage:
> * be told the nature and purpose of the programme, what the programme is about and be given a clear explanation of why they were asked to contribute and when (if known) and where it is likely to be first broadcast;

- be told what kind of contribution they are expected to make, for example live, pre-recorded, interview, discussion, edited, unedited, etc.;

- be informed about the areas of questioning and, wherever possible, the nature of other likely contributions;

- be made aware of any significant changes to the programme as it develops which might reasonably affect their original consent to participate, and which might cause material unfairness;

- be told the nature of their contractual rights and obligations and those of the programme maker and broadcaster in relation to their contribution; and

- be given clear information, if offered an opportunity to preview the programme, about whether they will be able to effect any changes to it.

(Section 7:2–7:4 2005)

The Code adds that if a contributor is under the age of 16 then consent needs to be obtained from a parent or guardian, and that they should not be asked to comment on areas likely to be beyond their capacity to answer properly. For example, it could be deemed unfair to have a 10-year-old giving their view on political matters. Most importantly the Code specifies that 'when a programme is edited, contributions should be represented fairly' (Section 7.6 2005) and that when material recorded for one purpose is used in a later or different programme, it does not create unfairness.

The aim of editing audio is to create a natural-sounding piece that flows well with a strong start and a memorable end. A certain amount of 'cleaning-up' of an interview by removing awkward pauses or where the interviewee has become tongue-tied is acceptable, especially at the start of a piece when many people respond to a question with superfluous words like 'well now, let's see . . .' before getting to the point. But removing all hesitations and pauses can also take away the drama of what is being said: sometimes the way something is expressed is as important as the words being used. As Martin Shingler and Cindy Wieringa point out, this is particularly true with political interviews; 'Here the producer can use such moments to suggest uncertainty, incompetence or, particularly, dishonesty' (1998: 98).

There are many different editing software packages available but they all work on the same principles. The audio is downloaded to the computer where it appears as a visual representation of the sound known as a waveform. This shows the peaks and troughs of the recording, and you edit by moving the cursor to the beginning of the piece you want to cut out, highlight the section and press the delete button so that it disappears. There is usually a zoom facility that allows you to enlarge the waveform so that your edit can be very accurate.

The system is very similar to the cut-and-paste facility on word processing packages. Its main advantage is that no matter how many edits you make the original recording remains intact, so a careless edit can be corrected easily and there is no degradation of the quality of the sound. Digital editing is also quite forgiving of poor recording: material recorded at low level can be boosted (within limits) so that the recording sounds clear and is at the same level as other audio. That said, very little can be done to rescue material that is distorted because it has been recorded at too high a level, and there is no substitute for having recorded at the correct level in the first place.

The systems used in most radio newsrooms have at least two channels and more usually four. This allows reporters to add sound-effects or music to packages, by recording them on different channels and mixing them together at the appropriate levels. It is possible to add music and effects to a single channel editing system, but it is easier if each sound source has a separate channel that can be individually adjusted before being brought together for the final mix-down. Once the piece is completed it is saved in a named file and stored in the appropriate news file.

Most news editors agree that digital editing is faster, easier to use and produces better quality audio than the old analogue system. But because it is a visual process as well as an aural one, there can be a tendency for every gap in the waveform to be edited out, which can make speech sound very stilted and unnatural. Reporters need to trust the way a piece *sounds* rather than how it looks on screen – after all, that is what the listener will be hearing. But computers are used in newsrooms for more than editing. They are also used for writing copy and cues, collating bulletins, researching stories and receiving audio and text from outside sources.

Most radio groups – like all BBC radio or all GCap stations (now Global) – have a system that allows play-out and editing as well as access to outside sources like the Press Association (PA), IRN and Sky news, and access to material produced by other parts of the group. All BBC newsrooms are connected to each other through ENPS (Electronic News Provision Service). Each local and regional station and each national news programme has its own folder that can be accessed through the system, allowing news editors in Bristol, for example, to see what stories are being covered in Newcastle, and if it is relevant they can then retrieve it for use in their programmes.

ENPS also connects newsrooms to various wire services like Reuters and PA as well as the BBC's Regional News Service that sends out summaries of the day's top news stories and copy and cues for use in bulletins. To make sure relevant stories are picked up, news editors list key words to be picked out on each service – usually the names of relevant towns, MPs, sports clubs, and so on. – and when a story appears it is flashed onto their computer screen for them to check.

Regular audio feeds from London with national and international material are sent to local newsrooms via satellite and stored on the station's main computer. Newsrooms use a system called Radioman to edit material, write copy and cues and compile bulletins and programmes. Through a combination of ENPS and Radioman the news editor is able to keep track of local and national events from one terminal. The system allows them to access work in progress as well as archive material. Every bulletin is electronically stored and is searchable through keywords, which makes compiling programmes like the end-of-year review much easier, and provides a useful database for background information on running stories.

As mentioned earlier, telephone and ISDN interviews are recorded directly onto computer, and newsrooms can also access audio from radio cars, or fed by reporters in the field via ISDN. Some BBC stations also equip reporters with E10s, which are small palmtop mobile phones that send back quality audio via WiFi. This can then be edited at the base and used in bulletins allowing reporters to move on to another interview without returning to supply their material in person.

Most commercial radio groups have similar systems. GCap (now Global) has a system called Splice that allows them to play out and edit audio. Through the Matrix system they have they can access PA and IRN and do keyword searches. Given that commercial stations tend to have fewer staff than BBC newsrooms, linking stations within a group effectively increases the number of voices available. This means that if no-one in your own newsroom is available to do a voice piece, another reporter in the group can do the job and send it down the line.

Microphones

There are three main types of microphone that each work in slightly different ways so is used in different situations. Generally the technical staff at a radio station will advise where and how each different microphone should be used, and what follows below is no more than a general description of the three main types of microphone.

The ribbon microphone: these mikes are bidirectional and pick up sounds within the range of a figure-of-eight. They are most commonly found in studios for interviews or discussions, either on a stand or suspended from the ceiling. Sports reporters use a specialised kind of ribbon mike called a lip mike which, as its name suggests, has a special bracket on it that allows it to be held against the mouth. Lip mikes pick up nearby sounds and so allow the reporter's commentary to be heard in noisy conditions.

Moving coil mikes: these can be either unidirectional – picking up sounds from in front of the microphone in a heart-shaped field – or omnidirectional – picking up sounds from all around. Mounted unidirectional mikes tend to be used in newsreading studios. Radio reporters tend to use omnidirectional mikes.

Capacitor mikes: these need their own power supply from either a battery or the recorder itself. They vary in the way they respond to sound and are most commonly used as tie-clip microphones for longer interviews outside the studio.

The type of microphone used depends on the situation and each situation has a set of procedures that should be carried out before broadcasting or recording to ensure a technically 'clean' programme.

Newsreading

It is the newsreader's job to ensure that the bulletin is broadcast at the correct level and with no other technical flaws. Ideally the newsreader should get to the studio a few minutes before the broadcast so that they sound relaxed and in control and not flustered. In many stations the entire bulletin is on computer and there are no paper scripts. The newsreader reads from the screen and 'fires' news clips stored on the computer using either a keyboard, mouse or touch-screen.

Once in the studio the newsreader should get into a position that allows them to access the computer and controls easily without moving away from the microphone. Where paper scripts are being used they need to be held so that when a story has been read it can be moved silently to one side. As mentioned earlier, most newsreading studios use a mounted unidirectional microphone. This should be positioned so that the bottom of the microphone is level with the end of your nose to avoid 'popping' caused by 'p' and 'b' sounds. Rather than talking directly into the mike you need to talk just below or just above it. The newsreader then has to set the level for their voice on pre-fade. The best way to do this is to read the first story as you will deliver it live and adjust the gain so that your voice peaks between four and six on the PPM meter.

Many news studios are designed so that the newsreader stands to deliver the bulletin, and voice coach Kate Lee recommends this especially for novice newsreaders because it allows them to project their voice more easily and use their diaphragm to add timbre to their voice (see Chapter 5 for tips from Kate Lee). But Nick Wilson,[1] news editor at Heart 106, says that when his newsreaders are presenting a 15 minute news magazine programme he tells them to take level from a position of sitting back in a chair to help them to sound more relaxed and conversational.

Having set the microphone level, the newsreader then has to check the level of all the news clips and jingles being used to make sure they all peak at between four and six as well. In most cases the levels on jingles and clips will have already been checked, but you should never assume that the desk has been left as it should have been so it is advisable to do a check yourself.

Once the news jingle has been fired, the newsreader should take a deep breath *before* opening the mike to do the introduction. Some newsreaders prefer to leave the microphone open throughout the bulletin, especially if the clips are very short, but the advantage of closing the mike during clips is that it allows you to take a deep breath, which gives your voice more resonance at the start of the next story.

Interviews

The general approach to interviews – preparation, handling interviewees, what kind of questions should be asked – is dealt with in Chapter 6. In this section the mechanics of different types of interviews are discussed.

One-to-one studio interview

Whether the studio interview is live or recorded it is most likely that a bi-directional microphone will be used, although there is usually a separate microphone for the guest. Where there are two microphones the job of setting levels is much easier – each microphone is set at the level of the person using it. Where there is a single bi-directional microphone it has to be positioned so that it is closer to the interviewee if he/she is softly spoken, and further away if they have a naturally loud voice.

Presenters usually combine setting microphone levels with putting their guest at ease by asking general questions – perhaps about their journey to the studio or the weather – that will give them a response to set the levels to. If it is a live interview there may not be much time to do this, and it is sometimes advisable to tell the interviewee what general area you are going to begin with so that they can collect their thoughts and give a coherent response to the first question. In any event, once the interview is underway you need to keep checking that the levels are stable. It is not unusual for softly spoken people to suddenly develop a booming voice when they realise they are on air or being recorded and you need to be alert to this and adjust the levels accordingly. That said, you will have a better interview if you can engage with your interviewee through eye contact, nodding occasionally and smiling, so resist the temptation to constantly scan the PPM meter. Listening to what is being said should alert you to a change in volume, so the occasional glance at the meter is all that is needed.

Discussion programmes

Discussion programmes will nearly always use bidirectional microphones but occasionally each participant will be fitted with a tie-clip mike. Again, using more than one microphone means each participant can have levels set individually. Where there is one microphone you may need to rearrange seating so that the microphone can be positioned in a way that lets everyone be heard at about the same level. Where clip mikes are being used you need to warn interviewees not to put their hands to their throat when talking as this will obscure their microphone or cause mike rattle.

Recording interviews in the field

Before going out for an interview you must check that your equipment is complete and working. Just as different stations use different editing and play-out systems,

Figure 7.3 A digital Marantz recorder

they also use a variety of different portable digital recorders from minidiscs to solid state digital Marantz recorders to Flashmikes that combine a microphone and a recorder in one. Each has different advantages and disadvantages but all produce high quality audio that can be easily transferred to a computer either by removing their flashcard (upon which the audio is recorded) and putting it into a card reader, or by a simple lead connected to the computer that allows you to access the files on the recorder and drag and drop them onto the computer for editing.

Most recorders work from ordinary batteries, but some have rechargeable packs. In either event, before leaving base reporters should check the battery level and if they are going to be recording for a long period take extra batteries with them. It is also advisable to test the microphone and lead on the recorder by talking into it to make sure it is all working properly. Most minidisc recorders and digital Marantz have an in-built microphone but they do not give broadcast quality sound so it is important to check that you have the recorder set for an auxiliary microphone, and that you have the microphone lead in the correct socket. Once you have listened back to your test remember to turn its speaker off otherwise you will have feedback when you switch it on to record at the interview. If the interview is being conducted outside microphones should be fitted with a wind sock even if it is not a particularly windy day – even a slight breeze can sound like a gale if it is picked up by the mike and that might render your interview unusable.

On arrival, the location of the interview needs to be assessed. Most locations outside a studio have some drawbacks that can cause distortion on the recording and you need to be aware of them so that they can be avoided and worked around. Offices, for example, can be a minefield because of all the electrical equipment in them. Where possible ask for computers to be turned off while you are interviewing, or at the very least move well away from them, otherwise the computer hum will be picked up by the microphone and sound very distracting when played back. Similarly you need to be alert to air-conditioning units and make sure you do not record near them. Wherever possible you should also ask for telephones to be unplugged or calls to the office stopped.

At the other extreme, large empty rooms with high ceilings and uncarpeted floors also cause problems because the sound bounces off walls, making the interview sound as if it were recorded at the bottom of a mine-shaft. If there is nowhere else for the interview to be done you need to try to dampen down the reflected sound as much as possible. One way to do this is to stand in a corner of the room and position yourself and the interviewee in a 'v' shape to trap the sound as much as possible. Where this is not possible you should try to sit as close as possible to the interviewee so that your bodies act as a shield for the sound.

In any event, even in the most accommodating setting, you need to be much closer to the interviewee than you would normally be were you simply chatting to them. This can be quite intimidating for the interviewee who may feel their personal space is being invaded, so sometimes just explaining that you need to be close to them to get a good recording will put them at ease. If the interview is being done standing, position yourself at right angles to the interviewee so that you are close but not 'in their face'. Standing directly in front of someone tends to make them take a step back and you can end up literally backing them against a wall, which is not the most relaxed way to conduct an interview. If you are sitting down for an interview, arrange the seats in an 'L' shape so that your knees are almost touching. If the interview is taking place at a desk or table, position the chairs at one of the corners. Never interview anyone across a desk – you will have to stretch too far with the microphone, which is not only awkward but risks one of your voices being off-mike. There is also more chance that moving the microphone will cause rattle on the interview.

Although reasonably robust, hand-held microphones are sensitive to movement especially where the lead goes into the mike and also where it connects to the recorder. The microphone should be held firmly with the lead looped once around your hand. Make sure that the lead connection to the microphone is not too taut and that you are not pulling on the connection to the recorder. The position you adopt for the interview should mean that there is minimum movement of the microphone.

Once in position you need to take level. It is important to get your levels right because an interview recorded at too low a level will have to be boosted for transmission. This not only means spending more time editing, but it also leaves an annoying hiss on the recording. Interviews recorded at too high a level will be distorted and not fit to be transmitted. As with studio interviews, you can use the chat needed to set levels as a bit of an ice-breaker to put the interviewee at ease.

Position the microphone about a hand-span away from the interviewee's mouth – any closer and it becomes intrusive and can distract them from what they are saying. The microphone should be roughly equidistant between yourself and the interviewee unless one of you has a louder voice in which case you will have to move the microphone until your voices are balanced. Resist the temptation to move the microphone between yourself and the interviewee. This can cause microphone rattle and it also risks one of you being caught off-mike. Instead tilt the microphone towards the person who is speaking. It is a good idea to start the recording with the interviewee giving their name and position as this helps to identify the recording later.

Most recorders allow you to either set the levels manually or use the automatic level control on them. The automatic level control works by keeping the signal below the point of distortion and boosting it when it falls too low. The problem is that to keep the signal even, the automatic control uses any background noise and boosts it to the same volume as the speech, which causes a 'surging' effect on the finished recording. Manual level-setting produces a better quality recording and gives you more control over it. For example, if you are doing a package about transport systems, you might want to interview a bus operator in the bus station to give the piece a sense of location and some colour. With the recorder on manual you can set your levels so that the bus station noises are in the background and your interviewee can be heard clearly above them. With the recorder on automatic, every pause in the interviewee's speech would be filled with bus noises at the same volume as their speech, which would not only be distracting when it is played back, but also sound very unnatural. Generally, automatic control should only be used in very quiet, near-perfect recording conditions.

At the end of the interview check that the piece has recorded *before* you leave. There is no need to play the whole thing back, but you should rewind and make sure it has recorded, then express your thanks and leave. It may be embarrassing to have to redo the interview if there has been an error, but getting back to the station with nothing on the tape is even worse! Before you leave you should also check that you have the interviewee's details – full name, proper title, and at least one contact number.

Finally, on the way back to the station it is a good idea to listen back to the full interview. This will remind you of exactly what has been said and allow you to do some mental editing so that when you get back you already know what your cue will be and what clips you will use.

Radio and technology

It should be clear from this chapter that technological advances have made radio broadcasting simpler: there is less equipment to learn about, and more ways to maintain the quality of sound, but it is still the skill of the presenter or reporter that differentiates good broadcasting from the mediocre or bad.

One disadvantage of computerised radio stations is that because every group has a different system, new recruits have to be trained to use a particular system before they can fully participate in the life of the station – a real problem for freelance presenters and reporters. However, the principles behind every system are similar enough to mean that being able to operate one makes it easier to understand all the others, and the best advice for would-be broadcasters is to get a thorough knowledge of whatever system is available to them through repeated use and practice.

Changes in technology mean radio output can be more creative in less time with a wider variety of voices and sounds. Radio is about communicating and as the following chapter examines, there are various forms of programming used to achieve this end. The technology behind the process should be used to improve the quality and range of what is being communicated rather than dominate it. It is not enough for the technology simply to make radio broadcasting faster – it should also be better.

8 Types of programming

···

All radio is about connecting with the audience but some programmes have a very direct connection. The phone-in, for example, needs the audience to take part for it to work, while during emergency situations many people rely on the radio to give them advice and information. Local radio also performs a service in covering elections: national radio can provide an overview of the election, but it is local radio that gives the detail and makes the election meaningful to its audience. Radio drama requires a different kind of connection from the audience. While most radio listening is a secondary activity, radio drama, whether it is a soap opera, a serial or a full length play, needs the listener to engage with it and be transported to another world.

This chapter will look at four widely used kinds of programming. It starts with the most popular form – the radio phone-in – then moves on to covering emergency situations and elections. It ends with an explanation of how to write drama for radio, and some advice for up-and-coming radio writers.

Phone-ins

·····························

Radio phone-ins in the UK began on BBC local radio in 1968 and were adopted by commercial stations when they came along in the 1970s. As phone-in presenter Brian Hayes notes, 'at that early stage they were novel but mostly dull' (1994: 42), partly because producers were wary about allowing the public on air and so kept to safe topics that were unlikely to cause controversy, and partly because listeners were not skilled in how to take part. As Linda Gage points out, 'over the years callers have come to understand the procedure and what is expected of them. They have learnt to be callers' (1999: 75). But for Trevor Dann,[1] the director of the Radio Academy, the public's new found ease with radio phone-ins makes them less interesting. 'I don't feel I'm hearing real people in quite the same way as I used to,' he says.

'What's happened in the last forty years of phone-ins is we've developed a phone-in mentality.'

From the beginning phone-ins were seen as a cheap way to fill air-time and for commercial radio, tied to a speech/music ratio by the terms of their licence, they were also an easy way to bring their speech content up to the required level. But it soon became clear that phone-ins also serve other functions. Through the phone-in stations can create a dialogue with listeners: the station not only talks to listeners, it also allows them to talk. The phone-in gives people who would not normally be consulted publicly a chance to express their opinion and enter the public debate. As Stephen Barnard notes, 'Encouraging listeners to take part in local or national debates is an important reputation enhancer; it enables stations to underline their own participation in and commitment to the democratic process' (2000:158).

Just how democratic phone-ins are in practice is another issue. The topic is usually selected by the phone-in producer and presenter, callers are screened before going on air, and if they deviate from the agreed subject they can be brought back to their point by the presenter, or even cut off. Ultimately the phone-in is controlled by the production team with the presenter setting its tone and steering the debate. Antony Bellekom,[2] the managing editor of BBC Radio 2 and 6 Music, says the production behind a phone-in is vitally important:

> There should be no such thing as an un-produced phone-in. You need to know where it's going, how long it's going on for, is it focused enough? How do we take the story that's been told by a caller forward? A phone in is not about throwing out some controversial point, waiting for the calls to come in and putting them to air in the order they come in. I would always say you'll be listening to what the caller has to say, to work out whether they're going to sound good, whether they've got something to say, and what coaching you need to give them so that they get to their message really quickly. If you listen to Jeremy Vine (on BBC Radio 2), the people who answer the calls are really skilled. They know how to get the point down really quickly. They know what coaching is needed so the person gets to the point rather than boring the nation. They'll go as far as saying 'Jeremy will say this to you' or 'you say this to Jeremy'. They'll actually take something they've said and use it as a way to introduce the caller without it always being 'how are you'. It's about retaining that critical facility. Listening to what the punters are saying and trying to have a direction to keep the thing moving forward.

As with every aspect of radio, the type of phone-in a station has needs to reflect its brand and research by the Broadcasting Standards Commission and the Radio Authority (now Ofcom) suggests that listeners expect phone-in participants to be aware of how they should behave and what sort of treatment they will receive from different presenters.

If presenters were known for the 'bad' treatment of callers, the caller should accept or expect that they were going to be treated badly. Some participants in the groups even went so far as to say that callers deserved *'everything they get'*. Others felt that if callers telephoned in then they should be clever or fast enough to *'give as good as they get'* so they do not open themselves up to mockery.

(Hargrave 2000: 20)

In the UK, American style shock-jocks like Howard Stern who use tactics like ridiculing callers and being deliberately outrageous did not really catch on. Nonetheless there are some controversial phone-in hosts who have developed their own particular style. talkSPORT's Jon Gaunt[3] hosts a topical phone-in every weekday morning and he is described on the station's website as 'one of the nation's most controversial voices' mainly because of his right-wing views and brusque attitude to callers. But despite his reputation he manages to connect with listeners, and in 2001 he and his team at BBC Three Counties in Luton where he worked at the time won three Sony gold awards for their coverage of the Vauxhall car plant closure:

If you want your listeners to share their most private things, you've got to give them something of yourself . . . We won the Sonys because those workers knew me and they'd phone up every day. They trusted me. So when Vauxhall took their jobs, who were they going to talk to first? It sounds condescending, but these guys don't know who their MPs are, they don't write to newspapers, they're not part of that process. And they're the ones I've always wanted to talk to.

(Quoted in Silver 2007)

So it would seem that the style of the presenter is less important than the expectations of the audience. Callers to BBC 5 Live, for example, expect the discussion to be well-mannered and balanced while those to stations like talkSPORT know that the presenters can be opinionated and abrasive. As the controller of 5 Live Adrian Van Klaveren admits, 'The role of a phone-in is always a hard thing to get exactly right. There's always a different opinion about how exactly you might have done it, and it often tends to be a negative one' (quoted in Plunkett 2008e).

Nonetheless, even the most opinionated and abrasive phone-in host has to operate within regulatory boundaries. One of the best-known phone-in hosts in the UK is James Whale who began his broadcasting career with a late-night phone-in on *Metro Radio* in Newcastle in 1974. While there he built up a loyal fan base with his 'no nonsense' approach to callers, which at the time was quite unusual in British broadcasting. In 1995 he joined what is now talkSPORT and became its longest serving presenter until May 2008 when he was sacked following complaints to Ofcom for urging voters in London to vote for Boris Johnson in the mayoral election. This breached the Ofcom Broadcasting Code regarding due impartiality. According to section 5.9 of the code 'presenters must not use the advantage of regular appearances to promote their views in a way that compromises the requirement for due impartiality. Presenter phone-ins must encourage and must not exclude alternative views'.

Stations like talkSPORT, which launched in 1995 as Talk Radio, rely heavily on phone-ins covering topics from politics to sport and their hosts are often very opinionated, and while it is all right for presenters to express an opinion they must allow alternative views to be heard in equal measure. Antony Bellekom, who worked at Talk Radio in its early days, says phone-in programmes tend to get a lot of complaints:

> Most commercial stations in those days would be quite unhappy if they had a complaint to the Radio Authority (now Ofcom) every year and I had to deal with something like 120 complaints a year. The reality was that only two or three were ever upheld and the reason given – it was a single phrase – was that it did not exceed the audience's expectations. And that I think is exactly the territory we're in. What does the audience expect? The complaints that were upheld by the Radio Authority in those days tended to be when a mild-mannered presenter did something wrong. It wasn't about James Whale being abrasive, it was about someone at three o'clock on a Sunday afternoon getting overly short with someone on air. So I think it's about creating and maintaining an expectation and that I think is the safest way of dealing with this sort of issue. There's no point in trying to break those boundaries – it can only go wrong on you.

The most popular phone-in format features a presenter and one or two guests to kick-start the discussion. Typically these programmes deal with topics related to news stories, consumer issues and advice lines. Some programmes like that of 5 Live's Victoria Derbyshire, which airs every weekday morning, demonstrate the flexibility of phone-ins by debating the big issues around the latest news stories, while others like BBC Radio 4's *Money Box Live*, which deals with personal finance issues, have a specific topic that is known about in advance by the listeners.

Having guests in the studio takes the pressure off phone-in presenters and producers if there are not many calls coming in because under the presenter's guidance they can stimulate the discussion. As well as phone calls programmes use texts and even emails to keep the discussion moving along. The use of texts in radio programmes broadens the range of people taking part in the phone-in as Antony Bellekom explains:

> You can make great use of texts sometimes. You can use something that someone has said who won't come on air or who maybe even inappropriate on air but through the text you get a really sharp message which helps take the

programme along. At the end of the day it's just another tool. A producer's just got a tool kit. It may be a box of records, it may be a good presenter, it may be news clips, it may be bulletins. The skill of the producer is just making the best possible use of the things they're allowed to play with.

That said the appeal of the phone-in for most listeners is to hear different voices giving their opinions, but putting the public live on air can be dangerous and for that reason almost all commercial radio stations use a delay system. The presenter is usually in charge of what is called the profanity button. This allows them to cut off any callers who start to swear or say something that could lead to a libel action. Even if the libel is unintentional, the station is responsible for broadcasting it, so extreme care has to be taken whenever a caller starts to mention brand names or particular personalities. The profanity button allows the station output to be broadcast with a delay of up to ten seconds so that if a presenter feels the need they can press the button before anything offensive goes out on air.

At the BBC there is no delay to calls going out on air, but as Antony Bellekom explains, the calls are moderated by producers and researchers before they go on air, and part of their skill is being able to recognise people who might abuse the situation. 'Of course once they get on air they can say what they like and you'd be foolish to have a producer or presenter who wasn't alert to that situation,' he says.

But as an organisation the BBC is aware of the potential hazards of phone-ins and its Editorial Guidelines (available at www.bbc.co.uk) give the following advice:

> phone-in programmes may use comments sent via text, email and the red button as well as talking to callers. The live nature of phone-ins means we should be alert to the possibility of contributors breaking the law or causing widespread offence. We should also be careful not to allow phone-ins to become a vehicle for the opinions of the presenter. The following best practice may help to minimise the risks:
>
> • contributors to phone-ins should normally be called back and if necessary briefed before they go on air:
> • content producers should read emails and texts before they are broadcast:
> • presenters should be adequately briefed on BBC Editorial Guidelines and the law and be able to extricate the programme from tricky situations with speed and courtesy:
> • when producing a phone-in on a difficult or controversial subject such as child abuse, the production team should be briefed on how to deal sensitively with contributors and support systems should be in place:
> • when a programme is contacted unexpectedly by someone wishing to share their difficult story, we should consider the implications and refer if necessary.

For many stations the most popular phone-in is about sport. The passion that major sports evoke mean these can be lively and even heated discussions so that even if you are not a fan they make compelling listening. Local radio stations in particular can use football phone-ins to good effect by giving fans of local teams which might not get coverage elsewhere a chance to air their views of their team's performance. Their popularity at a national level is also evident in the fact that 5 Live's *606* football phone-in started as a Saturday evening show and now runs three or four times a week.

But perhaps the most effective phone-ins are those where a breaking news story is happening and those directly involved in it call in, as happened on 7 July 2005 when London was hit by a series of terrorist bombs. Although reporters were soon at the scene, many eye witnesses, some still unsure of just what had happened, called radio stations to give their accounts. At the time Jon Gaunt was working for BBC London doing a morning phone-in. One of the station's employees had been on a bombed train and he called in making the station the first to get an eye-witness account on air (Hudson and Rowlands 2007: 377). As the morning went on and it was confirmed as a terrorist attack, more and more people called in with their stories, producing compelling radio. As Trevor Dann of the Radio Academy notes, 'Phone-ins work brilliantly where there's a piece of journalism and the caller gives you user generated content – that stuff is priceless.'

Emergency situations

As the example above shows, radio is at its best reacting to the unexpected. Its ability to change its entire output to react to a crisis makes it the medium most people turn to, at least in the first instance, at these times. Throughout the day of 7/7 stations across the country kept listeners informed of what was happening in London and allowed those directly affected to talk about their experience. The London stations in particular provided a vital service in keeping people informed and also comforting them by sharing what had happened. As Mark Dennison[4] of 96 Trent FM explains, 'At a time like that people watch the news and read the papers and although it sounds a bit cheesy, people look on their local radio station as a bit of a friend and that's where they go for a bit of support and reassurance.'

That was certainly the case in the summer floods of 2007 when thousands of people found themselves marooned in their homes with no drinking water or power. For people in Gloucester where the flooding was at its worst Severn Sound became a lifeline. As the news editor at Severn Sound, Duncan Cooke[5] was aware that the station had to help its listeners:

> People rely on local radio to tell them exactly what is happening where they live, as it is something they won't get from a national news provider. When the

initial floods started it was mainly affecting roads, so our job was to tell people which roads were closed and give out advice from police, highways agency and so on. When the emergency became more severe, we were informing people on the water shortage, where they could get bottled water and the latest advice on public health.

As the flooding took hold of the city the station found it was also affected as Will Nunan,[6] the station's charity manager, recalls:

The station's based right in the city centre and although we weren't flooded we had no water and no power. Obviously we couldn't broadcast without power so we switched to our generator that provides two hours of power. During that time the presenters and everyone else drove up to our sister station in Bristol and we set up there and presented from Bristol.

The station normally broadcasts hourly news bulletins from 6 am to 7 pm but for the two weeks of the crisis it extended its bulletins from 6 am to 10 pm and also ran updates every thirty minutes, which was a challenge for the news team of four. Duncan Cooke says that he based himself in Gloucester to cover the daily press conferences given by the emergency services, while two of his reporters covered the affected areas talking to flood victims, and the fourth team member read the bulletins. In common with most radio stations, Severn Sound already had a procedure worked out for how to deal with an emergency situation, and although it had never been put to the test before the floods, Duncan says it worked well:

We had a very positive response from people, who were grateful for the latest information, there was a real feeling of we're all in this together! We were able to provide a real service by taking their questions and concerns and then passing them onto the relevant authorities to get an answer. I think we all learnt a lot from the experience. As a news team it has made us stronger and given us plenty of ideas on how we would cover a similar event in the future, what went well and what we need to work on. We gained many new contacts as a result of what happened and it also strengthened our links with the police and local councils.

As well as extending the news service, Severn Sound used its promotional team, aptly named the Thunders, to go to badly affected areas and distribute bottled water and basic foodstuff like bread. There was also a helpline set up for listeners to call in with problems. Will Nunan was part of the team working on the helpline that took nearly 5,000 calls over the two week emergency period. He says the experience made him realise the strengths of local radio:

A lot of the calls were routine – when's my water coming on and how's the traffic doing – that sort of thing. But we also took calls from people who were badly affected and I remember there was one old lady of 90 who called and she said she'd had no water for five days and no-one had visited her and she didn't know what to do. It really gets you to know there are people depending on our service. We sent the Thunders straight down to her with bread and water and then we got in touch with her family and they went to get her. It could have been a nasty situation and it was good we were able to help out.

Will says a lot of people in the area used the station as a primary source of information because they had local information about things like where the nearest water bowser was, and when water and electricity could be expected to be restored. Even people who had no electricity could access the station by using battery powered radios. For those with power, the station's website came into its own, as Will explains:

We tried to put information online as soon as we got it. There's only so much we could say on air before it became repetitive and confusing so we directed people to our website and all the information was there as well as links to other websites that were providing support to people who needed it.

After the emergency, Tim Brain, the Chief Constable of Gloucestershire Police, publicly thanked Severn Sound for getting key messages out to the public, and local radio in general was praised in the Cabinet Office report into the floods:

The media, particularly local radio, has a pivotal role in passing important information to large numbers of people affected by flooding or loss of essential services . . . In many cases, the media acted as a 'friendly voice', listening to public concerns and providing a sense of reassurance, especially to people isolated by the floods and those living alone.
(Extract from the Pitt Review: Learning Lessons from the 2007 Floods.
Quoted in Action Stations 2008: 41)

Emergency situations like the floods show local radio at its best. The strengths of the medium in being immediate and portable, combined with the trust listeners have in their local station make it ideal for helping in a crisis, and like other stations who dealt with similar situations Severn Sound gained listeners for much longer than the immediate emergency period. Duncan Cooke says the aftermath of the floods was also important, and the station kept in touch with people evacuated to caravans to keep their stories in the news. But it was the two-week crisis period that he most remembers:

I remember it was an exhausting couple of weeks but also exciting, we were part of the emergency and eating and sleeping flood stories, so I would say it was one of the most incredible experiences of my career.

Elections

Covering elections – particularly general elections – can also be an adrenaline-filled experience for reporters, not only because of the passion of the event when the tension at a closely contested count is almost palpable, but also because elections are surrounded by a minefield of regulations. Because of this many music-based stations choose to restrict their coverage to reporting that the election has been called and giving the results at the end. Nick Wilson, the news editor at Heart 106 in the East Midlands, says for a regional station like his there are also practical considerations to take into account. Heart's transmission area covers 31 constituencies, making it difficult if not impossible to do all of them with a small newsroom. There is also a judgement to be made about how much your audience wants to hear about the election. 'In the last General Election we didn't cover the counts and decided to keep the election to headlines,' explains Nick Wilson.[7] 'People are voting for their local MP but ultimately they want to know who's going to be in overall power ahead of whether their local MP's changed.'

For other stations elections are periods of special programming both in the run-up to the day and following the count. Given the number of elections there are this can mean doing election coverage of one kind or another almost every year. General elections are held at least once every five years. Local councillors are elected for a four-year term: on some councils this means the whole council stands for election once every four years, but others hold an election three out of four years where a third of the council is up for election every year for three years with no election in the fourth year (election by thirds), and still others do election by halves where half the council is up for election every two years (election by halves). European Parliament elections are held every five years; and by-elections can occur at any time.

Broadcast media are subjected to more stringent restrictions during the election period than are the print media. Newspapers are able to favour certain candidates over others, campaign for a particular political party, and even run the results of an opinion poll on the day of polling. But under the combined effect of the 1981 and 1990 Broadcasting Acts, the Representation of the People Acts 1983 and 2000, and the Political Parties, Elections and Referendums Act 2000, television and radio must provide fair and balanced election coverage, and keep records to prove that this has been done. In particular stations and their presenters must never endorse a particular candidate or party on air. As mentioned earlier, phone-in host James Whale was sacked from talkSPORT in May 2008 for encouraging his audience to vote for Boris Johnson in the London Mayoral election. A complaint about his comments to Ofcom prompted an investigation by the regulator who fined the station £20,000.

Both the BBC's Editorial Guidelines (available at www.bbc.co.uk) and Ofcom's Broadcasting Code (available at www.ofcom.org.uk) have sections that deal with

how elections should be covered. These rules cover the period from the announcement of the election to the close of polls. Ofcom gives a precise definition of what
constitutes the election period:

> For a parliamentary general election, this period begins with the announcement
> of the dissolution of Parliament. For a parliamentary by-election, this period
> begins with the issuing of a writ or on such earlier date as is notified in the
> London Gazette. For the Scottish Parliament elections, the period begins with
> the dissolution of the Scottish Parliament or, in the case of a by-election, with
> the date of the occurrence of a vacancy. For the National Assembly for Wales,
> the Northern Ireland Assembly, the London Assembly and for local government
> elections, it is the last date for publication of notices of the election. For
> European parliamentary elections, it is the last date for publication of the notice
> of election, which is 25 days before the election. In all cases the period ends
> with the close of the poll.
>
> (Ofcom Broadcasting Code 2005)

Essentially the rules aim to give impartial, neutral and balanced coverage to each
political party taken over the whole election period. As the BBC Guidelines point
out:

> Previous electoral support in equivalent elections is a starting point for making
> judgements about the proportionate levels of coverage. However, other factors
> will be taken into account, including more recent evidence of variation in levels
> of support in elections since then, changed political circumstances (e.g. new
> parties, or party splits) as well as other evidence of current support.

The Guidelines go on to specify that balance must be achieved in three categories:
clips; interviews/discussions of up to 10 minutes; long form programmes, and
that:

> each strand (e.g. a drive time show on radio) is responsible for reaching its own
> targets within the week and cannot rely on other outlets at different times of
> the day (e.g. the breakfast show) to do so for it.

Understandably political parties monitor the coverage closely to make sure they get
equal exposure to other parties, and radio stations keep an election log to keep their
own record of coverage. In the past a candidate who refused to take part in a broadcast
report could effectively veto the entire report, but under the Political Parties,
Elections and Referendums Act 2000 as long as all candidates are given the chance
to take part in any report, their refusal to take part cannot stop the report going out,
as the Ofcom Code makes clear:

If a candidate takes part in an item about his/her particular constituency, or electoral area, then candidates of each of the major parties must be offered the opportunity to take part. (However, if they refuse or are unable to participate, the item may nevertheless go ahead.)

(Section 6:9)

This means that candidates can be used more freely than in the past, and according to Aeneas Rotsos, the news editor at BBC Radio Nottingham, it makes better coverage. 'Because of the changes our coverage of elections has become more interesting,' he says.[8] 'There's more of a build up now and we're able to reflect and debate issues of concern to the people of Nottinghamshire but previously it was more difficult to do that.'

The ubiquity of radio station websites has also meant that having to list all candidates standing in the election area is no longer necessary because listeners can simply be directed to the station website. The advice from Ofcom is clear:

Any constituency or electoral area report or discussion after the close of nominations must include a list of all candidates standing, giving first names, surnames and the name of the party they represent or, if they are standing independently, the fact that they are an independent candidate. This must be conveyed in sound and/or vision. Where a constituency report on a radio service is repeated on several occasions in the same day, the full list need only be broadcast on one occasion. If, in subsequent repeats on that day, the constituency report does not give the full list of candidates, the audience should be directed to an appropriate website or other information source listing all candidates and giving the information set out above.

(Section 6:11)

Audience interactivity can make lively and interesting broadcasting during an election period but care has to be taken that balance is achieved throughout. For phone-in programmes, for example, the BBC Guidelines say:

Callers to phone-ins must be checked to see if they are candidates. They can be encouraged to contribute, but the audience must be clear that they are speaking not as ordinary members of the public but as contributors with a stated political agenda.

The use of texts and emails in programmes must also be carefully monitored to make sure that there is balance in what is broadcast, rather than what is received by the programme from contributors. The BBC Guidelines warn that programme makers need to be alert to organised campaigns by parties or pressure groups that might distort the balance.

During this period [programme makers] should ask e-mail contributors to include their address and telephone number so that checks can be run if necessary where mass mailings are suspected. During the campaign we will not broadcast numbers received on either side of any issue.

Opinion polls are another fraught area during the election period. The BBC Guidelines acknowledge that opinion polls are 'part of the story' and audiences should be informed about them but they must be used carefully, and audiences need to be made aware that they can be wrong. 'Even when polls appear to be consistent, we should ensure the language and prominence of our reporting allows for the possibility that they may not be borne out' (BBC Editorial Guidelines 2008a).

Obviously stations that are more speech based will give more coverage to an election campaign than music-based stations, but Lewis Skrimshaw[9] from 96 Trent FM says even the music-based GCap stations (now Global radio) give more coverage to elections than they used to do by pooling group resources.

In the run-up to the general election the political battle buses are covered by the UK desk. What we do normally is a week of specials that we put into our extended bulletins. In 2005 we had a tightly edited montage of 20" from the three main candidates in every constituency in Nottingham saying what you would get if they were elected then a back announcement directing people to the website for the list of other candidates standing. The reporter set up the package with what the key issues for each constituency were and put it into context.

Polling day itself can be a bit of an anti-climax because it is an offence to broadcast anything about the way that people have voted in the election while the polls are open. This means stations can only refer to polling in a general way – giving weather conditions and whether polling is light or brisk – until the polls close at 10 pm. Then the real work for reporters begins in covering the election count. Once a count begins everyone in the counting area must stay there until the result is declared and if recounts are involved this can last many hours. As Aeneas Rotsos, news editor at BBC Radio Nottingham explains, reporters need to keep their wits about them during the count:

As a reporter you are very much the voice of the station at that count and you have to think on your feet a lot – you've got to find guests and find stories. You've got to find the latest story and the latest angle to make the count sound really interesting so it's a real challenge. As a reporter it's one of the most challenging things you'll ever face – you've got to think on your feet and find the stories to make that count come alive.

Stations doing election results programmes generally start them an hour after the polls close so that the first results occur quite early in the programme. The usual format is to have a presenter and some political analysts who can comment on important results and emerging trends, and the presenter has to keep the studio discussion going, announce the results as they come in, and go to live links when they are ready.

It is common practice for the count from several different areas to be held in a central location. Most of these places, like town halls or large sports halls, now have ISDN lines in place, which makes live links quite straight-forward. Reporters covering a count should use the time before the result is announced to get to know all the candidates and their agents and arrange interviews for after the result. If the announcement by the returning officer is needed, they need to make sure their microphone is in position in good time. They also need to keep an eye on how the count is progressing so that they can let the studio know when to expect a result.

Until recently all counts were done on the night of the election, which made it a long night for everyone involved, but meant that by the next morning almost all the results were known. Now several local authorities choose to do their count the next day, which often means any changes to the political landscape are not known until mid-afternoon of the following day.

But whenever the results are announced local radio has an important role to play in announcing them. Lewis Skrimshaw, from 96 Trent FM, says even with a small news team it is possible to give interesting coverage of elections:

> We only have four reporters so we're not about to man every count. What we do is collate results as they come in and try to cover one central location where there are several counts going on and do it that way. That enables you to have a bunch of candidates in one place for your field reporter to get. Then we can say this is how the political landscape has changed or not in Nottingham. Then we go for the GCap style which is – so what does this mean for the residents of Nottingham.

Being more speech-based and with more resources, BBC local radio tends to cover elections in more detail than commercial radio. Aeneas Rotsos, from BBC Radio Nottingham, says despite the challenge of doing an election special on the night of the election, and often spending most of the next day still gathering results, elections are important to both audiences and journalists, but he understands the constraints commercial radio works under:

> Commercial radio just don't have the staff in most cases therefore a duty falls on the BBC to make sure the elections are covered. I think it's a shame more commercial stations don't do it because local authorities affect everything that happens in their areas from policing right through to health care. It's also a good way of meeting new local councillors and it gives you a chance to make contacts.

But whether the coverage is in-depth or perfunctory local radio is the ideal medium to deal with elections: national coverage cannot explain the impact of the results for every area of the country, and local newspapers cannot provide the immediacy of radio. For these reasons elections are important events to local radio, albeit a time when newsrooms in particular breathe a sigh of relief when it is all over.

Radio drama

Radio drama[10] has a loyal following in the UK but unfortunately it is very much confined to BBC Radio 4 with some plays broadcast on BBC Radio 3. Nonetheless, radio drama is very popular, as the long-running soap opera on BBC Radio 4 – *The Archers* – shows. *The Archers* began in the early 1950s and tells the story of a group of farmers, farm workers and other people who live in the fictional village of Ambridge. Its 13 minute episodes are broadcast every day except Saturday, and it is one of the BBC's most popular podcasts. But despite drama having few other outlets on radio in the UK, radio dramatist Amanda Whittington[11] says the BBC is very supportive of new writing:

> In terms of the landscape of new writing, and I can only compare it with theatre
> – a regional rep may do one new play a year but I think Radio 4 can feature up
> to four new pieces of drama a day. So actually it feels that in this country because
> of Radio 4 we've got this amazing outlet for drama and it's the biggest employer
> of writers – certainly dramatic writers – in the country. If you're doing some

Figure 8.1
Radio playwright Amanda Whittington

interesting stuff Radio 4 is very open because they need that turn over of writers. In one way we're blessed because we have this fantastic institution that's producing drama at a rate of knots but it would be amazing to see that across the other networks because there really isn't that much apart from Radio 4. It works and people enjoy it because there's a great audience for Radio 4 drama. I'd love to see more opportunities but there seems to be a great deal more opportunities for writers in radio that there are in other mediums.

Amanda has written plays for the stage and also for the BBC *Afternoon Play* as well as serials for BBC Radio 4's *Woman's Hour*. While she agrees that radio can present some challenges for a writer, she also thinks it can be liberating:

Obviously the stage is a visual medium but on radio you're telling the story verbally. In some cases radio actually opens your writing up because the stage is a very practical medium: you have to think about getting actors physically on and off, and sets on and off. But in radio you can go anywhere really and you can have multiple locations. It's a bigger kind of toy box to play with in a sense so in a way it's more free than the stage.

It still has to be focused and it has to be a story that makes sense: it's not like you can pinball around locations that don't connect. You write shorter scenes as well. A woman's hour serial is 15 minutes and you might have 10 or 12 scenes within that whereas on the stage you can have one scene that lasts 15 or 20 minutes. So even though the story may be the same and the characters may be the same, the way you structure the story is completely different. And then you can have lots of stylistic differences. It's often very useful to have a character talking directly to the audience – a kind of a narrator – because in radio you really feel that you can get inside somebody's head whereas on stage that can feel a little bit odd. There's lots of stylistic things you can play with.

I find radio a fantastically creative medium to work in. I think you can get a bit hung up on sound effects in radio because actually it's best to keep it to the essentials – less is more really so to have just vital sounds. If the sounds are a part of telling the story and setting the location – things like if you're in a kitchen having the kettle boiling – something as simple as that can really set the location – you don't want five or six things going on at once. On stage to set a scene is an entirely different process.

I think what I've learned from working in radio is that it's absolutely about story and character, which is the same whether you're writing a novel or a play or anything. The medium is just a way of getting that story across – you don't want to be too bogged down by the medium itself.

Another interesting difference between radio and stage that I've found when adapting work is that obviously a stage play's written for an audience of may be five or six hundred people who will all see it collectively, whereas on radio people are generally listening individually on their own or maybe in ones and twos and that is a very different relationship as a writer. It just makes the writing more intimate. It means you can do things with more intimacy. You're very aware that a stage play is going out into a big space with several hundred people if you're lucky, but radio is going into someone's room or car with one person and that's an entirely different dynamic and that just allows you to be smaller and more detailed but often that detail is what makes something big. If you're writing a love story and there are tiny details that can actually make it quite epic. It's a really interesting dynamic that you play with – just because it's small and quiet and intimate doesn't mean the stories are small and quiet and intimate it actually can allow you to be quite bold and big.

Having written both longer plays for radio and serials Amanda has a lot of experience of the medium, and she warns that thinking every aspect of a story has to be illustrated with sound is a mistake. She believes the story and characters are the most important ingredients in a good radio drama, along with actors who understand the medium. She adds that the relationship between the writer, producer and actors is vital because there is not much time for rehearsal:

What's interesting about radio is you don't get much time to rehearse. Writing for Radio 4 you spend a long time on the script – maybe six months on the script – and then you have three days to record it. The cast comes together and at nine o'clock on day one – you'll read it and then at half past ten you'll be in the studio recording it. It demands of you as a script writer that you get everything exactly right. On a stage play you might have three or four weeks of rehearsal to get everything right. On radio you have to make sure that the script is really tight and really strong and then for the actors it's an incredibly demanding process in that sense because they perform it straight off. The actors have to understand the medium but equally it can be quite freeing because they have the scripts in their hands and they don't have to worry about their entrances and exits and their costumes and all that kind of stuff – it's just about character, voice, performance, story.

We recorded *Bollywood Jane* the *Woman's Hour* serial in three days which was really demanding but also such fun to do and very liberating. I think because you just have to hit the ground running and do it there's not enough time to really think about it.

Some of the sound effects for a drama, like traffic noise or general background atmosphere, are put in after the play has been recorded, but other effects, for example, the slamming of a door, are done live. And although there is no formal rehearsal, Amanda says each scene is usually done several times before the producer is satisfied:

You do a scene and maybe do three or four takes of that scene and the producer will kind of direct and change little things as you're doing it so there's a sense of rehearsal going on as it's being recorded. Then they might pick their favourite take or splice a couple of takes together so the editing process is quite clever. Often it's hard to tell the difference between takes but the producer will say right number three was brilliant that's the one we're using.

For a *Woman's Hour* episode it has to be something like thirteen and a half minutes – and it can't be 12 and it can't be 14 so to be that exact is really tough and often stuff is cut. The nightmare is when you have to fill it.

In the serials you try to leave each episode on a cliff hanger because there's the traditional thing of hoping people will tune in tomorrow. But that's quite fun as well – to create stories in bite-size pieces and its quite interesting when you sit down to write it to see how much ground you can cover in 13 minutes and how much story you can pack in.

A stage play is about two hours long so to do it for radio means your material becomes very compressed and stronger for it so you can find those little cliff hangers quite easily. I've also done afternoon plays and that's a very different shape because that's 45 minutes which would be only one half of a stage play. So again it's about playing with a different structure or shape. How do you tell your story and create something in that relatively short space of time.

Amanda's advice for new writers is to spend time listening to the Radio 4 output and to make a note of who has produced the work you like best, then directly contact that producer. 'Your way in to Radio 4 is through the producers,' she says. There are BBC in-house producers and also independent producers who make their pitch to commissioning editors about four times a year to try to get the work they are interested in commissioned and made. 'The key thing is to build a good relationship with the producer, then the producer will pitch your work and if it's commissioned then you're guaranteed that it's going to get broadcast,' she says. And because of the turn-over of drama on radio, Amanda believes producers are often open to new ideas:

I've found that generally speaking producers are interested and open to new ideas but you need to present your ideas in a constructive professional way. Rather than just 'I want to write for radio' say 'I listened to your show and I really like this and this is the kind of work that I'm interested in and this is what I've done'. You've got to sell your services and tell them what you can do for them rather than just expect them to open the door.

I've found there's a great openness there. If you haven't written anything before you need to write something that you can show to a producer to prove that you've got ideas and you've got potential. I think it's also about being open to the process. It's virtually unheard of that a completely unknown writer would write a radio script, send it in and they'd go 'oh this is brilliant we'll make it'. But that's a message of hope really – they're not looking for brilliant polished diamonds. What they're looking for is people and ideas with potential that they can work with. Get a piece of work together, send it in but then be very open to the development of it. And if they say 'that's not right but we like something in it' have three or four other ideas as well that you can pitch to them. It's a collaborative medium, if you can build relationships and be open to collaboration and be open to other people's input into your work that's how you'll move on.

What each of the four types of programmes looked at above show is that good radio is about connecting with the audience and involving them on an emotional level. As the next chapter examines, sport is another way that radio stations can form a bond with their audience.

9 Sport on radio

....

Sport works really well on radio whether it is to give the latest results or to provide commentary on a live event. The immediacy of the medium and its portability make it a natural choice for sports fans whether they are on the move, or attending an event and tuning in for the expert view on what is unfolding before them, or to catch the latest scores of rival teams. For national stations like BBC 5 Live and talkSPORT it is a core part of their output, but it is also important to local radio stations because by identifying with local teams they strengthen their links with the community they broadcast to and even people with little interest in sport want to know how local teams are doing.

Although specialist sports stations cover just about every sport, most stations tend to restrict their coverage to mainstream sports like rugby, cricket and of course football. GCap sports editor Phil Blacker[1] says the popularity of a sport determines how much coverage it gets:

> If we get the offer of a story from the badminton world championship or whatever we're not going to touch it because we don't have the time to. That's not to say it's not relevant, but to our main audience it's not as relevant to as many as football is. You're never going to get away from that because we've got to sell what we do in terms of bringing in the audience and bringing people in online and football is going to do that more than any other sport.

The first football match commentary broadcast in the UK was on a match between Arsenal and Sheffield United on 22 January 1927 from 'a wooden hut that largely resembled a garden shed' (Adams 2005) at the Highbury ground. According to BBC Sport's Audrey Adams, commentary would have started years before then but sporting bodies and newspaper owners thought the new medium would hit attendance at the games and newspaper sales and vetoed it. But when the BBC was granted its first Royal Charter in January 1927, it was also granted the right to broadcast major sporting events. The commentator for this historic broadcast was former Harlequin rugby player Henry Blythe Thornhill Wakelam, aided by a representation of the pitch published in the *Radio Times*. As Adams explains:

> The producer at the time, Lance Sieveking, devised a plan of the pitch divided into eight numbered squares, which was published in the Radio Times. The idea was that the listener at home could follow the play from his armchair using the grid on his lap. Many believe this is the origin of the phrase 'Back to Square One'.

The broadcast was a huge success, with the *Spectator* commenting that 'that type of broadcasting has come to stay' (ibid.), and by the end of the year a whole range of commentaries had been broadcast including the Grand National, the Boat Race, the FA Cup Final and Wimbledon.

Even in an age where television coverage of sport is extensive, radio is a natural partner for it, as GCap's Phil Blacker notes:

> Radio's a great medium for sport – especially live sport – it's so immediate. There's something almost romantic about it in that you can't see what's going on but someone is painting a picture for you and it's special in that way. It's much more intimate than television.

As mentioned before, sport – and most especially football – is important to local radio stations because it provides a way for stations to identify with the community, and also because it can attract a different audience. BBC Radio Nottingham, for example, provides commentary every Saturday afternoon for both local teams – Nottingham Forest and Notts County – using a split frequency. Editor Sophie Stewart[2] says that coverage widens their audience:

> Football's really important to us because it brings in a different audience that probably don't listen other than for sport on Saturday. The challenge is to bring that audience to the rest of the output. We use a lot of trails and promos for other programmes at that time. At half time it's important we have a lot of messages but they have to be done in a proper way. The way we do a trail for (inclusion in) sport on Saturday is different to other times because we want to be promoting things that this different audience can access easily.

BBC local stations tend to have their own sports reporters, but many music-based stations do not have that luxury, and stations in the GCap group (now Global Radio) use a London-based sports team for most of their coverage, as sports editor Phil Blacker explains:

What we try to do is complement local teams with all the national sport covering cup finals, premier league games, test matches – basically all the national sport. We're at those events plus we do day-to-day clips and audio and scripts of whatever's going on and we send it out via our internal system so its then up to the local stations whether or not they use it.

For big sporting events like Wimbledon or the Rugby World Cup the GCap sports reporters take requests from local stations to get interviews with players from their area that the stations can use either in bulletins or as part of programmes. Phil Blacker says the excitement around the 2007 Rugby World Cup meant his reporters were in great demand, doing regular two-ways into breakfast programmes around the country so that every station had a tailor-made segment. 'We did 36 two-ways in about two hours,' he says. 'It was literally three minutes dial up, dial in and do the same again with someone else.'

A similar arrangement was used by the BBC during the 2008 Olympic Games in Beijing when a small team of BBC sports reporters was sent to furnish local radio and television with interviews from local competitors. Ross Fletcher[3] from BBC Radio Derby was one of them, and he says it was a real challenge:

My remit was to interview competitors from all sports – all 28 sports or at least the ones that Great Britain had entrants in, not to duplicate what BBC Sport were doing during their live commentary – although we complemented them to a degree – but really to interview sports people who local stations had an interest in. We would tailor them for, for example, East Midlands Today television or BBC Essex, BBC Devon and so on. We'd have requests a day in advance and we would go and service that, but we'd also go to live events and interview competitors. For example we went to a rowing press conference pre the actual competition. There were 43 rowers and myself and my colleague managed to interview 27 of them. It was about providing material to all the different stations so that everyone got a slice of the Olympics and everybody's Olympic story was told on the BBC.

The growing importance of sport on radio was shown when the UK's first speech-based commercial radio station, Talkradio, re-launched in 2000 as talkSPORT shifting the emphasis of the station firmly towards sport. According to Antony Bellekom,[4] who was the station's programme director from 1998–2000, the change was the making of the station:

I think the strength of talkSPORT at its outset was that it did what commercial radio is supposed to do – it started from the position of its customer which unlike BBC radio is not its audience but its advertisers. That doesn't mean the radio was less good as a consequence – it just means there was a different driving force behind it. The driving force for talkSPORT was to turn from a loss making station to a profit making station by finding an audience that wasn't being served and that had money to spend. talkSPORT found a really niche hole in the market, somewhere not a huge distance from 5 Live but much freer in its approach and that's where it went. It went after the young male audience with some money in their pockets and a passion for sport.

Since the change talkSPORT has developed a growing audience, although its main rival, BBC 5 Live, has more than double the number of listeners. 5 Live was launched in March 1994 as a rolling news and sports station, but with a heavy emphasis on sport and that accounts for its audience profile, which is 72 per cent male with an average age of 47 (Plunkett 2008h). As well as the main station, there is a sister station, 5 Live Sports Extra, a part-time station that provides commentary for events not covered by 5 Live. According to its service licence, all of the digital-only station's output should be live sports coverage and it 'should aim to provide increased value for licence fee payers from the portfolio of sports rights already owned by the BBC by offering alternative coverage to that provided on other UK-wide BBC services' (BBC 5 Live Sports Extra Service Licence: July 2008). This means that when there are major sports clashes, or when a breaking news story is up against a major sporting event, 5 Live can switch its commentary to 5 Live Sports Extra.

But according to talkSPORT programme director Moz Dee BBC 5 Live's larger audience is purely down to it having more sports broadcasting rights (Plunkett 2008f). Coverage of most sporting events is determined by a contract with either the sport's governing body or individual clubs that dictates what can and cannot be broadcast. Separate rights are needed for each platform – radio, television, the internet and mobile phones. In Premier League football, for example, talkSPORT had the rights for 32 games a year against the BBC's 192 in a three-season deal signed in 2006. The BBC also paid £200 million for a five-year deal for the television, radio, online and mobile phone rights for Formula 1 motor racing, starting in 2009 (ibid.). Moz Dee says this is simply not fair:

> Clearly from this side of the fence the BBC is in a really dominant position. It insists that it's a competitive marketplace but it just isn't because the BBC, even through the woes of the past couple of years, are still minted. £200m for formula one? There always seems to be the cash there . . . it's not a fair fight.
>
> (Quoted in Plunkett 2008f)

Phil Blacker from GCap sport admits that the rights issue has changed the way radio in general deals with sport, particularly football. For premiership games commercial radio can still get access to do reports live from games by buying a one-off IRN licence at the start of the season. 'If someone else has commentary rights you can still go to that game as long as you buy a licence,' he says.

What's far more common now is for stations to concentrate on one club and try to appeal to those fans and say you'll hear every Arsenal game or Man United game here – that's basically all you can do. We're being much more selective because we have to be because of the rights situation.

(Phil Blacker, GCap Sport)

One way that stations, particularly music-based stations, can expand their sports coverage without alienating non-sporting listeners is through their internet sites. Most football clubs reserve the commentary rights for their matches for their own websites, but interviews and other material can be uploaded to station websites, as Phil Blacker explains:

The net is increasingly the place where we're looking to put a lot of our sports content now. Particularly for GCap stations where a lot of the target audience is mid twenties women that turn off when they hear sport. So for as many people who like sport – and there's a huge proportion of the population who do – as many people actively dislike it and turn off the radio. With the internet you've got choice. You're not losing people on FM but you're giving people an incentive to log on. We're increasingly putting interviews and full programmes like documentaries on the net. We're doing visual stuff as well. When you do an interview you can take a little camera and film it and put it on the website. It sits really well with radio. If you've got a clip of Arsène Wenger as your main sports story you'll put a little clip of Wenger into a two minute news bulletin and say you can hear that interview in full on our website and give the web address. They sit really well together.

Sports reporters need to have a wide range of skills. As well as covering sport they have to be able to source and carry out interviews with a wide range of people, and get their message across to diverse audiences. The nature of the job also means working long, unsocial hours. Phil Blacker explains:

If you want to do a Monday to Friday nine-to-five then this isn't the job for you. You've got to have a passion for sport. You need that thirst for knowledge which you don't have unless you have a passion for it. The bottom line is you've got to be a damn good writer because particularly here at GCap it's written not necessarily for the hard core sports fan. It's written for your average audience who've got a vague interest in sport or an interest in sport but they're not experts and they need to have things explained. You've not got a lot of time to do that so your writing needs to be bang on which is what most people find most difficult.

Presentation and commentary

Presenting a sports programme is one of the most demanding jobs on radio. In the first place, the audience is generally well informed about the subject and they expect programme presenters and reporters to have in-depth knowledge. And unlike other aspects of radio, sports programmes are not used in a secondary way as background to other activities: fans listen attentively to every word and many even have their radios tuned to commentary while they are at an event to get added information about the play.

With so much sport now tied up in exclusive deals many radio stations no longer have the traditional Saturday afternoon sports programmes based around live commentary. Instead, they have a studio-based programme with regular reports from important games to keep listeners up to date. Often these take the form of a presenter with one or two football experts who will have a studio discussion and take calls from listeners in between match reports and sports packages. But unlike news programmes, which can be carefully planned, sports programmes have to be able to change direction according to what is happening at the live event. For example, if five minutes from the end of a football match with the station's local team about to win promotion a goal is conceded, the whole tone of the next part of the programme would have to change from one of celebration to one of disappointment. Presenters have to be able to stay on top of what is happening and be ready to change the direction of the programme accordingly, taking advice from their producer via talkback or the studio computer and all the while adding to and steering the studio discussion.

But where commentary is possible it shows radio at its best: it is live and reactive, conveying not just what is happening on the pitch but also the reactions of the crowd and the atmosphere so that the listener shares the whole experience, as Phil Andrews notes:

> Radio can transport listeners to the scene of the action by using the sounds they would hear if they were there. Sound is all around us, and nowhere more than at sporting events: the roar of the crowd, the referee's whistle, the starting gun, galloping hooves, racing car engines, oars splashing in water, the sound of bat on ball, announcements over the public address system.
>
> (Andrews 2005: 121)

For Phil Blacker getting the atmosphere of an event across makes it come alive. 'You've got your microphones and you can hear the crowd in the background but you also need to get across the passion of the game,' he says. He also advises lots of preparation before a commentary:

> You need to do your research. I try to do a few hours stats before each match but you don't always get the time. It's harder doing European games because

the players aren't so familiar. So I'll sit down and go through the team and find out bits and pieces. As a matter of course I'll find out their age and appearances this season – that sort of stuff. Then you look for information that might be interesting for a quiet bit in the game. I don't get as much time as I'd ideally like to do that sort of thing. With doing the same club every week you really only need to do one team because I already know the other one.

Basically you're painting a picture. For radio a lot of it's very descriptive because obviously the listener can't see what you're talking about so you don't need as much added information on radio because you can just talk about what's happening on the pitch. But there will be times when there's not a lot happening – when they're just kicking it around and that's when you need to drop in added information to add to the commentary and make it a more interesting listen.

We also have a pundit – an ex professional player that we do the games with so you can just bounce off them and bring them in when it's quiet. The game dictates how much information you use. If it's a great game then you don't need anything else you can just talk about the game.

talkSPORT commentator Jim Proudfoot[5] agrees that you need to do research before a match, but warns that some commentators can give too much added information:

You can never have too many facts written down in front of you. Speaking from experience, something that I hope I don't do any more but I know I have in the past , is to say 'right – I've done lots of homework and I'm going to make sure you know I've done lots of homework and I'm going to tell you the biographies and vital statistics of all of these players'. You can only mention stuff when it's relevant. But you do need to know things because the game could be awful so you need to make sure you have something to say all the time. When it's radio the most important thing the listener wants to know is firstly – what's the score, and secondly – where's the ball. As long as you get the goal scorers right you can probably get away with making everything else up.

But BBC 5 Live commentator Alan Green[6] has a different approach to his commentaries:

A perfectly good radio commentary consists of certain basics – who's got the ball, where is it, how long have we played, what's the score – and if you keep on repeating that you will have a perfectly sound commentary. I have to say I disagree about doing research because I think it encourages the commentator to show off, to say 'look I know that's the fifth goal he's scored with his left foot on a Tuesday night since October'. Well who cares? Just be yourself and have fun and if it's poor enjoy saying how bad it is. The poor games are more difficult to do because you've got to find something else to say – but look around you. There might be somebody nodding off three rows to your left – mention him – and keep on mentioning him 'he still hasn't woken up'. It's fun, it's entertainment – but you've got to tell the truth. Don't say something that isn't happening. You must tell the truth because ultimately you want your audience to trust you implicitly and if they ever catch you not telling the truth it's gone and without trust you haven't got a commentary.

From this it is clear that there are many different ways to do a successful commentary, but everyone agrees that it is important not only to tell listeners what is happening but also to convey the passion of the sport. This can be difficult for radio commentators reporting on club matches: they need to engage with the game but not show bias to one side because to do so would immediately alienate half the audience. Jim Proudfoot acknowledges that allowing your emotions to come across in club games is not being professional. 'I couldn't do it on a club game because you'd be doing a disservice to a certain proportion of your audience,' he says, but he adds that commentating on England games is different:

I fully acknowledge that there will be people who don't want England to win a given football match but the vast majority of people who listen will want England to win and as a result I don't think that it's doing a disservice to the audience by being very pro-England. You're there as a supporter. The audience at home are supporters. They want a given result and as a result I think it's fair to try to put yourself into the position of a supporter and to portray the glory or the agony they feel.

BBC 5 Live's Alan Green agrees but adds that being passionate in your commentary is not the same as not criticising the play when the team is playing badly:

I think you must have passion but it must not take over your objectivity. I want England to win when I'm commentating on England but there's a difference between allowing the listener to know that and allowing it to affect what you're saying. You must never do that. I slaughter England at times – it hurts me to do it but I slaughter them.

Just as different fans support different football teams, they also tend to have their favourite commentators, and for Phil Blacker that is what makes radio commentating so rewarding:

If you build up a regular partnership with a club people associate your coverage with that club. It's not an easy thing to do and it can't be done in six months – it takes a lot of doing. But then people will tune in for that commentary or that pundit because they respect his view or they like listening to that particular coverage. On radio you can build up that sort of loyalty that you don't really get on television or anywhere else.

For many sports fans being a sports reporter appears to be the best job in the world, but as the profile below of BBC Radio Derby's Ross Fletcher shows, it takes dedication to get into and hard work to sustain.

Profile of Ross Fletcher

Twenty-eight-year-old Ross Fletcher's official job title at BBC Radio Derby is a broadcast journalist, but to most listeners to the station he is best known as the Derby County commentator. As well as presenting the station's drive-time programme every week night from 4–7 pm he also hosts a Derby County phone-in on Monday nights, and a sport and music show on Tuesday evenings.

Ross says he has always wanted to do sport on radio and realised he might have the talent to do so when he entered a competition on what was the old Radio 5 asking for budding sports commentators to try their hand.

I sent a cassette of my commentary as a 14-year-old to Radio 5 and a couple of weeks later I got a letter with a baseball cap from the show – Garth Crooke's

Figure 9.1 Ross Fletcher from BBC Radio Derby at the Derby County ground

Go radio show – and it said 'well done you're a runner up for this competition and even though I hadn't won I thought 'great – I haven't won but I might actually be all right at this'.

His chance came a few years later when he managed to get some work experience at Radio Derby:

I went in for three weeks on a Saturday afternoon to see what they did in the studio. I did three weeks and 12 years later I've still not left.

Gradually I did more and more but you have to be willing and able. When I was 19 I was doing some sports bulletins for the station and one of the sports producers was going to leave so I said to the editor at the time 'what do I have to do to get the sports job' and he said make yourself indispensable and I've always taken that piece of advice with me.

From 16 to 18 I worked unpaid for two years. Every Saturday I'd get the train from Loughborough to Derby and be in for five hours answering the phones, turning round half time reports, reading the ultra-local non-league scores on the radio at five to six. It was what you did to get a grounding and prove that I was worthy of being kept on.

I then went to university in Sheffield and they paid me a little bit to cover my expenses and I gradually did more and more stuff. I started to read sports bulletins at the weekend and in my final year at university, weekday sports bulletins in the mornings. Then I got my own show doing the pre-sports show on a Saturday – sport and music – and that gave me a great way in because when a job came up I was in a great position to go for it and here I am doing it full-time.

Like many sports reporters Ross is passionate about his job:

Best part of the job is being able to see live sports action and being the person who's painting the pictures. I'm an all-sports fan but football is my favourite and being able to go and watch my local team – Derby County – and being a commentator there to get caught up with the passion, the excitement, the intrigue, the sheer drama that football provides, and being able to tell that story as the eyes and ears of a listener is absolutely fantastic. It's still an adrenaline rush every day. Live sport for a sports reporter – it doesn't really get any better.

But although Ross is a Derby County fan he knows it is important not to gloss over the club's performance when they are not playing well:

We are partisan but we're not biased because in the BBC you have to be honest and impartial. What we like to say is that we'll tell it from Derby County's point of view. If Derby score a goal – wonderful. If they concede a goal or something bad happens then instead of saying 'great goal for Watford' for example, it'll be 'well Derby's defence let themselves down there because this because that'. We don't like to say Derby were unlucky because to me that's lazy sports journalism. If your team isn't doing well it's not because of some silly excuse it's because they're not good enough and the audience expect you to tell them why, otherwise I don't think there's any point in them listening to us. If we're going to be biased and make excuses for that team we're not telling the true story. We're not telling the whole story and we're letting the listener down. So in being partisan you're telling the whole story as you see it, but seeing it from one perspective. It's all right to criticise them when they deserve criticism. It's your job as a journalist. You're there as a sports reporter, as a journalist. Some people might think the lines are blurred that when you become a sports reporter you become biased and it's all about your team and how great it is – no. You've got to maintain your journalistic principles. You've got to be able to criticise as and when. You're there to look at the good the bad the ugly whatever it is – you've got to maintain those principles.

Ross says the build up to the weekend game usually starts on Thursday:

Typically on Thursday afternoon or Friday afternoon the football club will send out a media invite saying they're doing a pre-match press conference with the manager of Derby County and a player and that's an open invitation for all media to go to the training ground and get your five minutes with the manager and three or four minutes with a player. Then you use that for clips in sports bulletins leading up to the game and use the interviews in your Saturday two 'til three build up before the three o'clock kick-off. You'll always have a manager and a player to interview because they're integral parts of your build-up – they're the people the fans really want to hear from. We're quite lucky in Derby because on a Tuesday even if there isn't a match until Saturday the manager will also offer himself up to be interviewed so we can talk about the issues from the last weekend, issues from that week in football in general because our manager Paul Jewel[7] is very good like that, and also looking ahead to the weekend so it keeps things fresh.

And like most commentators Ross believes that research before the match is vital to do a good job:

If you don't prepare – yes you can go, you can do commentary but you might not pick up on a certain player's identity when the ball goes to him. If you haven't researched him, who he is, what he looks like, you'll be found out because if that player goes and scores a goal you need to instantly tell people who he is, who scored the goal. If you haven't done your research you might get away with it, then again if he's in a crowded penalty box it makes you look stupid. On a Friday morning I'll do two, maybe three hours research both on my team, Derby County, and as importantly, if not more importantly, the opposition so I know who they are and what they do.

Ross also finds it useful to spend the hour before he starts commentating watching the players warm-up. It is at this time that he can look for identifying characteristics like the colour of a player's hair or boots, and what sort of build they are – anything that will give him instant identification. This is also the time when any difficult names can be cleared up by chatting with the opposition commentator and practising pronunciation. Then it is on with the game, which Ross does with a regular summariser:

> I've been doing football commentary for five years now and I've had four different summarisers and each one has been very different in their approach but it's so important that you are a team and you understand each other. You don't necessarily have to get along but it helps because you are in tandem. You're two guys who're doing a pacey commentary who need to know when to interject, what to say, how to say it.
>
> As a commentator I'm the eyes and ears – I say what's going on. My summariser will say why it's going on because they've played the game at the highest level: they can provide the context to my explanation of what's going on. They will say this happened because x, y and z.
>
> With my first summariser, we were of different generations and I think that showed in our styles – they clashed a bit. But my next summariser was freshly out of football with a younger perspective. Me being a relatively young sports journalist we clicked and the banter was there and the audience really enjoyed the banter because as well as getting an accurate, passionate football commentary they also got to understand us as a double act. You're entertainment. You're also entertaining people because not everyone is there to learn the nuances of why the left back hoofed it 60 yards. They want to be entertained, and as long as you have a working relationship where you can banter and you understand each other then that really helps bring out the best in your commentary.

Once the final whistle goes there is still work to be done. After every match the manager will make himself available for an interview that can be used in bulletins over the rest of the weekend. 'Paul Jewel is very good,' says Ross. 'I can't remember a time he's shirked a post-match interview. He realises how important it is to get his message across to the fans.' Sometimes players will also give interviews, but Ross admits that when they win you get a better interview than when they lose.

Figure 9.2 BBC Radio Derby's Ross Fletcher at the Beijing Olympics

As well as covering every Derby County game, the station also has commentary rights for non-league Burton Albion, and in order to service both sets of fans they split their frequencies with mid-week Burton Albion games broadcast on AM and the internet, and Saturday matches on the internet only:

> We can't put Derby County commentary on our own website, however we have a deal with the club where they use our commentary through their own website. If anyone wants to listen to Derby County commentary they go through the club website but they will hear BBC Radio Derby. For Burton Albion, because it's a non-league side we can do the commentary on our website because there are no rights issues.

But despite his love of football Ross says his time in Beijing covering the 2008 Olympic Games, which he describes as 'the greatest sporting spectacle in the world' was a once in a lifetime experience – and a real challenge:

> It was high pressure. It was long hours and testing conditions with the heat and the humidity but you just had to be well prepared. Again it comes down to preparation and an ability to work in difficult circumstances with patience.

There was a lot of travelling involved and you had to be really well organised so you knew what time your bus was going. You had to be able to be a good communicator not only with your colleagues in the BBC but also with the Chinese authorities at which point not many of them spoke very good English – our Mandarin was terrible so we couldn't really argue on that – but you had to be very resilient and hard working and you had to know your stuff because you're doing 20 different sports that Britain was entered in. I probably covered about 15 different sports.

Ross' journey from being a Saturday afternoon phone-basher to covering the Olympic Games shows that determination and hard work can pay off – but it is not an easy road. You need to be passionate about sport, have near encyclopaedic knowledge, the ability to describe not only the sport but the atmosphere as well, and the willingness to work long hours not just covering events but preparing for them as well. But despite working six days a week Ross thinks he has one of the best jobs in the world, and he has this advice for those who want to follow his example:

I would say to students who want to get into sports journalism – just keep knocking at the door. Keep going at it and if you get a no don't let that put you off because although there will be 30 other people who want to do that job you've just got to keep offering yourself up. It's probably going to be a long and hard road and it's not fantastically paid to start with but you've just got to stay in there and prove you're good enough. If you're given a chance take it and don't take no for an answer.

10 Accountability

All broadcasters in the UK work within a framework of legal and regulatory constraints designed to uphold the existing law of the country, ensure levels of taste and decency, and prevent a concentration of ownership that it is believed would lead to a reduction in the range of available viewpoints. The purpose of this chapter is not to provide an exhaustive account of the laws and regulations governing radio, but to summarise the main areas of law that impinge on the day-to-day routines of programme making, some of which have already been discussed in other chapters, and outline the regulations for the medium.

Legislative controls

The purpose of legislative controls on radio is to ensure that broadcast material does not work against the interests of justice, unfairly represent a person or organisation, jeopardise national security, or cause offence to individuals or groups in society. In many cases these laws apply to all media, not just radio.

Defamation

The law of defamation is designed to protect the reputation of individuals and groups from unjustified attacks but because there is no absolute definition of defamation this can be a minefield for broadcasters who need to be aware that a careless comment about someone could land them in court.

Broadly speaking, defamation can be caused by written statements or pictures, in which case it is libel, or spoken statements where it is treated as slander. But under the Broadcasting Act of 1990 any defamatory statement made on radio or television is treated as libel. The problem comes in defining what is defamatory. Welsh, Greenwood and Banks give this guidance:

Judges tell juries that a statement about a person is defamatory of him if it tends to do any one of the following:

(1) expose him to hatred, ridicule or contempt;

(2) cause him to be shunned or avoided;

(3) lower him in the estimation of right-thinking members of society generally; or

(4) disparage him in his business, trade, office or profession.

(2007: 228)

That seems reasonably clear, but they go on to explain that the person suing does not have to show that the statement in question actually caused hatred and so on, simply that in the estimation of 'reasonable' men and women they could be regarded as defamatory and lead to hatred, ridicule and so on. Broadcasters also have to be aware of the context of what is being broadcast to make sure that background music on an item is not disparaging. Welsh, Greenwood and Banks cite a case where a holiday company won an out-of-court settlement from a television company who used the theme tune from *Colditz* under pictures of the size of rooms used by holiday makers (ibid.: 496).

But the real minefield for radio comes in live broadcasts where a studio guest or telephone contributor can say something defamatory about an individual or company. In cases like this both the person who spoke the words and the radio station would be sued. As mentioned before, most commercial radio stations use a delay on live phone-ins so that if something defamatory is said the presenter can use the profanity button to stop the remarks being transmitted. But where the words are broadcast, Welsh, Greenwood and Banks say 'The presenter should immediately dissociate himself and the station from the defamatory statement and should apologise without repeating the defamatory statement' (ibid.: 497).

Reporting restrictions and contempt of court

Restrictions on the reporting of court cases are covered by a series of laws but can also be ordered by judges in specific cases. One of the main reasons for imposing restrictions is to prevent media coverage from adversely affecting the outcome of cases. For example, the 1980 Magistrates' Courts Act restricts what can be reported about a preliminary hearing or committal proceedings to prevent prejudicing the full hearing. This limits these reports to specified facts: the name of the court and magistrates; the names, addresses and occupations of the parties and witnesses and the ages of the accused and witnesses; a summary of the offence; the names of counsel and solicitors involved; the decision of the court to commit the accused for trial, and any decision on the disposal of the case of any accused not committed;

where there is a committal, a summary of the charges and note of what court they are committed to; where there is an adjournment, the date and place of the adjournment; any bail arrangements; whether legal aid was given; and any decision of the court to lift or not to lift these reporting restrictions (Welsh, Greenwood and Banks 2007: 43).

There are also restrictions to prevent the identity of innocent parties involved in reported cases, such as the victims of sexual attack, rape or attempted rape, and those of juveniles (that is, those under the age of 18) accused or convicted of offences, and the identification of children involved in family proceedings.

Broadcasters could be regarded as being in contempt of court if their reports were likely to prejudice or give rise to substantial risk of serious impediment of a pending or current court case. This includes making any reference to previous convictions or any extraneous information that could be prejudicial where a case is to be tried by jury. The Contempt of Court Act 1981 not only covers broadcast reports but also the behaviour of reporters. For example, under Section 8 of the Act it is an offence to seek or disclose any information about the deliberations of a jury.

Official Secrets and DA notices

The disclosure of matters that are regarded as state secrets is covered by the Official Secrets Acts of 1911 and 1989. These are complicated Acts that detail what kind of information should not be reported, as well as restricting the disclosure of information obtained in certain ways, for example, if it has been given to the journalist from a Crown servant without lawful authority or in confidence.

Guidance on how certain types of information relating to national security should be reported or not reported is given to newsrooms in the form of Defence Advisory (DA) notices. These are issued by the Defence Press and Broadcasting Committee, which is made up of four senior officials of the Ministry of Defence, the Home Office, and the Foreign Office, and 13 nominees from newspapers, periodicals, news agencies, and broadcasting organisations. There are five standing DA notices that describe the broad areas that the committee has identified as being likely to require guidance to avoid damaging national security. These cover areas like defence plans and equipment, ciphers and secure communications, the identification of specific installations, and details about the intelligence service and Special Forces. Each notice describes what it is seeking to protect and why, but as Welsh, Greenwood and Banks point out:

> The system is advisory and voluntary and has no legal authority. Editors do not have to seek advice, nor do they have to take any advice that may be offered. In effect, the system is a code of self-censorship by the press in matters of national security.
>
> (Official Secrets: extended website chapter 19)

Obscenity

Prosecutions against a station for broadcasting material that may be considered obscene (Broadcasting Act 1990) or likely to incite racial hatred (Public Order Act 1986) can only take place with the consent of the Director of Public Prosecutions. What actually constitutes obscenity however tends to change according to the culture and the time: the definition of obscenity in Victorian times is quite different from that of today. In general, material that can be reasonably considered as being likely to deprave or corrupt an audience or incite racial hatred is covered by these Acts. Similarly a station can be prosecuted for blasphemy if an item uses language that vilifies the Christian religion or the Bible, or sedition if the item could cause a breach of the peace through the manner in which it is presented.

Regulatory controls

Historically broadcasting has always been more tightly regulated than other forms of media. This is partly because it is generally regarded as having a more direct impact on audiences than print, but also for wholly practical reasons connected to allocating the scarce resource of frequencies.

Radio in the UK is regulated by both Ofcom and the BBC Trust. Ofcom was created under the 2003 Communications Act to replace a series of industry-specific regulatory bodies like the Radio Authority and the Broadcasting Standards Commission. Its role is to regulate the UK's broadcasting, telecommunications and wireless communications sectors and enforce rules on fair competition between companies in those industries. Although Ofcom ultimately answers to the Government, it is independent from it and it is funded from fees from the industry charged for regulating broadcasting and communications networks and grant-in-aid from the Government.

Ofcom is responsible for licensing all UK commercial television and radio services including the existing analogue stations, digital radio stations, Restricted Service Licences (RSLs), and community radio (Ofcom 2008b). Through the Broadcasting Code (2005), it sets out rules and standards for all broadcasters, including the BBC. The Code deals with issues of Harm and Offense and aims to protect people under the age of 18 from material that is deemed unsuitable for them 'while allowing broadcasters an appropriate amount of creative freedom' (ibid.).

The BBC Trust was created under the BBC's Royal Charter of 2006 and it replaces the BBC Board of Governors. The Trust is independent from the BBC Executive and BBC Management so it does not have anything to do with the day-to-day running of the corporation. Instead it is there to represent the interests of licence payers to make sure the BBC delivers value for money, and monitor each service's contribution to delivering the overall BBC Public Purposes. As was noted in the Trust's first annual report:

As BBC Trustees our first duty is to guard the independence of the BBC against outside interference, whether political, commercial, or from any other quarter. The BBC can only be defended if it demonstrates impartiality, accuracy, high quality and good value for money. Our job as Trustees is to make sure that the BBC delivers these qualities.

(BBC 2006/07: 5)

As the 2006/07 Annual Report explains, the BBC Trust is a supervisory body with some regulatory duties. In some cases it works directly with Ofcom, for example, in the Joint Steering Group for market impact assessments. In other cases the two bodies have different responsibilities. So while the BBC is regulated by the Ofcom Broadcasting Code, the Trust regulates BBC output in terms of impartiality and accuracy and is the final arbiter within the BBC for editorial complaints (BBC 2006/07: 10).

The structure of Ofcom

Ofcom's structure is similar to that of many commercial organisations and in this way it is different from regulatory models of the past, which were often headed or overseen by a government appointed person or body. The structure of Ofcom aims to be transparent and far reaching. Ofcom has a Board with an Executive section headed by the chief executive officer Ed Richards, that runs the organisation and answers to the Board. The Board has up to ten members and is chaired by Lord Currie of Marylebone. As Ofcom's website explains, 'The Ofcom Board provides strategic direction for Ofcom. It is the main statutory instrument of regulation with a fundamental role in the effective implementation of the Communications Act 2003.'

The main work of Ofcom is done by the Content Board, which is a committee of the main Board that 'sets and enforces quality and standards for television and radio' and acts in the interests of the public (www.ofcom.org.uk). They also consider format regulation for radio. The Content Board has 12 members appointed by Ofcom and is chaired by the deputy chairman of the Ofcom Board, Philip Graf CBE:

The majority of Content Board members are part-time and drawn from diverse backgrounds across the UK, including both lay members and members with extensive broadcasting experience. Four are appointed to represent to Ofcom the interests and opinions of people living in Scotland, Wales, Northern Ireland and the English Regions.

(ibid.)

There are also a series of advisory bodies that work with Ofcom. These include advisory committees for England, Northern Ireland, Scotland and Wales to provide advice on matters of interest particular to each country; an Advisory Committee for Older and Disabled People to look after their interests; a Spectrum Advisory Board made up of people with particular technical knowledge and skills; and a Consumer Panel. The Consumer Panel is independent from Ofcom with its own budget to commission research. Its job is to raise issues of consumer interest including issues affecting rural communities and those on low income or otherwise disadvantaged.

The structure of the BBC Trust

The BBC Trust was formed under the Royal Charter that came into effect in January 2007. It replaces the former BBC Board of Governors and acts in the interests of licence fee payers to ensure that the BBC remains independent from Government or commercial pressures, that it provides value-for-money and high quality programmes, and contributes to the economy and culture of the UK. The Trust has a total of 12 members, including the chairman, Sir Michael Lyons, who are appointed by the Queen on advice from Ministers. As detailed in Chapter 1, the BBC Trust does not have anything to do with the day-to-day running of the BBC, but acts as a watchdog for the BBC, to ensure it meets the requirements of the Royal Charter.

As the first annual report of the Trust notes 'we are the sovereign body of the BBC, its independent Trustees acting in the public interest' (BBC 2006/07: 9). So as well as making sure the BBC is doing its job properly, the Trust 'set the framework within which the Executive handles complaints and, where appropriate, we hear appeals' (ibid.: 10).

Under the Royal Charter of 2006 the BBC is required to have Audience Councils, 'the purpose of which is to bring the diverse perspectives of licence fee payers to bear on the work of the Trust, through the Councils' links with diverse communities, including geographically-based communities and other communities of interest, within the UK' (Royal Charter: Section 39). There is an Audience Council for Northern Ireland, Scotland and Wales, which each have 12 members, including the chairman who is the BBC Trust member for that nation. The Audience Council for England is different because its members come from a network of Regional Audience Councils – one for each of the broadcasting regions in England. According to the Royal Charter (2006) the role of audience councils is:

(a) to engage with licence fee payers including geographically-based communities and other communities of interest;

(b) to be consulted on all relevant proposals that are required to be subject to a Public Value Test by virtue of any Framework Agreement;

(c) to be consulted, as part of any review of service licences, which the Trust undertakes in accordance with the requirements of any Framework Agreement, on the content of the service licences and the performance of the services to which the review relates;

(d) to be consulted on the BBC's performance in promoting the Public Purposes;

(e) to submit a report to the Trust each year on the BBC's performance in each nation and advise on issues arising; and

(f) to publish an Annual Review Report each year in the nation concerned, assessing how well the BBC is meeting the needs of licence fee payers in that nation.

(Section 39: 6)

According to the BBC Trust website 'council members are recruited to ensure they reflect the diversity of the UK, have connections with communities and are able to take a view on how the Public Purposes should be promoted'.

As well as consulting closely with audience councils, the Trust also carries out its own research. One of the first pieces of research it undertook was in February 2007 when it commissioned an audience survey of 4,500 adults, which revealed that while the BBC's approval rating is steady, only a minority of people feel it caters equally for all regions of the UK (BBC 2006/07: 26).

The Ofcom Broadcasting Code

The Ofcom Broadcasting Code provides broadcasters in the UK with a set of principles, meanings and rules that they need to follow to meet accepted standards in programming, sponsorship, fairness and privacy. The code covers ten areas: protecting the under-18s; harm and offence; crime; religion; due impartiality and due accuracy, and undue prominence of views and opinions; elections and referendums; fairness; privacy; sponsorship; commercial references and other matters. But although the Code has clear rules, it also attempts to give broadcasters more freedom of expression than in the past by taking into account the Human Rights Act 1998 and the European Convention on Human Rights:

> In particular, the right to freedom of expression, as expressed in Article 10 of the Convention, encompasses the audience's right to receive creative material, information and ideas without interference but subject to restrictions prescribed by law and necessary in a democratic society.
>
> (Ofcom: Legislative Background to the Code)

To that end the Code explains that broadcasters 'should be aware that the context in which the material appears is key' (Ofcom: How to use the Code). In other words, material should be suitable for the intended audience. For example, under Section One: Protecting the under-18s, the Code explains that children (defined as people under 15) should be protected by appropriate scheduling from material that is unsuitable for them. The Code then goes on to clearly define 'appropriate scheduling' as referring to the nature of the content, the likely number of children listening, the time of the broadcast, and the nature of the station and the likely expectations of the audience. In particular it points out that a time when children are likely to be listening 'particularly refers to the school run and breakfast time, but might include other times' (Section 1).

Section 2 of the Code then goes on to explain the meaning of 'context':

> Context includes (but is not limited to):
>
> • the editorial content of the programme, programmes or series;
>
> • the service on which the material is broadcast;
>
> • the time of broadcast;
>
> • what other programmes are scheduled before and after the programme or programmes concerned;
>
> • the degree of harm or offence likely to be caused by the inclusion of any particular sort of material in programmes generally or programmes of a particular description;
>
> • the likely size and composition of the potential audience and likely expectation of the audience;
>
> • the extent to which the nature of the content can be brought to the attention of the potential audience for example by giving information; and
>
> • the effect of the material on viewers or listeners who may come across it unawares.
>
> (Ofcom 2005: Section 2)

By providing clear definitions the Code allows broadcasters the chance to transmit material that in the past may have been considered offensive by some, provided it is editorially justified and where appropriate warnings are given to the audience.

Most sections of the Code deal with the affect of programmes on listeners, but Section 7: Fairness and Section 8: Privacy (which also apply to the BBC) are concerned with the way broadcasters deal with individuals directly involved in programmes, and both have a section providing 'practices to be followed'. In Section 7 the Code explains that broadcasters should avoid unfair treatment of individuals or organisations making a contribution to a programme:

> Where a person is invited to make a contribution to a programme (except when the subject matter is trivial or their participation minor) they should normally, at an appropriate stage:
>
> • be told the nature and purpose of the programme, what the programme is about and be given a clear explanation of why they were asked to contribute and when (if known) and where it is likely to be first broadcast;

- be told what kind of contribution they are expected to make, for example live, pre-recorded, interview, discussion, edited, unedited, etc.;

- be informed about the areas of questioning and, wherever possible, the nature of other likely contributions;

- be made aware of any significant changes to the programme as it develops which might reasonably affect their original consent to participate, and which might cause material unfairness;

- be told the nature of their contractual rights and obligations and those of the programme maker and broadcaster in relation to their contribution; and

- be given clear information, if offered an opportunity to preview the programme, about whether they will be able to effect any changes to it.

(Ofcom 2005: Section 7.3)

The Code goes on to say that if a contributor is under-16 then consent should be obtained from a parent or guardian, and that under-16s should not be asked their views on matters beyond their capacity to answer properly without such consent. In the case of persons over 16 who are not in a position to give consent, a person of 18 or over with primary responsibility for their care should normally give it on their behalf. In particular, people not in a position to give consent should not be asked for views on matters likely to be beyond their capacity to answer properly without such consent.

The Code also advises that in edited programmes contributions should be represented fairly, and where contributors have been guaranteed confidentiality or anonymity, these should normally be honoured, and it warns that care also needs to be taken with material recorded for one purpose and then reused in a later programme.

The Code goes on to deal with giving people involved in factual programmes a chance to respond, and to make sure that dramas and factually-based dramas are fair to individuals and organisations. It also has a section dealing with 'deception, set-ups, and 'wind-up' calls, saying that broadcasters should not normally obtain audio through the use of 'misrepresentation or deception', but:

- it may be warranted to use material obtained through misrepresentation or deception without consent if it is in the public interest and cannot reasonably be obtained by other means;

- where there is no adequate public interest justification, for example some unsolicited wind-up calls or entertainment set-ups, consent should be obtained from the individual and/or organisation concerned before the material is broadcast;

- if the individual and/or organisation is/are not identifiable in the programme then consent for broadcast will not be required;

- material involving celebrities and those in the public eye can be used without consent for broadcast, but it should not be used without a public interest justification if it is likely to result in unjustified public ridicule or personal distress. (Normally, therefore such contributions should be pre-recorded.)

(Ofcom 2005: 7:14)

Section 8 of the Code, which deals with privacy, is similar in many ways to what is said under the section on fairness (above), but it does have specific advice on recording and broadcasting phone calls:

Broadcasters can record telephone calls between the broadcaster and the other party if they have, from the outset of the call, identified themselves, explained the purpose of the call and that the call is being recorded for possible broadcast (if that is the case) unless it is warranted not to do one or more of these practices. If at a later stage it becomes clear that a call that has been recorded will be broadcast (but this was not explained to the other party at the time of the call) then the broadcaster must obtain consent before broadcast from the other party, unless it is warranted not to do so.

(Ofcom 2005: 8:12)

However, it then goes on to say that recorded 'wind-up' calls for the purpose of entertainment may be warranted if it is intrinsic to the entertainment and does not amount to 'a significant infringement of privacy such as to cause significant annoyance, distress or embarrassment' (Ofcom 2005: 8:15).

When members of the public think that the Broadcasting Code has been breached they can make a complaint directly to Ofcom who will investigate and publish their findings along with the reasons the Code has been breached in regular Broadcast Bulletins that are published on their website (www.ofcom.co.uk). When a broadcaster deliberately, seriously or repeatedly breaches the Code, Ofcom may impose statutory sanctions against the broadcaster including heavy fines (see Phone-ins in Chapter 8 for specific examples).

'Sachsgate'

The way that regulatory codes impact on broadcasters can be seen most clearly in an episode involving broadcasters Russell Brand and Jonathan Ross in October 2008. Brand's regular BBC Radio 2 programme was broadcast on a Saturday night between 9 pm and 11 pm. Going out at that time on a Saturday night meant that the audience could reasonably be assumed to be adult and therefore the use of offensive language and 'adult' humour would be allowed to some extent. But the programme broadcast on 18 October, which had Jonathan Ross as a guest, was widely regarded as having 'the almost complete absence of anything resembling good taste or judgment' (Hewlett 2008) and ended up with 42,851 complaints to the BBC (BBC 2008e)

The focus of the complaints was a series of messages left on the answer machine of 78-year-old actor Andrew Sachs, best known for his role as Manuel in the television comedy *Fawlty Towers*, who had been due to take part in the show but had to cancel due to unforeseen circumstances. Brand had previously had a relationship with Sachs' granddaughter Georgina Baillie, and when it emerged that Sachs would not be taking part in the show it was decided that Brand and Ross should leave a message on his answer machine. During the first message Ross swore and said that Brand had slept with Sachs' granddaughter. This was then followed by three more messages where Brand and Ross apologise for the first message but end up making further lewd comments about Georgina Baillie.

Ironically the show was not heard by Andrew Sachs or his granddaughter until it was pointed out to them by the *Mail on Sunday* who contacted Sachs' agent for a comment about it. This led to the actor making a complaint to the BBC and the story being picked up by other media and dubbed 'Sachsgate'. As more and more people heard about the prank, and duly watched it online, it caused a storm of complaints with the Prime Minister Gordon Brown stepping into the row ten days after the broadcast to say that the programme was 'clearly inappropriate and unacceptable behaviour', and the leader of the Conservative party, David Cameron, questioning why it had been allowed to be broadcast when it was pre-recorded (BBC 2008c).

For most people it was the fact that the programme had been pre-recorded and still aired that was most perplexing. Section 2 of the Ofcom Broadcasting Code, which deals with Harm and Offense, is quite clear:

> In applying generally accepted standards broadcasters must ensure that material which may cause offence is justified by the context . . . such material may include, but is not limited to, offensive language, violence, sex, sexual violence, humiliation, distress, violation of human dignity, discriminatory treatment or language (for example on the grounds of age, disability, gender, race, religion, beliefs and sexual orientation).

That alone should have alerted producers, but Section 8 of the BBC's Editorial Guidelines also gives advice:

> Any proposal to use the most offensive language . . . must be referred to and approved by a senior editorial figure or for Independents by the commissioning editor and then also approved by the relevant output controller for television, radio, online and any other service.

Moreover, it appears that the rules for following the BBC guidelines were not followed. Normally, following the recording the producer would fill in a compliance form. This gives details of the programme's content to alert senior executives to potentially offensive material under headings including strong language, sexual content, violence, impartiality:

> For every box ticked on the form, an explanation must be given as to why the producer feels the audience may be offended, and also why the content is justified.
>
> Subsequent questions ask whether there should be an announcement before the programme is broadcast – and whether there are any legal issues that need to be checked by the BBC's lawyers.
>
> The form is then signed both by the producer and a more senior editorial person. In the case of Radio 2, this would generally mean an editor or commissioning editor.
>
> ('How does the BBC vet its shows?', available at bbc.co.uk)

The BBC Trust Editorial Standards Committee investigation into the matter found that the programme was 'so grossly offensive that there was no justification for its broadcast' (November 2008: 3) and it identified three failures in procedure: 'a failure to assert editorial control by Radio 2, a failure to follow the compliance systems in place and a failure of editorial judgement' (ibid.: 4). In other words, had the editorial guidelines been followed in the first place then the recording would have been stopped and not used. And if the compliance system described above had been followed then the recorded programme would not have been allowed to be broadcast. And if the BBC's Editorial Guidelines regarding privacy had been adhered to then the programme would not have been allowed to go out.

The Trust investigation revealed that the programme's producer, who was employed by the BBC but accountable to Vanity Productions – part owned by Russell Brand – had telephoned Andrew Sachs following the recording, and he believed the actor had given his consent for the piece to be broadcast. This is disputed by Andrew Sachs. The producer then contacted the head of compliance for Radio 2 and alerted him to the content of the programme, in order to get permission to broadcast it. The head of compliance then emailed the controller of Radio 2 recommending that the programme be allowed to be aired with a strong language warning. The Trust found that both the head of compliance and the controller were at fault:

> The Committee agreed that whilst the Controller of Radio 2 could not have anticipated that the Head of Compliance for Radio 2 had made a severe error of judgement the words of the email sent to her should have nonetheless alerted her to the possibility that the material she was being asked to clear contained unacceptable material . . .

The Committee concluded that the decision to authorise broadcast with a strong language warning was a serious misjudgement by the Controller of Radio 2. The Committee agreed that the sexual use of the f word in relation to an identifiable individual should have raised alarm bells.

(ibid.: 7)

To some extent Sachsgate was less about that particular programme, and more about the fact that the BBC is funded by public money and so it should ensure that its programmes fully comply with regulations. There was also a degree of anger that one of the offenders was Jonathan Ross who became the BBC's highest paid broadcaster when he signed a three-year deal in 2006 worth £18 million. The programme also came in the same year that the BBC was fined £400,000 by Ofcom after it admitted it had misled audiences by 'faking' phone-ins on several programmes (Gibson 2008b) and the Brand programme was seen as another example of the Corporation being out of control.

In the end, Russell Brand resigned from the BBC a few hours after being suspended, and the next day the Radio 2 controller Lesley Douglas also resigned. Jonathan Ross was suspended from the BBC for 12 weeks without pay. Many people felt that Lesley Douglas should not have had to resign, but as the Trust's investigation showed, she had the final decision to air the show, and as the BBC Editorial Guideline on Harm and Offence shows, this means the material should have been checked by Douglas before it was aired if only because of the swearing involved. Mark Thompson also made this clear in a statement about the matter:

The ultimate editorial responsibility for BBC programmes lies with producers and editorial managers. The consequences of errors of editorial judgment are therefore more serious for managers . . . We agree that nothing like this must ever happen again and that tight discipline will be required for the future.

(Quoted in Gibson 2008b)

What the incident also shows is that even the most carefully constructed procedures can fall down, and that is why broadcasters at every level need to be constantly updated on law, regulatory codes and procedures for following them.

11 Getting started in radio

··

The radio industry in the UK employs over 22,000 people[1] doing a vast array of jobs from producing content, to technical support, to admin, marketing and sales. But to work on air most stations expect some previous experience and at least basic technical skills. There are many ways to get this experience, as this chapter examines, but all the radio professionals interviewed for this book agree that enthusiasm, commitment and a knowledge of the medium will go a long way to getting you that first job in radio.

A good place to start is the Skillset website (www.skillset.org). Skillset is an independent organisation, owned and managed by the audio visual and publishing industries, that works with both the industry and government to identify and tackle the skills and productivity needs of these industries throughout the UK. Although they do not provide training, they do fund training through approved partners, and they also have occasional bursary schemes to help individuals get training, and have information on how to get work experience. One successful scheme they run is called 'Route into Radio'. This involves a three-month placement at a radio station with on-the-job training to help work towards a City and Guilds Media Techniques qualification.

Another organisation that is worth checking out is the Broadcast Journalism Training Council (BJTC). This industry body oversees the training of journalists going into radio and television and it is responsible for accrediting courses in further and higher education. Standards for these courses are set by the industry through the Council, and both the BBC and the commercial sector through RadioCentre, hold directorships on the BJTC and play an active part in setting and maintaining standards, visiting courses and making decisions as to whether they are good enough to be accredited. The BJTC website (www.bjtc.org.uk/) has a list of accredited courses at postgraduate and undergraduate level, and it also covers other courses like those run by the National Broadcasting School in Brighton. The site also has a student section which has useful information about bursaries, contacts and training materials.

The Radio Academy is a registered charity that promotes excellence in UK broadcasting and audio production. It brings together the BBC and commercial radio, representing broadcasters from national networks to individual podcasters to outside bodies including the government (www.radioacademy.org). It runs a series of 'master classes' in many aspects of broadcasting at centres across the UK. These events are usually day-long conferences that have seminars, hands-on skills sessions and lectures from experts in the industry. The classes are open to members of the Radio Academy, but complementary membership is available to anyone who already works at a station that sponsors the Academy,[2] as well as active participants in student radio, hospital radio and community stations licensed by Ofcom. Their website also has information on getting a placement at a radio station and a 60 minute MP3 file called 'Getting into Radio' that has an introduction by the late John Peel and information on other aspects of radio including engineering, production, journalism and presenting.

The director of the Radio Academy, Trevor Dann,[3] says if you want to get into radio it is vital to get some real experience either on or off-air at a student, hospital or community station:

> Write to stations you've actually heard and offer to help where you know they need it. Get some experience yourself that stations will want to use. Make sure the demo you send is relevant to the station you're approaching. Never write 'To Whom It May Concern' or 'Programme Director'. Get a name and focus on a personal approach. Make your pitch stand out from the pile – be bold and different.

As well as giving you valuable experience and skills, working for hospital, community or student radio can raise your profile and bring you to the attention of mainstream broadcasters. Presenter Philippa TJ was spotted after her shows on student radio won her a Gold in the Best Specialist category and the Best Female award at the Student Radio Awards. Philippa[4] explains how it happened:

> 6Music were changing the presenter of the 6 Music chart and approached the production company who organise the audio entries [for the Student Radio Awards] for suggestions of young talent who might be appropriate. Wise Buddah forwarded my demos to Ric Blaxill and off the back of this, he invited me to London to record a demo show. Luckily he liked it and he asked me to come and do the show. This turnaround was about two weeks so as you can imagine it was completely out of the blue and entirely surreal.

The 6 Music chart was an hour-long show that played tracks from albums that were just outside the official Top 40 album chart. The chart was compiled by the Official Chart Company and included artists who are still alive, have never been in the top 40, and who have released an album in the past year. Philippa says:

From this strict and bizarre criteria we get to play a wide range of eclectic music from hip-hop, drum and base, folk, electronica, heavy metal, indie – you name it and it's in there! It's a fast paced show with links that are based on the information surrounding the album or artist. At the end of the show we count down the top ten albums and play a track from the number one album.

Unfortunately, 6Music decided that the format for the show was too complicated and they scrapped it in 2008, ending Philippa's contract with them – but she is undeterred:

My intentions are still to be a broadcaster as it's what I love doing and perhaps 6Music was the wrong time and wrong place for me. It was certainly an interesting experience and all presenters have to start somewhere and I do not regret the decision they made. I am still going to pursue my musical ambitions – this is merely a sideways step to where I want to be. I'm proud of what I achieved. What I have learnt is that it is not a straight swap for student radio to the mainstream and you do have to put up a fight in order to retain your place by proving yourself on every level.

She also learned that being a music presenter is not always as glamorous as it sounds, and while working for 6Music she had a full-time job to support herself. 'You have to be prepared for randomness and waiting until something pops your way or you pop into something's way,' she says. 'After working in the industry I'd say that being passionate, determined and natural are really important things to retain.'

Lewis Skrimshaw[5] from 96 Trent FM agrees that you need to persevere in your attempts to get a job or work experience, but he also advises newcomers to put some research into their chosen station before making contact:

The there are the little things like knowing the name of the news editor when you make an enquiry – whether it's on the phone, email or a letter. Making sure you get their gender right if it's a name that could be a man or a woman. And when you come to meet that person come with some recently gleaned knowledge or observations about their product, because they'll want you to have shown interest and they'll want to know what you think of their product to test you probably, and at least know that you've bothered to listen to their output before you turn up on their door asking for a job or a placement or freelance work.

A good voice in commercial radio is crucial so if you're on an undergraduate or postgraduate course and you're offered voice training grab as much as you can. Practice reading bulletins and reading out loud – reading to children helps – just get comfortable reading out loud.

It's most important that you know about the news but it helps to have listened a bit more widely. Knowing what the breakfast show's latest stunt is and what they talked about that morning won't do you any harm – having an understanding of how other departments fit in within the station and work with and influence the news will all help.

Aeneas Rotsos,[6] news editor at BBC Radio Nottingham, says if you want to work as a radio journalist you must have a passion for all news:

People who are keen on news and devour it – listen to local news, read local newspapers as well as nationals, watch TV news – that's a big tick. Another big tick is to be keen and interested in what people are saying – people have to have an inquisitiveness. Another plus point is to have an enthusiasm for news and broadcasting in general – if they don't have that they're going to find it hard to convince someone that they want to be a newsroom journalist.

On a practical level, Jim Latham,[7] the secretary of the BJTC, admits that getting into radio is more difficult now than ever before – particularly in the commercial sector. He says good written and spoken English is vital and having a driving licence is a distinct advantage, but he adds that nowadays if you want to work in radio you must also be able to work on multi-platform output because of media convergence:

You'll need to be able to shoot and edit video and stills, as well as audio, to operate in website templates as well as having some understanding of how to design your own.

You need to understand the demands of a modern, converged newsroom – different deadlines and priorities, choices and decisions to make for the different platforms, news-flows, how to manage your time to deliver on all those platforms – and still have the extra, special, spark of creativity and originality, to make the different angles you choose for each platform stand out from the others – and the competition.

You need to understand the nature of radio – what an intimate, personal medium it is, that even newsreaders need to connect with their audience, show evidence of a shred of human warmth, how important your voice is and how you use it, that a radio audience is only ever one person, not a crowd, the importance of sound and how to use words and sounds to create pictures in listeners' minds.

And of course you need those traditional, core journalism skills and knowledge – knowing what a news story is, recognising it when it happens, how to research it accurately and safely, how to distinguish truth from fiction, fact from fantasy, how to pitch it to your editor, how to find interviewees, pictures and audio, how to interview, how to do all this and remain safe and healthy, how to handle risk assessment and dangerous assignments.

Then there's the knowledge – without the crucial background of the law, ethics and industry regulation, you're dangerous. No employers are taking risks these days – not with seven figure Ofcom fines and highly public criticism in the offing.

You need to understand the concepts of fairness, objectivity and trust, what they mean in modern broadcasting and why they're so vitally important.

And because politics and government are the source of so much news, you need to understand how Government works at every level, which department's responsible for which role, who the players are at every level.

While that may seem a daunting list to accomplish, no employer expects all those skills in a work experience candidate, but they will expect some research to have been done about the station and its target audience, and an enthusiastic approach.

It is also important to put some research into any course that you are considering. There are a wide range of degrees, college courses and vocational courses available and it is important to select a course that is relevant to the area you want to work in, and wherever possible select one that has a nationally recognised qualification and is accredited by the industry. You also need to consider:

- How the course is assessed. Is it theory-based or does it give practical training as well?

- What equipment is used? Will it give you skills that are relevant to the broadcasting industry of today?

- Who teaches the course? Do the tutors have radio experience themselves or is it 'second-hand'?

- What links does the course have with industry? Courses that have industry links provide valuable contacts for their students for both work experience and future employment.

- What is the employment record? A good indication of the relevance of the skills being taught is the number of students who go on to work in radio.

Jim Latham of the BJTC says work experience is critically important:

Every BJTC accredited course tries to replicate real life in the industry as closely as possible – up to and including running their own training radio stations.

But getting out there, actually experiencing the real thing is different again – the importance of close contact with and learning from a working news team and with a real audience cannot be over-emphasized.

Frequently your first job will develop through that work placement. If they like you, offers of paid relief/freelance work may follow, and you and what you're capable of will be known by the news editor, when the next vacancy arises.

The BJTC has a range of formal and informal deals with the BBC and commercial sector for proper work placements – not sitting in a corner, making tea, sorting the post – working as a real radio reporter.

The explicit deal with the industry is that they offer such work placements so that they can review a beauty parade of the next generation of talent.

Unfortunately, not all stations take an ethical approach to work experience candidates, and there are tales of students being asked to work unpaid for weeks on end 'to get to know the job'. Jim Latham says this only happens on a few stations but the rules are that if you are on an accredited training course employers are entitled to take you on a work placement for a total of four weeks in any year without paying you. After that they are supposed to pay you the minimum wage rate. But because students are keen to get as much experience as possible, and hard-pressed stations need the extra pair of hands, the guidelines are often blurred. As Jim Latham says, 'There's a fine line between learning on the job and exploitation, and many students go along with this because they're desperate for a job.' He advises students who feel they are being exploited to contact either the BJTC or the National Union of Journalists.

As Jim Latham notes 'it's a tough world out there – and getting tougher' but as broadcasters from Jeremy Vine to Philippa TJ know, working in radio can be one of the most fulfilling jobs around and well worth the sacrifices and effort it takes to get there.

Glossary

actuality – the live or recorded sound of an event or interview on location, i.e. as it 'actually' happens.

ad – advertisement or commercial.

ad lib – unscripted, improvised speech.

AM – see *frequency*.

analogue broadcasting – non-digital broadcasting, e.g. on AM or FM.

as-live – an item pre-recorded to sound as if it is happening live.

atmosphere or 'atmos' – background noise that provides a sense of location to interviews or voice pieces. The 'natural' sound of a location, e.g. pubs, schools, countryside. Can be used as a 'bed' for studio links to provide continuity for packages. Also known as 'wild track'.

audio – literally sound. Material from an interview or a live or recorded voice piece.

audio feed – sound bites and other material sent to studios or stations.

automatic level control – (ALC) a device on portable recording machines and studio desks that maintains a standard recording level.

back-anno, B/A – an announcement at the end of a piece of music or an interview that gives details of what has been heard.

base – the location of the on air studio.

bed – a recording of music or actuality played under speech to provide continuity or atmosphere. For example, the music played under a news bulletin on commercial stations is known as the 'news bed'.

bi-media – describes any operation that involves both radio and television. The BBC, ITN and Sky have reporters that produce material for both radio and television.

bulletin – a report containing the latest information on a topic such as news, travel or weather.

cans – headphones.

catchline – a word at the top of a script that identifies the story or item; also known as a slug.

clip/ cut – an extract from an interview or other recording.

commentary – a report broadcast from an event as it is happening, e.g. a sports match or state funeral.

copy – written information read by a presenter or newsreader. News copy tells the story without any audio.

cue – 1. the written introduction to a piece of audio that is either live or recorded. 2. a signal either by hand or by light for the next item to begin. 3. programme or audio played into a person's headphones that introduces or indicates when they should start broadcasting, e.g. from a studio to an outside broadcast unit, or someone down the line.

DAB – Digital Audio Broadcasting. The system of digital radio transmission adopted by the UK.

DAB+ – An alternative system to DAB for delivering digital radio that uses a different codec (method of decoding the digital signal).

delay system – electronic device that delays the transmission of a live broadcast by three to ten seconds, used mainly in phone-ins to override libels or profanities.

demographic – the profile of a station's average listener based on age, gender, race, profession, etc. This is very important to advertisers who want to target a particular audience.

desk – the control panel in a studio that mixes different sources for transmission.

Digital Marantz – a portable digital recording machine.

digital platform – method for transmitting and receiving digital programming, e.g. DAB, digital television, mobile phones.

Digital Radio Development Bureau – organisation owned by the BBC and commercial radio set up to promote DAB.

Digital Radio Mondiale, DRM – an alternative system to DAB for delivering digital radio that uses AM transmitters.

Digital Radio Working Group – group formed in 2007 from representatives of the radio industry and related stakeholders to promote digital radio and increase its penetration, working towards a switchover date for radio in the UK to move from analogue to digital.

double-header – item or programme presented by two people.

drive – to drive a desk is to operate a studio desk.

drive-time – the late afternoon rush-hour period when a great number of listeners are in cars going home from work. One of the peak listening times of the radio day.

dub – to copy audio from one source to another, e.g. an audio recorder to a computer.

duration – the length of time to the nearest second of a piece of audio or written text (cue or copy line).

edit – to make audio ready for transmission. At its simplest this involves finding an appropriate start and end point, but it can also involve removing unwanted material to help the piece to make sense or flow better.

embargo – request not to release information until a specific date or time.

ENPS – Electronic News Provision Service. The computerised newsroom system used by the BBC to manage audio and text.

fader – the slide mechanism on a studio desk that opens an audio channel and controls the volume.

feature – a prepared item for a radio programme usually consisting of interviews, actuality and links.

feed – a supply of audio from an outside source, e.g. IRN feeds news clips to various commercial radio stations for them to use in their bulletins.

feedback – also known as 'howl round'. The effect produced when the signal from a microphone is transmitted through a nearby speaker, which is in turn picked up by the microphone producing a high-pitched howling sound. It can also be caused if a phone-in contributor has a radio tuned in to the programme that is near to the telephone.

fixed spot – an item that features regularly in a programme at a particular time, e.g. travel news at breakfast and drive-time.

FM – see *frequency*.

format – 1. the agreed style of programming for a radio station regarding the speech/music ratio, genre of music played, style of delivery. 2. the structure and presentation of individual programmes regarding, for example, the number of time checks in any hour, use of jingles and idents, duration of links.

frequency – the measurement of analogue radio waves. A station's frequency denotes its position on the dial. Frequencies on the AM waveband (amplitude moderation) are expressed as kHz (kilohertz) including medium- and long-wave transmissions, and on the FM waveband (frequency modulation) as MHz (megahertz).

FX – sound-effects used to bring colour to features or packages.

GTS – Greenwich Time Signal. Now no longer from Greenwich but generated by the BBC, this is six pips broadcast at the top of the hour to give an accurate time-check.

IBA – Independent Broadcasting Authority. The body that regulated all non-BBC broadcasting from 1973 to 1990. Its radio monitoring activities were taken over by the Radio Authority, which was then replaced by Ofcom in 2003.

idents – a way of identifying the station to listeners usually in the form of a jingle.

ILR / IR – Independent Local Radio/ Independent Radio. All commercial radio covering national, regional and local stations.

ISDN – Integrated Service Digital Network. A system of providing high-quality digital audio signals through telephone lines.

jingle – a short musical piece used to identify the station or a particular programme or presenter.

landline – a cable capable of carrying a high quality signal used for outside broadcasts before ISDN.

lead – the first and most important story in a news bulletin; also refers to an electrical cable from one piece of equipment to another.

LED – Light Emitting Diode. A meter that indicates volume through a series of lights.

level – the volume of recorded or broadcast sound as registered on a meter; also a pre-recording check on a speaker's voice, known as a 'level-check'.

link – any speech between items that introduces or sets up the item for listeners; also refers to the words between interview clips in a package that connects the clips.

log – a recording of a station's output that is required to be kept for a minimum period in case of legal disputes; also refers to a note of all music played by the station for notification to the Performing Rights Society so that royalties can be paid.

meter – a device for monitoring audio level. The VU (volume unit) meter gives the average reading of the audio, the PPM (peak programme meter) measures the peaks of the audio.

mike rattle – noise caused on a recording when the microphone cable is moved during the recording.

minidisc recorder – digital recording machine that uses a miniature compact disc.

mixing – combining two or more audio sources. Used in making packages when interviews and links are combined with music or sound effects.

needletime – the amount of time a station may use to play commercially produced music.

news agency – an organisation that provides news stories on a commercial basis for use by other news media.

news release – also known as a press or media release. Information prepared by an organisation to inform news organisations of their activities. This can be to promote a new venture by an organisation, or to provide a statement about an ongoing story, for example, a crime story or industrial action.

NVQs – National Vocational Qualifications, known as SVQs in Scotland. A vocational award to a nationally set standard of skill. Standards for radio broadcasting are set by Skillset.

OB – outside broadcast.

off-mike – noise not fed directly through the microphone but audible in the broadcast.

out – the last few words of a piece of audio, written on the cue as a warning that the piece is about to end.

Output – the sound that is heard by listeners.

package – a recorded item combining interviews, links, and/or music and effects, prepared for broadcast with a cue.

popping – distortion caused by the rush of air in 'p' and 'b' sounds usually caused by the presenter or interviewee being too close to the microphone.

PPL – Phonographic Performance Ltd. Represents record companies and licenses the broadcasting of music.

ppm – peak programme meter. Measures the peaks of audio. See *meter.*

pre-fade – facility on a studio desk that allows a presenter to listen to an audio source (live or recorded) and adjust the level before it is broadcast.

prof – also known as 'in profanity'. When the station's output is in delay, for example, during a phone-in, to prevent profanities or libels being broadcast.

promo – a promotional spot for a forthcoming programme; also known as a 'trail'.

prospects – a list of news stories expected to be covered that day.

PRS – Performing Rights Society. Represents the interests of musicians, composers and publishers and acts as a clearing-house for the use of their material both live and recorded.

psa – public service announcement. Any item that provides information in the public interest, e.g. travel news, notification of charity events, police appeals.

Q and A – an item where the reporter is questioned by a presenter about a story they have been following; also known as a two-way.

Radio Authority – the body that licensed and regulated radio in the UK from 1990 to 2003. Now replaced by Ofcom.

RadioCentre – body that represents the interests of commercial radio in the UK. Formed in 2006 from a merger between the Commercial Radio Companies Association and the Radio Advertising Bureau.

RAJAR – Radio Joint Audience Research. The body owned by the BBC and the RadioCentre that measures audiences for all stations in the UK.

reach – the percentage of total listeners in the TSA (Total Service Area) who tune in during a specified period.

royalties – fee paid to the Performing Rights Society based on the amount of recorded music played by a radio station.

RSL – Restricted Service Licence. A licence from Ofcom for special events broadcasting over a limited geographical area for a specified time, usually 28 days.

running order – the planned order of items in a programme.

schedule – the planned sequence of programmes throughout a week.

Selector – a software system that selects tracks from a pre-entered base of music. The music is categorised in various ways, for example, artist's name, title, chart position, mood, tempo, etc. and the system provides running orders that take account of the time of day of the programme and the required frequency of play, and makes sure the tracks 'flow' together in pace and mood.

share – the total listening time achieved by a station expressed as a percentage of the total amount of time spent by people listening to all radio services in the same transmission area.

simulcasting – the practice of broadcasting the same output on different frequencies, e.g. when analogue stations broadcast their output on a digital frequency.

slug – word or words used to identify an item; also known as a catchline.

sound bite – brief extract from an interview.

soc – standard out cue. An agreed form of words used by a reporter at the end of a report, e.g. 'John Smith for IRN at the Old Bailey.'

stab – a short jingle or ident.

sting – a brief burst of music sued to punctuate output, often including the station name.

stringer – a freelance reporter covering an area where there is no staff reporter available.

talkback – off-air communication system linking studios, control rooms, or OB locations.

tease – a short advert for something coming up later in the programme.

tec. op. – technical operator. Someone who drives the programme from outside the studio.

top and tail – basic edit to make the start and end of a piece of audio 'clean' so that the item starts and ends at the correct point.

Trail – a promotional advert for a forthcoming programme.

transmission area – a geographical area served by a station. This may not be the same as the area the station can be heard in, but it is the area used by RAJAR to measure a station's audience, and the one referenced in its output. This is also known as the TSA (Total Survey Area) in RAJAR terminology.

two-way – another name for a Q and A. An interview between a presenter and reporter to provide information and analysis of an event.

Voicebank – system used by the emergency services whereby information is recorded for journalists to access.

voice piece – a scripted report of a story read by the reporter, used with a cue read by the newsreader.

vox pop – literally 'voice of the people'. A series of responses from people in the street to a specific question, edited together in a continuous stream. Used with a cue read by the newsreader.

VU – Volume Unit meter. This measures the average volume of sound.

waveform – the visual display of sound on a computer in digital editing systems.

wild track – the recording of background noise or ambient sound on location, used for editing into a recorded piece to provide atmosphere.

windshield – a foam 'sock' used over a microphone to prevent wind noise on the recording.

wire service – national and international news stories sent by news agencies to newsrooms, usually electronically.

wrap – a news item where the reporter links an interview, literally 'wrapping' their voice around an interview clip.

Notes

....

1   The renaissance of radio

1   All quotes from Trevor Dann from author interview February 2008.
2   For more on the definition of PSB see Harrison 2006.
3   All quotes from Antony Bellekom taken from author interview June 2008.
4   Russell Brand resigned from his BBC Radio 2 show in October 2008 following a public outcry over a prank call. See Chapter 10 for details.
5   BBC Asian Network is available on DAB digital radio and other digital platforms as well as on some AM and FM frequencies across the country. It has a primary target audience of British Asians under 35 (BBC Asian Network Service Licence 2008).
6   All quotes from Sophie Stewart from author interview April 2008.
7   The first national commercial station to go on air was Classic FM in September 1992, followed by Virgin 1215 in April 1993, then Talk Radio (now talkSPORT) in February 1995.
8   The last new FM licences in the UK were awarded by Ofcom in 2007.
9   In August 2008 the Office of Fair Trading announced that it would allow Global to retain its ownership of all five London stations.
10   All quotes from Mark Dennison from author interview March 2008.
11   Their suggestion had been for a minimum of three hours a day of local programming on weekdays with seven hours a day for larger stations (Ofcom 2007: 4).
12   All quotes from Tim Humphrey from author interview April 2008.

2   Radio revolution

1   All quotes from Andy Puleston from author interview April 2007.
2   All quotes from Trevor Dann from author interview February 2008.
3   According to the DRWG Final Report, advertising revenues for 2008 fell by 15 per cent (Foreword to the report).
4   All quotes from Stuart Cosgrove taken from author interview February 2008.
5   Full details are available in *RSLs: Notes for Applicants* available from Ofcom. In 2008 the fees for short-term RSLs ranged from £25 per day for AM to £70 per day for FM broadcasts above 1W.

3   You radio

1   All quotes from Antony Bellekom taken from author interview June 2008.
2   All quotes from Trevor Dann from author interview February 2008.
3   Any community radio station with a coverage area that overlaps by 50 per cent or more with a commercial radio station with a Measured Coverage Area (MCA) which contains more than 50,000 adults and no more than 150,000 adults will not be allowed to take any advertising or programme sponsorship. This restriction was placed in the Order to protect small Commercial stations (www.commedia.org.uk).
4   iTunes has various guides available online to help people make and upload podcasts and to guide users through selection and downloading.
5   All quotes from Andy Puleston from author interview April 2007.
6   All quotes from Ben Cooper from author interview April 2007

4   Radio style

1   All quotes from Phil Dixon taken from author interview October 2007.
2   All quotes from Mark Dennison from author interview March 2008.
3   All quotes from Sophie Stewart taken from author interview April 2008.
4   All quotes from Antony Bellekom from author interview June 2008.
5   According to the service licence for BBC Local Radio, stations should have a 60 per cent speech output for their 'core hours' but over the course of 24 hours this balances out at around 70 per cent speech and 30 per cent music.
6   The rules can be found at the Broadcast Committee of Advertising Practice (BCAP) Radio Advertising Standards Code.
7   GCap is now part of Global Radio but at the time of interview it had not been taken over.
8   All quotes from Phill Danks from author interview April 2008.
9   For more on internet radio see Chapter 2.
10 All quotes from Tim Humphrey from author interview April 2008.

5   The voice of the station

1   All quotes from Trevor Dann from author interview February 2008.
2   All quotes from Mark Dennison from author interview March 2008.
3   All quotes from Kate Lee from author communication August 2008.
4   This section deals with broadcast scripts in general. For information on writing for news see the section in Chapter 6.
5   All quotes from Piers Bradford from author interview April 2007.
6   All quotes from Sophie Stewart from author interview April 2008.
7   All quotes from Antony Bellekom from author interview June 2008.
8   All quotes from Ben Cooper from author interview April 2007.
9   All quotes from James Wood from author interview April 2007.
10 All quotes from Andy Puleston from author interview April 2007.
11 All quotes from Piers Bradford from author interview April 2007.

6   The role of news

1   All quotes from Lewis Skrimshaw taken from author interview November 2007.
2   All quotes from Nick Wilson taken from author interview November 2007.
3   All quotes from Aeneas Rotsos taken from author interview March 2008.
4   At the time of interview Heart 106 in the East Midlands broadcast three extended news shows from Monday to Friday at 6 am, 1 pm and 6 pm. These were 15 minutes long including a commercial break. This was due to a 33 per cent speech commitment under the original licence, which Ofcom allowed to be changed in February 2008.

7   The tools of broadcasting

1   All quotes from Nick Wilson from author interview November 2007.

8   Types of programming

1   All quotes from Trevor Dann from author interview February 2008.
2   All quotes from Antony Bellekom from author interview June 2008.
3   Jon Gaunt was sacked by talkSPORT in November 2008 for calling a London councillor a 'Nazi' during a row about a ban on smokers being allowed to foster children.
4   All quotes from Mark Dennison from author interview March 2008.
5   All quotes from Duncan Cooke from email interview February 2008.
6   All quotes from Will Nunan from author interview April 2008.
7   All quotes from Nick Wilson from author interview November 2007.
8   All quotes from Aeneas Rotsos from author interview March 2008.
9   All quotes from Lewis Skrimshaw from author interview November 2007.
10   There are several excellent books about radio drama that give more detail than this short section. Among them are *Radio Drama* edited by Peter Lewis; *British Radio Drama* edited by John Drakakis; and *Radio Acting* by Alan Beck. See bibliography for details.
11   All quotes from Amanda Whittington from author interview November 2008.

9   Sport on radio

1   All quotes from Phil Blacker from author interview February 2008.
2   All quotes from Sophie Stewart from author interview April 2008.
3   All quotes from Ross Fletcher from author interview September 2008.
4   All quotes from Antony Bellekom from author interview June 2008.
5   All quotes from Jim Proudfoot taken from the Radio Academy podcast May 2008 available at www.radioacademy.org.uk.
6   All quotes from Alan Green taken from the Radio Academy podcast May 2008 available at www.radioacademy.org.uk.
7   Paul Jewel resigned as Derby County manager in January 2009.

11 Getting started in radio

1   According to Skillset (www.skillset.org.uk) in November 2008.
2   A full list of patrons of the Radio Academy is available at their website, but most UK stations are covered.
3   All quotes from Trevor Dann taken from email interview November 2008.
4   All quotes from Philippa TJ from email interviews in February and November 2008.
5   All quotes from Lewis Skrimshaw from author interview November 2007.
6   All quotes from Aeneas Rotsos from author interview March 2008.
7   All quotes from Jim Latham from email interview November 2008.

Bibliography

Adams, A. (2005) 'Radio football down the years', available at http://news.bbc.co.uk/sport2/hi/football/1760579.stm.

Allan, S. (1999) *News Culture*, Buckingham: Open University Press.

Allen, K. (2008) 'GCap to pioneer "listen and buy" radio for iPods', *The Guardian*, 11 February 2008.

Andrews, P. (2005) *Sports Journalism: A Practical Introduction*, London: Sage.

Baehr, H. and Gray, A. (eds) (1996) *Turning it On: A Reader in Women and Media*, London: Arnold.

Barnard, S. (2000) *Studying Radio*, London: Arnold.

BBC

—— (2006) Royal Charter, available at www.bbc.co.uk.

—— (2006/07) BBC Annual Report, available at www.bbc.co.uk.

——(2007/08) BBC Annual Report, available at www.bbc.co.uk.

—— (2008a) Editorial Guidelines, available at www.bbc.co.uk.

—— (2008b) BBC Radio Service Licences, available at www.bbc.co.uk.

—— (2008c) 'Brown speaks out over prank calls', BBC news online, Tuesday, 28 October 2008.

—— (2008d) 'Timeline: Russell Brand prank calls', BBC news online, Friday, 31 October 2008.

—— (2008e) BBC Trust Editorial Standards Committee Report, November 2008.

Beaman, J. (2000) *Interviewing for Radio*, London: Routledge.

Beck, A. (1997) *Radio Acting*, Oxford: A & C Black.

Berry, R. (2006) 'Will the iPod kill the Radio Star? Profiling Podcasting as Radio', *Convergence*, 12 (2): 143–62.

Boyd-Barrett, O. and Newbold, C. (1995) *Approaches to Media*, London: Arnold.

Boyle, R. (2006) *Sports Journalism: Context and Issues*, London: Sage.

Briggs, S. (1981) *Those Radio Times*, London: Weidenfeld & Nicholson.

Carter, C., Branston, G. and Allan, S. (eds) (1998) *News Gender and Power*, London: Routledge.

Chambers, D., Steiner, L. and Fleming, C. (2004) *Women and Journalism*, London: Routledge.

Collins, R., Curran, J., Garnham, N., Scannell, P., Schlesinger, P. and Sparks, C. (1986) *Media Culture and Society: A Critical Reader*, London: Sage.

Commedia (2007) *History of Community Radio in the UK*, www.commedia.org.uk.

Crisell, A. (1986) *Understanding Radio*, London: Methuen.

—— (1994) *Understanding Radio*, 2nd edn, London: Methuen.

—— (1997) *An Introductory History of British Broadcasting*, London: Routledge.

Curran, J. and Gurevitch, M. (2000) *Mass Media and Society*, 3rd edn, London: Arnold.

—— and Seaton, J. (1991) *Power without Responsibility*, 4th edn, London: Routledge.

—— and —— (1997) *Power without Responsibility: The Press and Broadcasting in Britain*, 5th edn, London: Routledge.

Digital Radio Development Bureau (DRDB) (2009) http://www.drdb.org.

Dougray, G. (1994) *The Executive Tart and Other Myths*, London: Virago.

Drakakis, J. (ed.) (1981) *British Radio Drama*, Cambridge: Cambridge University Press.

Evans, E. (1977) *Radio – A Guide to Broadcasting Techniques*, London: Barrie & Jenkins.

Everitt, A. (2003) *New Voices: An Evaluation of 15 Access Radio Projects*, London: UK Radio Authority.

—— (2005) *New Voices: An Update*, London: UK Radio Authority.

Feldman, S. (1999) 'Twin Peaks: The Staying Power of BBC Radio 4's Woman's Hour', paper delivered at the Radiodyssey Conference, Cardiff, November 1999.

Fogg, A., Korbel, P. and Brooks, C. (2005) *The Community Radio Toolkit*, Manchester: Radio Regen.

Ford, S. (2007) *Writing News for Local Radio*, Nottingham: Booklaw Publications.

Gage, L. (1999) *A Guide to Commercial Radio Journalism*, 2nd edn, revised by L. Douglas and H. Kinsey, Oxford: Focal Press.

Gibson, O. (2008) 'BBC funding: the public's verdict', *MediaGuardian*, 18 August 2008.

—— (2008b) 'BBC battles to calm prank storm', *The Guardian*, 31 October 2008.

Goatley, M. (2007) *The Community Radio Sector: Looking to the Future*, London: Department of Culture, Media and Sport.

Graff, V. (2008) 'An unlikely comeback' in *MediaGuardian*, 20 October 2008.

Hargrave, A.M. (2000) *Listening 2000*, Broadcasting Standards Commission and the Radio Authority.

Hayes, B. (1994) 'The Role of the Public Voice in Present-day Radio', in A.M. Hargrave (ed.) *Radio and Audience Attitudes: Annual Review – 1994 – Public Opinion and Broadcasting Standards Series*, London: John Libbey.

Hewlett, S. (2008) 'Brand damage and the cost of Ross', *MediaGuardian*, 3 November 2008.

Hospital Broadcasting Association (2009) 'History', www.hbauk.co.uk/public/about/.

Hudson, G. and Rowlands, S. (2007) *The Broadcast Journalism Handbook*, Essex: Pearson Education.

Johnson, B. (2006) 'DAB gets a poor reception', *The Guardian*, 9 October 2006.

Kelner, M. (2008) 'Heard the same song three times today? Blame the craze for "testing" tunes', *The Guardian*, 19 May 2008.

Kiss, J. (2007) 'We've given music a home', *The Guardian*, 4 June 2007.

Lewis, P. (1981) *Radio Drama*, London: Longman.

McLeish, R. (1988) *The Technique of Radio Production*, 2nd edn, London: Focal Press.

—— (1994) *Radio Production*, 3rd edn, Oxford: Focal Press.

McNair, B. (1994) *News and Journalism in the UK: A Textbook*, London: Routledge.

McQuail, D. (1994) *Mass Communication Theory: An Introduction*, 3rd edn, London: Sage Publications.

Milmo, D. 'Merger costs push GCap into £48m loss', *The Guardian*, 25 May 2006.

Mitchell, C. (ed.) (2000a) *Women and Radio: Airing Differences*, London: Routledge.

—— (2000b) 'Sound Advice for Women Who Want to Work in Radio' in C. Mitchell (ed.) *Women and Radio: Airing Differences*, London: Routledge.

Mitchell, C. and Michaels, K. (2000) 'The Last Bastion: How Women Become Music Presenters in UK Radio', in C. Mitchell (ed.) *Women and Radio: Airing Differences*, London: Routledge.

Ofcom (2004a) *The iPod Generation*, www.ofcom.org.uk.

—— (2005) Ofcom Broadcasting Code, ibid.

—— (2007a) *The Future of Radio: the next phase*, ibid.

—— (2007b) *Illegal Broadcasting: understanding the issues*, ibid.

—— (2007c) *Illegal Broadcasting: Annex 1*, ibid.

—— (2007d) *Illegal Broadcasting: Annex 2*, ibid.

—— (2007e) *Illegal Broadcasting: Annex 3*, ibid.

—— (2007f) *Illegal Broadcasting: FAQs*, ibid.

—— (2008a) *The Communications Market 2008*, ibid.

—— (2008b) *Ofcom: a short guide to what we do*, ibid.

—— (2008c) Restricted Service Licences: Notes for Applicants, available at www.ofcom.org.uk/radio/ifi/rbl/rsls/rslapps/rsl_notes010808.pdf

Plunkett, J. (2007a) 'Radio days are here again as Britons tune, click and plug into the digital age', *The Guardian*, 17 August 2007.

—— (2007b) 'Will radio ever get on the same wavelength?', *The Guardian*, 16 July 2007.

—— (2008a) 'Radio fined record £1.11m for phone-in scam', *The Guardian*, 27 June 2008.

—— (2008b) 'GCap Digital Stations for the chop', *The Guardian*, 11 February 2008.

—— (2008c) 'Pagers have been ditched and it's back to radio diaries to measure listening', *The Guardian*, 28 April 2008.

—— (2008d) 'Digital radio attracts more listeners', *The Guardian*, 1 May 2008.

—— (2008e) 'It's all or nothing', *The Guardian*, 21 April 2008.

—— (2008f) 'A man for all seasons', *The Guardian*, 7 April 2008.

—— (2008g) 'A poor reception', *The Guardian*, 11 February 2008.

—— (2008h) 'A different hand on the dial', *The Guardian*, 3 March 2008.

—— (2008i) 'IRN drops ITN for Sky News', *The Guardian*, 15 October 2008.

Price-Davies, E. and Tacchi, J. (2001) *Community Radio in a Global Context: A Comparative Analysis*, Sheffield: Community Radio Association.

Radio Advertising Bureau (2006a) *Discovery and Recovery: the complementary roles of radio and iPod*, www.rab.co.uk.

—— (2006b) *Multi-platform radio*, www.rab.co.uk.

—— (2007) *Radio and the Digital Native*, www.rab.co.uk.

RadioCentre (2006) *An Introduction to Commercial Radio*, www.radiocentre.org.uk.

—— (2008) *Action Stations: The Output and Impact of Commercial Radio*, www.radiocentre.org.uk.

RAJAR (2008a) *Podcasting and Radio Listening via Internet Survey*, January, www.rajar.co.uk.

—— (2008b) *Podcasting and Radio Listening via the Internet Survey*, June, www.rajar.co.uk.

Robinson, J. (2008) 'Channel 4 bid to rule airwaves my just be pie in the sky', *The Observer*, 24 August 2008.

Robinson, P. (2007) 'Gaydar finds that listeners will dance to its different tunes', *The Guardian*, 2 July 2007.

Rudin, R. (2006) 'The Development of DAB Digital Radio in the UK', *Convergence*, 12(2) 163–78. London: Sage.

Scannell, P. (1991) 'Introduction', in P. Scannell (ed.) *Broadcast Talk*, London: Sage.

—— (1996) *Radio, Television and Modern Life*, Oxford: Blackwell.

Schofield, J. (2007) 'Ofcom is still clueless when it comes to DAB radio', *The Guardian*, 10 May 2007.

Shinglewr, M. and Wieringa, C. (1998) *On Air: Methods and Meanings of Radio*, London: Arnold.

Silver, J. (2007) 'Licence to shock', *The Guardian*, 1 October 2007.

Starkey, G. (2004) *Radio in Context*, Basingstoke: Palgrave Macmillan.

Sweney, M. and Holmwood, L. (2008) 'BBC fined £400,000 over unfair phone-ins', *The Guardian*, 31 July 2008.

Welsh, T., Greenwood, W. and Banks, D. (2007) *McNae's Essential Law for Journalists*, 19th edition, Oxford: Oxford University Press.

Whelan, S. (2007) 'Why internet explorers are all ears', in *Radio Reborn*, a special supplement from *The Guardian* and RadioCentre, 5 November 2007: 7.

Wilby, P. and Conroy A. (1994) *The Radio Handbook*, 1st edn, London: Routledge.

Winston, B. (1995) 'How Are Media Born and Developed', in J. Downing, J. Mohammadi and A. Sreberny-Mohammadi (eds), *Questioning the Media: A Critical Introduction*, 2nd edn, London: Sage.

Winter, A. (2008) 'Getting the business of radio audience measurement right', RadioCentre: Radio Research, available at www.radiocentre.org.uk.

Index

....

eBooks – at www.eBookstore.tandf.co.uk

A library at your fingertips!

eBooks are electronic versions of printed books. You can store them on your PC/laptop or browse them online.

They have advantages for anyone needing rapid access to a wide variety of published, copyright information.

eBooks can help your research by enabling you to bookmark chapters, annotate text and use instant searches to find specific words or phrases. Several eBook files would fit on even a small laptop or PDA.

NEW: Save money by eSubscribing: cheap, online access to any eBook for as long as you need it.

Annual subscription packages

We now offer special low-cost bulk subscriptions to packages of eBooks in certain subject areas. These are available to libraries or to individuals.

For more information please contact webmaster.ebooks@tandf.co.uk

We're continually developing the eBook concept, so keep up to date by visiting the website.

www.eBookstore.tandf.co.uk